W9-ABY-278

"A Different Sense of Power"

"A Different Sense of Power"

Problems of Community in Late-Twentieth-Century U.S. Poetry

Thomas Fink

Madison • Teaneck
Fairleigh Dickinson University Press
London: Associated University Presses

Associated University Presses
440 Forsgate Drive
Cranbury, NJ 08512

Associated University Presses
16 Barter Street
London WC1A 2AH, England

Associated University Presses
P.O. Box 338, Port Credit
Mississauga, Ontario
Canada L5G 4L8

The paper used in this publication meets the requirements
of the American National Standard for Permance
of Paper for Printed Library Materials Z39.48–1984.

Library of Congress Cataloging-in-Publication Data

Fink, Thomas.
  A different sense of power : problems of community in later twentiety-century U.S. poetry / Thomas Fink
      p. cm.
  Includes bibliographical references (p.   ) and index.
  ISBN 0-8386-3897-X (alk. paper)
  1. American poetry—20th century—History and criticism. 2. Social problems in literature. 3. Literature and society—United States—History—20th century. 4. Power (Social sciences) in literature. 5. Community in literature. I. Title.
PS310.S7 F56 2001
811'5409358—dc21   2001023156

PRINTED IN THE UNITED STATES OF AMERICA

for Nikken Shonin

Contents

Acknowledgments

From *Borderlands/La Frontera: The New Mestiza,* copyright 1987 by Gloria Anzaldúa. Reprinted by permission of Aunt Lute Books.

"Fingering the Jagged Grains" appears in *Change of Territory* (University of Kentucky, 1983), "Heartbeats" and "Aunt Ida Pieces a Quilt" appear in *Love's Instruments* (Tia Chucha, 1995), and "I'll Be Somewhere Listening for My Name" is an adaptation of a keynote speech delivered at OutWrite '92 and printed in *Sojourner: Black Gay Voices in the Age of AIDS* (Other Countries, 1993). This work has been reprinted with the permission of the Estate of Melvin Dixon.

Grateful acknowledgment is made to Denise Duhamel for permission to quote from her books, *Smile!* (Warm Spring, 1993), *The Woman with Two Vaginas* (Salmon Run, 1995), *Girl Soldier* (1996), and *Kinky* (1997).

Grateful acknowledgment is made to Martin Espada for permission to quote from his book, *The Immigrant Iceboy's Bolero* (Cordilera, 1984; Waterfront, 1986).

Grateful acknowledgment is made to Bilingual Press/Editorial Bilingue (Arizona State University, Tempe, Ariz.) for permission to quote from *Trumpets from the Islands of Their Eviction* by Martín Espada, copyright 1987 by Bilingual Press/Editorial Bilingue.

Grateful acknowledgment is made to Curbstone Press for permission to quote from *Rebellion is the Circle of a Lover's Hands* by Martín Espada, copyright 1990 by Martín Espada.

From *City of Coughing and Dead Radiators* by Martín Espada. Copyright 1993 by Martín Espada. Used by permission of W. W. Norton & Company, Inc.

From *Imagine the Angels of Bread* by Martín Espada. Copyright 1996 by Martín Espada. Used by permission of W. W. Norton & Company, Inc.

10 ACKNOWLEDGMENTS

Excerpts, as submitted, from "The Colonel" from *The Country Between Us* by Carolyn Forché, copyright 1981 by Carolyn Forché. Originally appeared in *Women's International Resource Exchange*. Reprinted by permission of HarperCollins Publishers Inc.

Excerpts totalling about 135 lines from *The Angel of History* by Carolyn Forché, copyright 1994 by Carolyn Forché. Reprinted by permission of HarperCollins Publishers Inc.

Excerpts from *Human Rights*, copyright 1998 by Joseph Lease, Zoland Books, Cambridge, Massachusetts.

Grateful acknowledgment is made to Stephen Paul Miller for permission to quote from his book, *Art Is Boring for the Same Reason We Stayed in Vietnam* (Domestic, 1992).

Excerpts "Birmingham Brown's Turn," "Interpretation," and "The Lynching" from *Rainbow Remnants in Rock Bottom Ghetto Sky* by Thylias Moss. Copyright 1991. Reprinted by permission of Persea Books, Inc. (New York).

"For Hagar" and "Crystals" from *Last Chance for the Tarzan Holler* by Thylias Moss. Copyright 1998. Reprinted by permission of Persea Books, Inc. (New York).

Excerpts totalling about 91 lines from *Small Congregations: New and Selected Poems* by Thylias Moss. Copyright 1983, 1990, 1991, 1993 by Thylias Moss. Reprinted by permission of HarperCollins Publishers, Inc.

Grateful acknowledgment is made to John Yau for permission to quote from his book, *Crossing Canal Street* (Bellevue, 1976).

Excerpts from "Genghis Chan: Private Eye" and "No One Ever Tried to Kiss Anna May Wong," copyright 1989 by John Yau. Reprinted from *Radiant Silhouette: New and Selected Work 1974–1988* with the permission of Black Sparrow Press.

Excerpts from "Genghis Chan: Private Eye," copyright 1992 by John Yau. Reprinted from *Edificio Sayonara* with the permission of Black Sparrow Press.

Excerpts from "Genghis Chan: Private Eye" and "Peter Lorre Dreams He is the Third Reincarnation of a Geisha," copyright 1996 by John Yau. Reprinted from *Forbidden Entries* with the permission of Black Sparrow Press.

I would like to thank Tuzyline Jita Allan, Charles Altieri, Lakshmi Bandlamudi, Mark Blasius, Gerald Johnson, Mary Ann Mason, Eric Monder, Shivaji Sengupta, Eleanor Q. Tignor, and Phyllis van Slyck, all of whom have offered valuable commentary on sections that became part of this book.

"A Different Sense
of Power"

Introduction

A *DIFFERENT SENSE OF POWER* TREATS WRITERS OF VARIOUS RACES/
ethnicities and geographical locations in the U.S. who speak directly
(though utilizing divergent aesthetic strategies) to issues of community that are central to our sociocultural moment. These issues
include the notion of visibility/invisibility, the erasure and reconstruction of history, coalition, and the expansion of collectivity.

Typically, writers of books about contemporary American poetry
concentrate primarily on authors—for example, Adrienne Rich, Audre Lorde, John Ashbery, A. R. Ammons, Robert Creeley, Amiri
Baraka, Allen Ginsburg, and James Merrill—born before 1935. While
major critics like Charles Altieri, Marjorie Perloff, and Helen Vendler
have devoted substantial attention to younger poets,[1] I believe that
it is time for a book that exclusively concerns a group of writers who
came to maturity in the past twenty years. Eight of the poets discussed
herein were born between 1950 and 1961, and one (Gloria Anzaldúa)
was born in 1942. Except for Melvin Dixon, who died in 1992, all are
in midcareer.

Marjorie Perloff, George Hartley, Linda Reinfeld, and others have
developed cogent, sustained analyses of the leftist group of experimental writers known as "the Language Poets," most of whom were
born after 1940 and came to prominence in the late seventies and
early eighties.[2] Such Language Poets as Charles Bernstein, Susan
Howe, Bruce Andrews, Ron Silliman, Lyn Hejinian, Michael Palmer,
Bob Perelman, and Myung Mi Kim have made distinct contributions
to the elucidation of the problematic of representation in current
American poetry and poetics. Of the nine poets considered in the
chapters that follow, four (John Yau, Carolyn Forché, Joseph Lease,
and Stephen Paul Miller) are experimental writers who, though not
associated with the Language group, are engaged in parallel theoreti-
cal and aesthetic concerns.[3] While Language Poets' prose critiques of

13

"traditional" "bourgeoise" forms of representation, addressed briefly in chapter 2, are heuristically valuable, I will suggest that their implicit proscriptions regarding poetic practice may unnecessarily foreclose possibilities of social articulation that, I believe, many Language Poets would endorse.

Although "marketplace" evaluations of literature should not be taken too seriously, the current reception of the poets I treat deserves a brief assessment. In the mainstream poetry scene, Martín Espada, Carolyn Forché, Thylias Moss, and John Yau are deemed prominent "voices." Forché, currently published by HarperCollins, won the Yale Series of Younger Poets competition and the Lamont Prize for a second book of poems, which established her reputation with a searing portrayal of political conditions in the war-torn El Salvador of the late seventies and early eighties. Moss's fourth book won the National Poetry Series open competition. Her *Selected Poems* (from the Ecco Press) appeared when she was under forty, and she has won many awards, including a Guggenheim Fellowship and the MacArthur "Genius" Grant. Espada's prizes include two fellowships from the National Endowment for the Arts, a Paterson Poetry Prize, and a PEN/Revson Fellowship. His last two books were published by Norton. Yau, who has published eleven books of poetry—most recently with Black Sparrow Press—and six books of art criticism, has earned numerous fellowships and awards, including a Lavan Award from the Academy of American Poets. As a cultural critic who combines genres, including poetry, and as an anthologist of radical feminist women of color, Gloria Anzaldúa is frequently cited with enthusiasm and respect by feminist critics and postcolonial scholars. Her work has been analyzed in several books. Melvin Dixon's important second book of poems was published three years after his passing, and the influence of his poetry—as well as his novels—is likely to grow in the coming years, especially since the field of African-American literary studies is beginning to note the contributions of gay authors.

Both Joseph Lease, published by Zoland, and Denise Duhamel, author of five books and one poetic collaboration between 1993 and 1999 and now published by Southern Illinois University Press, seem on the verge of entering the "front ranks." Lease has earned the praise of Robert Creeley, Michael Palmer, Frank Bidart, and other prominent poets, and Duhamel's work has garnered the approbation of Edward Field, Colette Inez, and Jean Valentine. Duhamel and Lease have published various poems in leading magazines. Long a "coterie" poet on Manhattan's Lower East Side and recently emerging as a cultural critic in the area of American studies, Stephen Paul Miller is the author of a 1992 book-length poem that, regrettably, was not widely distributed.

IN/VISIBILITY

Since the publication of Ralph Ellison's *Invisible Man* in 1952, the issue of in/visibility has held a prominent place in American literature. At the beginning of the book's prologue, the first-person narrator patiently and ironically demonstrates that the "invisibility" of a living human being—in this case, an African American—is not a paradox, but an unsettling displacement of the literal by figurative elements. While calling himself "a man of substance, of flesh and bone," as well as "a mind," the narrator insists that he is "invisible, . . . simply because people refuse to see [him]."[4] The narrator's "invisibility" is constituted by others' highly selective perception, including frequently arbitrary superimpositions of what is external to him onto the "field" that he embodies: "Like the bodiless heads . . . in circus sideshows," he seems "surrounded by mirrors of hard, distorting glass" (1). Other people perceive his "surroundings, themselves, or figments of their imagination." Ellison's narrator blames his invisibility on "the construction of [the] *inner* eyes" (3) of those who look at him. Even if the narrator knows that these "*inner* eyes" are not working properly, his own self-perception is at least somewhat adversely affected, because he must continually encounter human "mirrors" that "surround" him and whose "distorting glass" paradoxically "presents" his "invisibility" to him.

As the unfolding of the novel's plot suggests, the confluence of ideology and individual desire for power often shapes the phenomenon of the narrator's invisibility. Late in the novel, contemplating his "invisibility," the narrator reflects upon how men he had encountered "merge into one single white figure," because each had tried "to force his picture of reality upon" the invisible man and did not give "a hoot in hell for how things looked to [him]," since he was seen merely as an exploitable "material" (497). What Ellison describes as "invisibility" can be termed *false* or *distorted visibility* promoted by the dominant culture's *exclusion* of the marginalized individual or group's *self-representation*. In *Orientalism* (1978), Palestinian-American cultural critic Edward W. Said places Ellison's narrator's remarks in the context of European "Near Eastern Studies": "The exteriority of the representation is always governed by some version of the truism that if the Orient could represent itself, it would; since it cannot, the representation does the job, for the West, and . . . for the poor Orient."[5]

Two lesbian-feminist writers who have written poetry and prose that exerted a strong influence on younger social poets of the past two decades have refashioned Ellison's trope of invisibility in their own discourse. In a 1977 speech published in *Sister Outsider* (1984), Audre Lorde, speaking of the "distortion of vision" caused by notions of "racial difference" in the U.S., declares that "black women . . . have always been highly visible," yet "have been rendered invisible through the depersonalization of racism."[6] Lorde adds that, even within the white-dominated feminist movement, African-American women "have had to fight, and still do, for that very visibility which also renders us vulnerable, our Blackness" (42).[7] In a 1984 essay, "Invisibility in Academe," Adrienne Rich addresses the prohibition of self-representation for lesbians and others by "those" in U.S. society who possess the authority to legislate what comprises social reality and thus to "choose not to see . . . or hear" others or include them in a description of the world.[8] The "moment of psychic disequilibrium" for the excluded, Rich states, is like "a game with mirrors" in which one "looked into a mirror and saw nothing" (199). In the game of the "closet," woman-identified women "must pretend to be heterosexual in order to hold jobs" and perform numerous other acts that heterosexual women take for granted (198). Rich calls "invisibility . . . the attempt to fragment you, to prevent you from integrating love and work and feelings and ideas" and, thus, from achieving "empowerment" (199).

In *Borderlands/La Frontera—The New Mestiza* (1987), a book that combines poetry, historical writing, autobiography, and critical theory, Chicana (or more properly, mestiza) lesbian-feminist poet Gloria Anzaldúa problematizes the in/visibility of lesbian experience.[9] In "*La conciencia de la mestiza*: Towards a New Consciousness," the most widely read essay in *Borderlands,* Anzaldúa implicitly criticizes Chicano patriarchy's effort to render the lesbian invisible or cast her outside *la raza*'s social sphere: "As a *mestiza* I have no country, my homeland cast me out; yet all countries are mine because I am every woman's sister or potential lover. (As a lesbian I have no race, my own people disclaim me, but I am all races because there is the queer of me in all races)" (80). Even if there seems to be an advantage to the lesbian's disinheritance—admission to a transnational or transethnic "queer" sisterhood—Anzaldúa refuses to concede that the Chicano/a spirit is essentially patriarchal. The poetry and prose of *Borderlands* poses a challenge to the Chicano people, themselves rendered invisible in the United States, to bring those made peripheral within *la raza* to the center.

"Interface," a sci-fi poem in which the woman speaker has a relationship with a "noumenal" "alien," is an allegory of the problematic in/visibility of lesbian existence in U.S. society at large *and* in Chicano culture. The poem's opening lines do not indicate that the speaker's "space alien" beloved has suddenly walked into her life but that "she'd always been there / occupying the same room" (148). This sentence suggests that the potential for making the "invisible" and extraordinary qualities of loving interaction "visible" and accessible to the desiring self resides within the subject's power to perceive "margins," interstices, rather than to be stuck in the socially conditioned and habitual: "It was only when I looked / at the edges of things / my eyes going wide watering, / objects blurring" that mere "empty space" was revealed as "layers and layers," thickened "air." "Spiritual being" appears "behind" the speaker's "eyelids a white flash / a thin noise."

At times, the new mode of perception causes a shock to the psychic system, and the speaker shies away from contact: "Once I accidentally ran my arm / through her body / felt heat on one side of my face. / She wasn't solid. / The shock pushed me against the wall. / A torrent of days swept past me / before I tried to 'see' her again" (148). At the beginning of their time together, when the lovers are only able to "see each other" *between* their two realms—"on the border between / the physical world / and hers"; "there at the interface"—each desires to inhabit the other's territory:

> I wished I could become
> pulsing color, pure sound, bodiless as she.
> It was impossible, she said
> for humans to become noumenal
>
> What does it feel like, she asked
> to inhabit flesh,
> wear blood like threads
> constantly running?
>
> (148–49)

Later, when the speaker realizes her lover—whom she has "named . . . Leyla, / a pure sound"—is "changing," the former reports: "A yearning deluged me— / her yearning. / That's when I knew / she wanted to be flesh" (149). The speaker's desire to be "bodiless" is a trope for the desire to enter the lover's consciousness so thoroughly as to transcend anything so "separate" or "borderline" as empathy or sympathy. Perhaps the remarkable frissons of their erotic encounters depend on each calling upon the other, not only to provide what is lacking, but to supplant familiar features of identity with sublimely alien ones. In exploring each other's difference, their psyches experience a departure from the quotidian world: "We lay enclosed by margins, hems, / where only we existed" (150).

Leyla marvels at human "solidity, / the warmth of . . . flesh, its smell"; she is like a heretofore cerebral person—perhaps a woman who is becoming aware of her lesbian desire—suddenly shocked by the intensity of corporeal sensuality. On the other hand, in a long passage of remarkable sensory acuity, the speaker describes how she is flooded by complex effects of synesthesia that accompany varieties of touch, opening, penetration, and interpenetration:

> Fog, she felt like dense fog,
> the color of smoke.
> She glowed, my hands paled then gleamed
> as I moved them over her.
> Smoke-fog pressing against my eyelids
> my mouth, ears, nostrils, navel.
> A cool tendril pressing between my legs
> entering.
> Her finger, I thought
> but it went on and on.
> At the same time
> an iciness touched my anus,
> and she was in
> and in and in
> my mouth opening
> I wasn't scared just astonished
> rain drummed against my spine
> turned to steam as it rushed through my veins
> light flickered over me from toe to crown.
>
> (150)

After the seemingly orgasmic, magical transformation of "rain . . . to steam," the speaker "notices" the most "alien" image of their coupling: "Looking down my body I saw / her forearm, elbow and hand / sticking out of my stomach / saw her hand slide in" (150). Her experience has been so intense, so transgressive of thresholds, that she "started hurting a little," then "started cramping," so Leyla "pushed out / her fingers, forearm, shoulder" and "stood before" her as a material presence, as though their lovemaking had enabled the speaker and Leyla to experience and reexperience the process of giving birth and of being born respectively.

Perhaps to stress that no love relationship can exist in isolation, apart from the less than perfect social sphere in which it occurs, the speaker rapidly teaches Leyla rudiments of functioning in the human world—including, ironically, an appreciation of "how humans love, hate" from TV—and "soon Leyla could pass, / go for milk at the bodega, count change" (151). Poignantly, her lover feels a loss of intensity in their relationship now that their meeting at the "interface"—and now, the coldness of the computer term can be appreciated—of two distinct subjectivities reveals less obvious, dramatic differences in their qualities: "But no matter how passionately we made / love / it was never like before / she'd taken on skin and bone" (151–52). Nevertheless, their meetings in the middle have not resulted in an obliteration of all differences. As the penultimate strophe reveals, the "alien" can still perform magical acts that enliven her lover's daily experience: "She had snow in the livingroom / and a tree in the bathtub" (152). Frustrated that she is not tall enough to reach "a high shelf," the speaker finds that Leyla has levitated her: "When my head touched the ceiling / I had to yell at her to stop, / reverse. / How do you do it, I asked her. / You do it, too, she said, / my species just does it faster, / by thinking it." Indeed, the poem's quirky narrative thrust playfully promotes a kind of "thinking" that would enable a dismantling of sociopolitical barriers to occur more quickly.

In the final strophe, when the speaker flies across the U.S. to "speak at a conference" yet is "short on cash" to bring her lover along, Leyla manages to maintain the illusion of her invisibility: "She walked past the flight attendants / didn't even have to hide in the lavatory. / She laughed at my amazement, said / humans only saw what they were told to see" (152). According to this perspective, the "interface" between the physical and the noumenal, between ordinary visibility (sanctioned by dominant social constructions) and that which is extraordinary and seemingly invisible, has constituted the love relationship since the beginning of the poetic narrative. The binary opposition between the two terms/realms is not an objective truth but a limiting construct. Challenging the opposition in a way parallel to lesbians' contestation of heterosexist demarcations of normal/abnormal, Leyla has "told" the speaker "to see" and feel an approximation of her own subjective reality without resorting to the distortion and reification of a fixed, abstract conceptual framework for it.

Given the abundance of critical ink spilled on the problematic of representation and the instability of "selves" or "subjects" in the past two decades, poets must be aware that the cultural force of their sincere attempts at *accurate visibility* can be appropriated, recontextualized (in distorting ways), and used against them and their communities by those who wish to preserve unequal power relations. Illustrating a (post-)colonialist dynamic in anthropology that informs numerous disciplinary and other social realms, Vietnamese-American critical theorist/filmmaker Trinh Minh-ha, who has cited the influence of Lorde on her thinking,[10] analyzes how the visibility produced by a "native's" self-representation can be (ab)used by colonizers who "desire 'to grasp the native's point of view' and 'to realize *his* vision of *his* world,' "[11] a "*knowledge*" of self that "the other" "cannot, supposedly, have" (66). Striving to fulfill the desire "to *own* the others' *minds*" and to provide the "others" "with a standard of self-evaluation on which they necessarily depend" (66), the anthropological seeker, Trinh states, must train "disciples" or "ideal Insiders" who will "busy themselves with [his] preoccupations and make themselves useful by asking the right kind of Question and providing the right kind of Answer" (68). This "ideal Insider" informant serves to comfort "the Master's self-other relationship in its enactment of power relations, gathering serviceable data, minding his/her own business-territory, and yet offering the difference expected" (68).[12]

My first chapter, "Problematizing Visibility: Thylias Moss, John Yau, and Denise Duhamel," explores poetic speculations about the subtle and unsubtle dangers, as well as the opportunities, of visual representations, whether they are being produced by marginalized groups or those who would assert their power over them. Like Trinh, who is hesitant to endorse the task "of merely 'correcting' the images whites have of non-whites" (72), since even relatively "accurate" visibility can be misused by dominant forces, Moss, Yau, and Duhamel do not attempt to argue for the validity of any fixed visual representations; instead, they engage, as Trinh puts it, in the labor "of tracking down and exposing the Voice of Power and Censorship . . . in whichever side it appears" (73). The destabilizing critique of a "gamut of fixed notions" based on a version of "essential difference"—which constitutes "censorship" of the fluid, untotalizable processes of self-elaboration of "othered" individuals and groups—challenges distortions without offering positive formulations.

Although Moss and Duhamel, unlike the even more experimentally inclined Yau, make extensive use of sensory description and relatively coherent storytelling, the strategic questioning of the discourse of visibility in their work is probably fueled by a skepticism about the possibility that a "true representation" of individual (or community) identities can exist. Calling the distinction between representations and misrepresentations "at best a matter of degree," since all "are embedded first in the language and then in the culture, institutions, and political ambience of the representer," Said in *Orientalism* holds that "some common history, tradition, universe of discourse" defines their "common field of play" (272–73). Moss, Yau, and Duhamel examine, parody, and demystify images forged in the seductive institution of U.S. pop culture. However, none of these poets seem tempted to measure these unsatisfactory and often ludicrous images against the norm or standard of a "true," complete picture.

HISTORY, EFFACEMENT, (RE)-TRACING, RECONSTRUCTION

The poetry discussed in chapter 2, "The Effacement, (Re)- tracing, and Reconstruction of History: Carolyn Forché, Joseph Lease, Martín Espada, and Gloria Anzaldúa," thematizes the erasure of histories of injustices against specific communities, the struggle to represent traces of what cannot be fully recovered, and the effort at overall restoration of community histories. Especially in the work of Forché and Lease, there is a dynamic interplay between the notions of erasure and trace. No matter how devastating, effacement is never total, and poets labor to discern, interpret, and make affirmative use of residues of history for the benefit of oppressed or war-stricken communities. While striving to recognize what cannot be recuperated—and Forché and Lease in particular make fragmentary aspects of their chosen aesthetic forms faithful to the actuality of erasure—the poets also seek to place traces in historical context, to recover bits of narrative or fuller narratives from other points of history to draw parallels between disparate experiences. They wish to facilitate acknowledgment of psychic wounds, empathic solidarity with those who share their losses, and a commitment to the vigilance that the work of freedom requires.

When I speak of poetic "reconstruction" of history, this involves both the *restoration* of history that others have tried to efface and the *reinterpretation* of historical material that dominant narratives have distorted. Espada and Anzaldúa both concentrate on violent displacement, discrimination, and economic disenfranchisement *and* on practices of resistance. The poets are aware that, if oppression is represented as all-pervasive and unremitting in a group's past and recent history, then readers within the marginalized community lose the hope that conditions could be improved, and so they take great pains in the ways they articulate resistance and, occasionally, something akin to "prophecy."

An early poem by Melvin Dixon, "Fingering the Jagged Grains," cogently illustrates the project of historical recovery through poetry.[13] Dixon's poems about his travels to Africa and about African-American cultural figures—predominantly in his first book, *Change of Territory* (1983)—reflect his own creative contribution to the ongoing project of the (re)construction of memory and the elaboration of alternative histories. "Fingering the Jagged Grains" assesses the cultural significance of the blues in light of the critical and creative work of three of Dixon's aesthetic forebears, Ralph Ellison, Albert Murray, and Romare Bearden, who "play on" each other like "a three-note chord. / Triptych and three part harmony" (55).

The poem's title and epigraph are taken from Ellison's essay "Richard Wright's Blues." Ellison calls "the blues . . . an impulse to keep the painful details and episodes of a brutal experience alive in one's aching consciousness, to finger its jagged grain, and to transcend it"; he adds, in a clause not cited by Dixon, that this transcendence involves "squeezing . . . a near-tragic, near-comic lyricism" from such suffering.[14] In the poem's fourth section, Dixon also quotes a clause from Ellison's 1968 essay "The Art of Romare Bearden": "Ellison on Painting: The problem for the plastic artist / is not one of telling but of *revealing* . . ." (55), which continues " . . . that which has been concealed by time, custom, and our trained incapacity to perceive the truth."[15] In Bearden's case, Ellison asserts, revelation is through "a reassembling" in forms which convey the "truth" of "the depth and wonder of the Negro American's stubborn humanity" (690) and the "ceremonial continuity" of "the Negro American community" as evidenced by "rituals of rebirth and dying, of baptism and sorcery" (691).

Dixon, again in his fourth section, cites Albert Murray's *Stomping the Blues*: "Stomp, stomp, stomping the blues. / 'Young men who become the heroes / do so by confronting and slaying dragons. /

Improvisation is the ultimate skill' " (55). Underscoring Ellison's notion of blues transcendence, Murray holds that the "most immediate concern" for one afflicted by the blues "is how to dislodge" these feelings through improvisation "before the botheration degenerates into utter hopelessness."[16] Though concerned "with the most disturbing aspects of life," blues music, Murray asserts, is supposed "to make people feel good" by inducing the pleasures of "dance movement" (45). In "The Visual Equivalent of the Blues," an essay on Bearden, Murray suggests that "A Bearden" is "emblematic" of "the fundamental rituals of the blues idiom and the way it conditions one to survive" with "one's humanity" and "sense of humor intact."[17] He praises Bearden's expression of "flexibility through elegant improvization" as a "stylishly heroic method of survival . . . under the pressure of all tempos, in response to all disjunctures and even in the face of impending nothingness" (26).

The first section of Dixon's poem shows how Murray, Bearden, and blues musicians' "discourses" on trains (and the blues urge toward transcendence) play off one another: "Blue notes from Baltimore and Charlotte, N.C. / Albert Murray riffing on Bearden's / long vamp to his own fast train, / a whistling northbound steel-smoking hound" (51). As Murray notes in *Stomping the Blues*, African-American blues music and dancers' "locomotion" have been influenced not only by the form and spirit of strivings for transcendence at "the downhome church" but also by "the old smoke-chugging railroad-train engine," which evokes, among other major American images, "the mostly metaphorical Underground Railroad that the Fugitive Slaves took from the House of Bondage to the Promised Land of Freedom" (124). Murray, who met Bearden in Paris in 1950, engaged in several collaborative efforts with the artist.[18] For example, in 1978, when Bearden developed a collage series inspired by "anecdotal memories of his childhood in Mecklenburg County and his youth in Pittsburgh," he and Murray, reports Myron Schwartzman, "collaborated on a series of short narratives . . . which Bearden would write on the walls of the large . . . gallery" (264). Murray developed "a narrative style for" Bearden's "recollections of specific people and scenes"; one narrative includes lines cited by Dixon about the notion that "passenger trains" were considered "good trains."[19]

Alluding to Bearden's 1981 Brooklyn Museum retrospective and the musical performance at the opening reception,[20] Dixon conveys the excitement of African-American collaboration and cultural cross-reference:

Teddy Wilson and son heat up on piano
and bass, fingering Ellington's A train
back through Catfish Row. Upstairs the melody
is Bearden playing Bearden: *Out Chorus, Tenor Spot,*
Stomping at the Savoy and *Carolina Shout,*
calling up J. P. Johnson and baptism in the Pee Dee.

(51)

Bearden Plays Bearden is a 1980 documentary film on the artist produced by Third World Cinema.[21] Just as Bearden is "calling up" the
spiritual acuity of masterful blues and jazz musicians—for example,
"stride pianist" J. P. Johnson[22]—in numerous artworks, including
the ones that Dixon lists, musicians (and the music scholar/critic
Murray) return the favor, and the poet imagines the performance of
a musical ensemble consisting of "fast-tracking Scooter" as conductor, Maudell Sleet, the women from Bearden's childhood whom he
painted several times, as singer, and Ellison's character Rinehart in
Invisible Man "[soloing] up from underground" (51).

Troping on Murray's statement about "the prevalence of ritual,"
Dixon indicates how the three cultural figures he is honoring have
participated elegantly in a collective project, the ritual that gets hold
of the blues and, in so doing, celebrates the capacity of African
Americans to transcend it: "It is the elegance of ritual: Bearden,
Ellison / and Murray cutting the jagged grains: patchwork / figures
in silhouette, blue notes in calico / and quilting under glass. *What*
did I do / to be so black and blue?" (52). Bearden's part in the ritual is
the labor of collage, linked here and in part 2 with the traditional
African-American (women's) art of quilting:

Electric blue, fire
and fuschia in the sky. Lightning, lonesome blue.
Cut out legs, fingers and bebop eyes
shape the uncreated features of face and race.
Found objects of the territory:
Mecklenberg County to Harlem and back.
Cloth and color in piano stride.

(52)

Bearden literally "cuts" and artfully reassembles—on "grainy"
wood or canvasboard—"found objects" that figure "the jagged grains"
of his experiences in black communities, from the North Carolina of
his early childhood, to Harlem, where he grew to adulthood, "and

back." (Material elements of the composition often have "jagged" edges.) Dixon's description of color, especially the powerful "fuschia in the sky," evokes *Carolina Shout* (1974), in which eight figures crowd around each other, uniting in jubilant song, and *Solo Flight* (1979), which, as Schwartzman states, renders "a valve trombonist in profile" (275).[23] Although the only thing a "black" person in the U.S. must "do" to be "blue" is to have "lived," the energy evinced by Bearden's vibrant color combinations, his ensemble of textures, and the vibrant rhythm of the spatial arrangement of collage elements, including "bebop eyes," make "the jagged grains" erupt in song.

In the poem's second section, Dixon "riffs on" how Bearden's representation of women like Maudell Sleet, whose collaged hands are supernaturally gigantic, literally illustrates the principle in the poem's title. Not only do Bearden's collages and photomontages include "faces cut from Benin masks with jaws / carved out of hunger and loss and joy," but the African-American "women in gardens, bathing from washtubs, / or just making love with those great huge hands" elegantly produce their own regenerative blues forms out "of Carolina quilting and African weaves" (53). In such masterful collages as *Patchwork Quilt* (1970) and the mural *Quilting Time* (1985),[24] the cosmopolitan artist influenced by (predominantly male and European) modernist contributions to the visual arts pays tribute to the equally powerful aesthetic influence of his African-American females.

Analyzing *Invisible Man* in his book of criticism, *Ride Out the Wilderness* (1987), Dixon contrasts African-American life "aboveground, where it is subject to societal guises such as those adopted by Rinehart,"[25] and the protagonist's profound "underground" experience. "The boomerang," for Dixon, is "a metaphor for the passage and progress of the hero" (73). In the third section of "Fingering the Jagged Grains," Rinehart, who is always "round the corner and back again" (54), himself stands as a figure of the performance of "boomerang." As a trickster, Rinehart offers a response to the blues that parallels, if somewhat sinisterly, the collagistic, improvisatory sensibilities of the cultural figures whom Dixon has been lauding and the strategies of the poem itself: "Faceless picaro cool-strutting through collage, / you smoked glasses and high-water threads, / fedora hat and patent leather dogs, you midnight / indigo of mood and magic, act cut from sack-cloth / shadow: Ellison playing Bearden playing Ellison" (54). Rinehart's movement is as unpredictable as the next pattern in a blues or jazz riff. *Invisible Man*'s protagonist muses about Rinehart's ability to assume multiple identities like "Rine the runner and Rine the gambler and Rine the briber and Rine the lover and Rine the Reverend," to "be both rind and heart"—indeed, to make "his world . . . possibility" (486–87).

Affirming the "world" of African-American artistic "possibility," Dixon's fifth section reiterates his thesis about the multisensory experience of aesthetic "ritual" that re-presents and struggles heroically to "prevail" over a collective history of blues: "Those hands cut from paper bag groceries and grace, / those hands opening like lips on a blues, / finger the jagged grains of a long, long, long / remembered time" (56). The poet urges the reader to engage fully with this tradition, with African-American history, and the final alliteration evinces once more a belief in the powerful confluence of individual psychological and moral strength, cultural awareness, and aesthetic strategies of assemblage: "Rinehart, Scooter, and Maudell Sleet: / Character, Consciousness, and Collage." This is a potent retort to "well-meaning" people who see African-American history *solely* as one long string of dehumanization, battering at the hands of racist violence, and reactive protest, or to those who dismiss black American culture.

The challenge to reconstitute largely erased or marginalized histories—which, for African Americans, as Vincent Harding notes, "has always been created and renewed in the matrix of" their "freedom movement" from the time "men and women were telling and retelling their stories" in preparation for "rebellions on the slave ships and prison ships of the Middle Passage"[26]—was brought to unprecedented public awareness in the U.S. through the events leading to the founding of ethnic and women's studies programs and the rise of these programs in the early seventies. In 1967, recalls Japanese American historian Gary Y. Okihiro, "on the campus of the San Francisco State College, black and other minority students" entered into sixteen months of fruitless negotiation with administrators about their demands for a Department of Black Studies, and then, along with "Chicano, American Indian, and Asian American students," initiated a "strike"—soon supported by numerous members of the community, including whites—"in protest of the historic and systematic exclusion of minorities from higher education, both in admissions and in the curriculum."[27] They insisted that "the study of American history and society . . . must . . . derive from the perspective of those" excluded "communities" (4). After several months, the administration relented.

A similar struggle (and victory) occurred at the University of California, Berkeley, in early 1968, and activist students at various other campuses followed suit. Carlos Muñoz Jr. states that "the first Department of Mexican American Studies in the nation was created in the fall of 1968 at California State College, Los Angeles, as a result of demands by" a Chicano group "on that campus," and "even before" the celebrated 1969 Santa Barbara "conference," where a plan for Chicano political struggles and goals for empowerment within academia was devised, "student activists, working with sympathetic faculty and staff," established a basis for "Mexican American or Raza [Race] Studies programs at several California campuses during the 1968–69 academic year."[28] Glòria Anzaldúa's later literary efforts to challenge distortion of Chicana/o history might well be traced to what was accomplished in Chicano Studies during this period. Although Martín Espada was not yet in high school in 1970, the development of Puerto Rican Studies on the other coast was surely an enabling factor in the development of his poetic thinking about Puerto Rican history. Josephine Nieves and five coauthors write, "in 1969, in the wake of campus upheaval, a New York City Board of Higher Education resolution conceded" that the City University would establish Black and Puerto Rican Studies programs.[29] Nieves et al. note that Puerto Rican Studies is deeply informed by "the context of the Island's colonial relationship to the United States" and its impact on migration to urban areas.

African-American feminist historian Darlene Clark Hine cites the year 1970 as a profound point of transition, since, after National Guards killed students at Kent State, "the American educational enterprise experienced the greatest student and faculty strike in its history," and "the education industry," facing the specter of "possible student rage" *and* "the violence of unchecked state power," "confronted its weaknesses and admitted vulnerability."[30] These events engendered "a decade-long negotiation" by "students, faculty, and administrators" about "structure, nature, and content of the curriculum" that made possible "a proliferation of black studies, women's studies, and ethnic studies programs, departments, and centers" (7). Chinese American historian Sucheng Chan states that "in the late 1960s and early 1970s" Asian American Studies programs "were started at several dozen colleges and universities on the Pacific Coast."[31]

Because advocates for such new programs as Asian American and Women's Studies, as Chan observes, sought curricula involving "an incisive analysis of the history of racism, sexism, and class oppression in the United States; an accurate portrayal of the contributions and struggles of people of color; and practical training to enable graduates to bring about fundamental social change in their ethnic communities as well as in society at large," these "programs encountered stiff resistance from curriculum and personnel review committees. A number folded, while others managed to stay afloat but did not grow" (181).[32] Often, university management used the rationalization of budget constraints to assail such programs.[33]

While Hine points out that "the fiscal crises of the 1980s triggered the demise of many of the new programs" and the refusal of traditional scholars to tenure "many black, women, and minority faculty" (8), she perceives, in the nineties, a powerful "impact of feminist and black scholarship"—and, work by other people of color—on the discipline of history, which now "pays considerable attention not only to women but also to social relationships and the construction of gender systems, to issues of race, to the concerns of the poor" (9–10), and so on. (The same point applies to various other disciplines in the humanities.) According to Chan, "in the late 1980s," a resurgence of Asian American Studies programs was occasioned by "students at an increasing number of colleges . . . demanding a more multiethnic curriculum" (181). "Young Asian Americans," she says, wish to "articulate sensibilities that arise directly out of the historical experience and contemporary life circumstances of Asians in America," and "Asian American Studies courses" comprise the locus where such an articulation is made manifest and "encouraged." Henry L. Minton asserts that "gay and lesbian studies," already embodied in the work of significant practitioners in the seventies, "is coming of age in the 1990s"; he points to a recent abundance of research in the area and to the establishment of Lesbian and Gay Studies Centers at Yale in 1986 and the City University of New York in 1990, and a department at the City College of San Fransisco in 1988.[34]

Some measure of the cultural influence of those struggling for the recuperation of previously occluded histories can be located in conservative (and sometimes neoliberal) resistance to their projects. As Japanese American historian Ronald Takaki states in a 1993 article, "conservative critics" like Allan Bloom, Arthur Schlesinger Jr., and Dinesh D'Souza utilize "McCarthyite tactics" of precritical name-calling and vague evocations of "intellectual freedom and excellence" that impose "their own intellectual orthodoxy" and bespeak an unwillingness "to open the debate and introduce students to different viewpoints."[35] Takaki observes how "conservative foundations" tend to finance "projects to promote their own political agenda" on U.S. campuses" (118). In the eighties U.S. cultural sphere, President

Ronald Reagan's media presence and foreign and domestic policies had a pervasive impact on the rejuvenation of the erasure of history. Arguing that "the Reagan regime put America back together again by exploiting and disavowing the 1960s," Michael Rogin identifies the deployment of a "covert spectacle" that "reflects the persistence of dreams about American dominance in the face of the erosion of the material and ideological sources for American preeminence in the world."[36] Prior to the late eighties' improvement of relations with the Soviet Union, the administration pursued costly "efforts at symbolic recovery that center[ed] around military and national security" (116).

Since, as Rogin argues, "theatrical events—Grenada invasion, Libyan bombing, Persian Gulf flagging, Honduran 'show of force' " and the paradoxical "covert spectacle" of U.S. aid to the Nicaraguan contras were "staged for public consumption" (116), President Reagan needed to combat evidence of imperialist dimensions of past and present U.S. foreign policy, as well as proof of long-standing inequalities in the nation's internal affairs, that would undermine the equation of U.S. military strength with moral rectitude. (This is also true of President Bush, whose rhetoric during the U.S.-Iraqi War will be examined briefly in chapter 3's discussion of Stephen Paul Miller.) In his January 1989 "Farewell Address to the Nation," Reagan lauds "the new patriotism," a "resurgence of national pride" that occurred "in the past eight years," but then calls for a "reinstitutionalization" of this "spirit": "We've got to do a better job of getting across that America is freedom—freedom of speech, freedom of religion, freedom of enterprise. And freedom is special and rare."[37] To combat the threat of "an eradication of the American memory that could result, ultimately, in the erosion of the American spirit," Reagan calls for the teaching of "history based not on what's in fashion but what's important: Why the Pilgrims came here, who Jimmy Doolittle was, and what those thirty seconds over Tokyo meant" (417). For Reagan, teaching history would involve the tendency that Howard Zinn finds (in so many of his fellow European-American historians) to include scattered historical details or observations that mark a ruling class's atrocious conduct "and then bury them in a mass of other information" that admits that "mass murder took place, but it's not that important—it should weigh very little in our final judgments; it should affect very little what we do in the world."[38] In his insistence upon the equation of "America" and "Freedom," Reagan must ignore "fierce conflicts of interest (sometimes exploding, most often repressed) between conquerors and conquered, masters and slaves, capitalists and workers, dominators and dominated in race and sex" (9–10).[39]

COALITION AND COMMUNITY

As my discussion of President Reagan's speech on the teaching of history suggests, the president attempted to formulate a sense of American community by masking the disunities in U.S. political life— that is, the conflicts among various groups. For example, in keeping with his attacks on affirmative action and government spending on social programs, his public pronouncements, like those of his successor George Bush, tended to assert that racism is a thing of the past. In the prefatory comments to the published version of a 1983 speech on Martin Luther King Jr., Reagan argues that "national black leaders" who support "big-government . . . thinking" have hindered "the independence and aspirations of many black Americans" (163). In the speech itself, Reagan states that King "tumbled the wall of racism in our country" and adds that the Civil Rights leader "in many ways, . . . freed the white man" by teaching "the principles of love and non-violence" (166). Reagan camouflages the "wall," the persistance of racism, which has not "tumbled."

Some might argue that, in the pragmatic politics of Bill Clinton's centrist neoliberalism, a similar silencing of racial issues in the name of American community has occurred. Always a pragmatist, Clinton has been saddled throughout his presidency with either a Republican majority in both houses of Congress or enough Republicans to block the passage of traditionally "liberal" measures that he might have otherwise supported. Further, his capitulation to the other party's pressure for "welfare reform" might be considered a way of warding off the passage of even more conservative measures. The point relevant to the context of U.S. social poetry is that, in the nineties, the Reagan/Bush concept of "American community," which ironically excludes the concerns of many who are nominally deemed part of it, retained much of the cultural force that it possessed in the previous decade.

The poets treated in my third and final chapter, "Probings of Coalition and Broad Community: Melvin Dixon, Joseph Lease, Stephen Paul Miller, and Gloria Anzaldúa," not only stand in opposition to the right-wing sense of "American community," but ponder how communities seeking a greater share of power in U.S. (and world) society can test the viability of strategic alliances with other groups, as well as the vision of a truly inclusive sense of collectivity. Cultural theorist Lisa Lowe, finding both strengths and "limitations inherent in a politics based on cultural, racial, or ethnic identity,"[40] stresses "incommensurate and heterogeneous" aspects of "the Asian American community and other racialized and immigrant communities" to suggest that "cultural politics" can be recast "so as to account for a multiplicity of various, nonequivalent racialized groups" (70). While "Asian Americans can" collectively "articulate distinct challenges and demands based on particular histories of exclusion and racialization," Lowe holds that "the redefined lack of closure" emphasizing "differences" of class, gender, and other variables, "opens political lines of affiliation with other groups in the challenge to specific forms of domination insofar as they share common features."

Judith Butler cautions against the project of figuring "the . . . form . . . of an emerging and unpredictable assemblage of positions"—for example, among diverse feminists—"in advance."[41] Butler questions "efforts to determine . . . the true shape of a dialogue, what constitutes a subject-position, and, most importantly, when 'unity' has been reached" (14), since "a coalition" might need "to acknowledge its contradictions and take action with those contradictions intact"; further, "dialogic understanding" might include "acceptance of divergence, breakage, splinter, and fragmentation as part of the often tortuous process of democratization" (14–15). Butler argues for "the assumption of [the] essential incompleteness" of the category of "woman" and against a "unity" which would engender intricate disagreements that threaten to postpone broad collective action (15). Therefore, "provisional unities might emerge in the context of concrete actions" not focused on "identity," and "an open coalition" can "affirm identities that are alternately instituted and relinquished according to the purposes at hand"; "multiple convergences and divergences" may occur "without obedience to a normative telos of definitional closure" (16).

Perhaps Butler's notion of the temporary character of alliances and the apparent absence of an enduring ideological common ground would destabilize a "critical mass" needed for a thorough, progressive social transformation. Charles Altieri seeks the correlation of "a strong sense of individual will with a model of social alignment that provides an alternative to seeing society as the irreducible clash among wills to power."[42] Altieri adds that "we . . . find almost

inescapable the hope that we can develop the framework necessary for making . . . disparate wills intelligible to one another and
assessable by one another" (129). Cornel West valorizes the figure of
the "jazz freedom fighter" who practices "an improvisational mode
of protean, fluid, and flexible dispositions toward reality," and who
fosters an "interplay of individuality and unity" embodying "conflict
among diverse groupings that reach a dynamic consensus subject to
questioning and criticism"; "*creative* tension with the group . . . yields
higher levels of performance to achieve the aim of the collective
project."[43]

For bell hooks, the project's aim is "a culture where *beloved community*"—as broad a conception of community as possible—"flourishes
and is sustained."[44] Calling upon people "who know the joy of being
with folks from all walks of life, all races, who are fundamentally antiracist in their habits of being . . . to give public testimony" and illustrate "conditions of change that make such an experience possible,"
hooks declares that the "generous spirit of affirmation" of differences "gives" those committed to "*beloved community*" "the courage
to challenge one another, to work through" racial and other "mis-
understandings" (272). "Profound commitment to a shared vision"
and the celebration of "cultural hybridity" can create a "solidarity and
trust" to withstand fragmenting forces that stem from unequal power
relations. Democratic social transformation, then, can come from
the multiplication and linking of small communities based on strenuous effort to put an ideal into practice: "If that longing guides our
vision and our actions, the new culture will be born and antiracist"—
and one might add, anticlassist, antisexist, and antiheterosexist—
"communities of resistance will emerge everywhere."[45]

In the eighties, the presidential candidacy of Jesse Jackson and
the concept of his "Rainbow Coalition" may be seen, by some, as
close to Lowe or Butler's sense of coalition and, by others, to hooks's
notion of *broadly inclusive community-building*. According to Sheila
D. Collins, "the emergence of the Jackson campaign in 1984 as a
progressive, black-led, multiracial, anticorporate, and anti-imperialist
movement that took an electoral form must be appreciated as a daring and visionary innovation," especially since "it occurred during"
the Reagan years, "a time of resurgent racist violence and public
retrenchment."[46] In a campaign speech, Jackson draws inferences
that no Democratic or Republican presidential candidate of the
eighties (and few in the nineties) would dare express; he attributes
devastating U.S. unemployment trends to the fact that "multinational

corporations . . . have sought higher profits elsewhere at the expense of your communities."[47] "*Our present foreign policy,*" he exclaims, "*serves no one but multinational corporations seeking cheap labor markets abroad*" (314). He also notes that "today 1 percent of all manufacturers control 88 percent of manufacturing assets and make 90 percent of all manufacturing profits," that "last year 90,000 corporations that made profits paid no taxes," and that, whereas "before World War II, corporate income taxes accounted for 34 percent of all federal receipts," the current figure is "no more than 13 percent" (313).

Thylias Moss's poem, "Tribute to Jesse and Then Some," which appears in *Small Congregations,* provides an excellent illustration of how Jackson raised vital issues of coaliton and community in the eighties. In the first two strophes of the poem, Moss portrays drastic economic distinctions and presents an implicit seconding of Jackson's critique of corporate irresponsibility that is intentionally somewhat crude and yet discerning:

> Sometimes the only dignity is in walking the streets
> in Goodwill shoes that once upon a time transported
> other feet to club dates and charity luncheons
> where the future is at the discretion of stock brokers
> who treat the crystal ball, fragile as the world,
> like a piñata at a Mexican theme benefit. They say
> *ole* and *salud* when they toast. The light, dim
>
> as their idea of poverty is yellower, antique
> when the vintage alcohol glazes the blood coursing
> like liquid rats. This is called a buzz. This
> is likened to the charitable work of bees, pollen
> pushing, a powder fine as dream sugar, that soft
> palette of heroin or innocent double, Block Drug
> Company's BC powders folded into waxed paper sleeves
> and so suspicious you're better off feeling the neuralgia,
> keeping sciatica's ache[48]

Moss plays on the similarity of "the future" and "futures," uses the term "stock brokers" to refer, not merely to literal agents of (ex) change, but to financial power brokers in a broader sense, alludes to the notion of "discretionary income" through the future-linked noun "discretion," and creates a visual/conceptual analogy among the abused piñata, the spherical trope of financial (and other) speculation, and the environmentally polluted world. Through all of this complex troping, Moss follows Jackson's much more specific analyses, not only in making causal connections among spheres of endeavor and social conditions that Reaganites would keep hidden, but in giving voice to deep frustration felt by those wearing others' "Goodwill shoes," as well as the frightened working and middle classes, about a small corporate plutocracy's indifference to their needs. Like Jackson, the only candidate in 1984 who assailed U.S. corporations' investment in South Africa's apartheid-tainted regime,[49] Moss indicates through such tropes as the smashed piñata that a Eurocentric arrogance—a cultural and economic imperialism—informs multinational corporate instrumental reason. Her corporate luminaries flit through their "theme benefits" with amused condescension toward the appropriated postcolonial ("third world") cultures whose economic resources they exploit. Troping deftly on the cliche, "drunk with power," the poet likens these privileged individuals' "idea of poverty" to the impairment of judgment resulting from the pleasure of "vintage alcohol." Due to the exposure of a phonological reason for a tropological pattern, this pleasurable "buzz" is connected to the hard work of drones, a labor ironically termed "charitable" because it is meagerly compensated.

The poet's reading of the working poor's involuntary "charity" to the rich (in the eighties economic scene) seems to fit Immanuel Wallerstein's contention that practitioners of "the endless accumulation of capital," the "law" of "historical capitalism," have increasingly created "conditions wherein the others have been forced to conform to the patterns or to suffer the consequences."[50] Whereas plutocrats, according to Moss's speaker, express their largesse ("Goodwill") by making voluntary charitable contributions to "causes" as a perfunctory afterthought, or for tax breaks, many low-income workers responsible for basics of production have the nonchoice of dronish, physically debilitating labor or unemployment (and even greater poverty). Moss's reversal exposes a "flood-up" actuality behind the Reaganomic "trickle-down" theory. Against the conservative notion of welfare as undeserved charity, Moss exclaims: "Welfare is about as charitable as America gets / with its limbo stick rules of income to make you / crawl" (121). The welfare recipient has to diminish her/himself by "crawling" under the "limbo stick" of income limits that are often harshly unrealistic, especially in times of inflation. Due to scant job opportunities and other social factors affected by racism, s/he is placed in a "limbo" from which escape can be extremely difficult.

Next, the speaker commences her "tribute" to the first major

African-American presidential contender by reporting to the reader
and "the king" what "Jesse said":

> . . . that *Jesus was born homeless*
> *to a single mother* like her counterparts
> cloistered in the projects, alleys, subway tunnels,
> forsaken buses, tenement nunneries, the order of Mary,
> all of them with God-solicited child again and again,
> *our father still art in heaven* so he can't pay child
> support but *thy will be done* anyway.
>
> (121)

First admiring how Jackson plays on a typically dehumanizing image
of an African-American female welfare recipient by placing her in the
context of a Christian image exalted by many Americans,[51] Moss's
speaker reveals a previously repressed feminist implication of the
story. A poor, single mother is often victimized by the fact that the
father of the child is "in heaven" because of inner city violence,
in the pseudo-"heaven" of drug addiction, or any form of escape
made attractive by harsh living conditions and the difficulties of
finding "the work that deserves / pride, that doesn't depend on
people spending, using / wasting, destroying" (121–22). Troping on
"immaculate conception" and indicating Joseph's peripheral status,
Moss asserts that, since Mary is not privileged by God but cut off
from economic support that a present, employed "husband" would
provide, this narrative situation reflects Christian institutions' patriarchal biases. (Jackson, on the other hand, sees no conflict between a
socially redemptive version of Christianity and feminist values, since
he is a Christian minister.)

Turning to the short-term hedonism of drug use and its deadly
depletion of African-American resources, Moss's speaker laments the
many "pipers in the neighborhood" who make "every child . . . likely
to hear the music he can't resist / and groove and hip hop his way
into stone, the mausoleum / of a mountain" (122). This reference
pays implicit tribute to Jackson's role in raising this concern;[52] Moss
parodies his rhymes about location denoting elevation—for example,
"run from the outhouse to the statehouse to the courthouse to the
White House"[53]—with a series of nouns of location denoting a downward spiral about "everyone want[ing] to go home, to the sweet, the
humble, / the whorehouse, crackhouse, poorhouse." Since corporate
manipulation of consumer culture breeds self-defeating behavior by
preying on otherwise positive values like psychological uplift and the

seeking of "roots," the speaker recycles a hollow advertising phrase and again puns on the term "stock" (including self-examination, general value, and "stock brokers'" profiteering at the expense of countless others): " . . . grab some gusto if you can, and if you take stock / in gusto. Otherwise, forget it."

The concluding strophe of Moss's "Tribute" resounds with a set of grim ironies that elude the dangers of manufactured "gusto":

> Sometimes scrubbing the rounded front end of the toilet
> is like polishing a trophy, a miniature of the winning
> yacht. Flush and there's even tides. Steady, steady—
> good; the boat doesn't budge, the anchor is mighty, of
> brooding iron clenching river bottom dirt that's
> being worked on by the water, readied for the making
> of men, the hope of all dirt since that first time. And
> no, hope is not better than nothing; they're about
> the same. But keep it alive anyway, vegetative, attached
> to a machine.
>
> (122)

The wonderfully farfetched yet visually apt analogy between the lofty "yacht" and debased "toilet" shows a quixotic straining to overcome constipated possibility, ceaseless drudgery, and severe social barriers through fantasy. Mimicking fifties' and sixties' advertising pitches for domestic products, the speaker parodies the expectation that middle-class housewives should repress anger at their second-class citizenship and be grateful for modern technology that would save them so much time and energy and help them fulfill their roles.

Echoing Jackson's call to "keep hope alive" during his 1988 Democratic Convention address,[54] the speaker expresses pessimism about the dream that U.S. society will transform lopsided power relations into anything resembling equality. While some patients in a "vegetative" state are eventually restored to a modicum of health, this "miracle" is rare. If "hope" depends upon the whims of a political "machine," and if grass-roots movements have scant influence on national politics, then perhaps "hope" is "about / the same" as "nothing." For Moss, writing near the end of twelve years of conservative Republican control of the White House, bell hooks's notion of "*beloved community*" is distant. However, this "tribute to Jesse" leaves open the possibility that many might come to endorse and join further efforts to use the "water" of compassion and left-liberal ideology to rid the U.S. *socius* of racist, sexist, and classist "dirt." And Moss's poetic resistance to established hierarchies proclaims that psychopolitical euthanasia is not in order.

Like Moss, the poets whose work is examined in chapter 3 are ever mindful of the polarizations of the current sociopolitical climate and the burdensome accretions of history, and so they do not muster the utopian zeal of some literary proponents of the sixties' counter-culture. Instead, sometimes sharing hooks's "longing" for "beloved community," they carefully and lucidly question how a fundamental core of shared ideology can (and cannot) be conceptualized, rhetorically situated, put into circulation, and constituted as a basis for transformative action.

1

Problematizing Visibility: Thylias Moss, John Yau, and Denise Duhamel

THE RECENT WINNER OF A COVETED MACARTHUR "GENIUS" GRANT, Thylias Moss has written a body of tropologically complex and unsettling, wickedly humorous poetry that contests the absurdly inadequate ways in which her fellow African Americans have been represented in U.S. pop culture, Christian religious institutions, and elsewhere, and situates visibility as a problem that relative accuracy might not solve. Born in 1954, the year of the Supreme Court's landmark verdict *Brown vs. Board of Education,* Moss has published six books of poetry. Her first collection was *Hosiery Seams on a Bowlegged Woman* (1983), and her most recent books are *Small Congregations: New and Selected Poems* (1993), and *Last Chance for the Tarzan Holler* (1998). She has also authored a memoir, *Tale of a Sky-Blue Dress* (1998).[1]

Moss tends to choose pop culture topoi from the first half of the twentieth century as material to confront in her poetry, since those earlier tropes and images have continued to affect the U.S. collective psyche. After the promise of the Civil Rights movement and Black Power and Black Arts, social setbacks for a majority of African Americans during the Reagan/Bush era seem to have occasioned a return, in black letters, to the problematic of in/visibility found, not only in Ellison's great novel, but in works ranging from W. E. B. DuBois's *The Souls of Black Folk* (1903) to Nobel Laureate Toni Morrison's *The Bluest Eye* (1970).[2] In "Lessons from a Mirror"—a poem in *Pyramid of Bone* (1989) not reprinted in *Small Congregations*—Moss probes the uses of "Snow White" as a heavy-handed advertisement for Caucasian supremacy and African-American women's invisibility.[3]

We do not know whether Moss is alluding to the Grimm Brothers' nineteenth-century text about Snow White, the twentieth-century American appropriation which has come to overshadow it, or both.[4]

However, the second possibility is a stronger one, since, as Patricia A. Turner shows, the Disney version transforms the Grimm tale by developing imagery that deploys the racially charged binary opposition that Moss's poem critiques. Whereas the Grimm text has "references to dark colors," the Disney movie features the treacherous stepmother wearing "a flowing black cape . . . and a black turban," and during the audience's first glimpse of Snow White, she "is surrounded by white doves. Soon 'her Prince' rides up on a white horse."[5] Turner adds that "the light/goodness and the dark/evil pattern continues throughout the movie," especially with the drastic contrast between what goes on in "the bright light of day" and "the dark forest" (110), and observes the ubiquity of such patterns in the Disney establishment's subsequent work and that of its many imitators (112).

In "Lessons from a Mirror," Snow White's "nudity," resulting from the illusion of white-on-white (as though *living* Caucasians' skin really resembles snow!), is the figure for a unification of visual effects that unsubtly promotes the cherished value of "whiteness" and its dramatic difference from "blackness" in the socially fabricated aesthetic pattern: "Snow White was nude at her wedding, she's so white / the gown seemed to disappear when she put it on. // Put me beside her and the proximity is good / for a study of chiaroscuro, not much else" (3). The speaker is exasperated at the overkill in the compressed simile "Snow White" because it links white skin, purity, and beauty. The seemingly empirical notion of "appearance" is tied to the imposition of cultural regularities that would make African Americans insubstantial afterthoughts of Euro-American "substance": "Her name aggravates me most, as if I need to be told / what's white and what isn't. // Judging strictly by appearance there's a future for me / forever at her heels, a shadow's constant worship." "Judging strictly by" this "appearance" is not natural or imbued with common sense, and the speaker's rhetorical question—"Is it fair for me to live this way, unable / to get off the ground?"—rejects a "shadow" status, a "flattened" representation that helps keep her people as a whole on the socioeconomic "ground."

The speaker can imagine "turning the tables," a reversal of the pernicious hierarchy, but realizes that it "isn't fair unless they keep turning." While some might consider individual financial and social "destinies" in the U.S. a matter of chance like "the danger of Russian Roulette," the African-American speaker perceives her "disadvantage: nothing falls from the sky to name me" (3). One who is figured as an absence because of the cultural uses made of visibility must contest the ludicrously arbitrary figuration of the celestial association that bolsters "white" skin privilege, and, in the last three couplets, the speaker does so by "turning tables," dramatically shifting *all* attention away from Snow White and toward herself. The "tongue" of demystifying language "rushes to fill" the "vacancies"—gaps in understanding and foolish racist images—that the speaker "can't stand": "I am the empty space where the tooth was, that my tongue / rushes to fill because I can't stand vacancies. // And it's not enough. The penis just fills another / gap. And it's not enough." Discourse is "not enough" since it may lack the "teeth," the psychological and political solidity to break down the damage done by an egregious flood of cultural advertising like the Disney *Snow White,* and the presumption that the gap in equality experienced by women can be "filled" by sexual intercourse with a man is absurd.

When Moss's speaker concludes the poem by refusing to name what is missing from others' perception of her, she ironically tropes on her prior assertion that she "can't stand vacancies" by *not* filling one for the reader: "When you look at me, / know that more than white is missing" (3). If various significances of "black" and specific characteristics of the speaking subject are "missing" "when" others "look at [her]," she will not assume the task of developing and positing her own construction of her visibility as an "authentic," accurate totality; this, too, is vulnerable to disfiguring misprision, amid a plethora of others' cultural misrepresentations. Thus, the "lesson" in "Lessons" may involve the practice of an ongoing suspicion about how unequal power relations influence the functioning of "mirrors," of *the discourse of visibility.*

In "A Little Something for Buckwheat and Other Pickaninnies," a poem first published in *At Redbones* (1990), Moss turns to a well-known emblem of the defacing visibility of African-American children in the U.S. mainstream at midcentury.[6] Not only does Moss play on the connection between the name of this token black character in the popular TV series *The Little Rascals* and the breakfast food advertised on television, but she stresses how the media's visual representation of Buckwheat—"sometimes . . . a girl and ugly. / Sometimes . . . a boy and ugly"—is intended to inculcate the idea that blackness is an eternal confinement and liability and to encourage whites to laugh at this pathetic "fact":

> Look at the kite strings of your hair
> tied into knots like balls and chains.
> Does Mammy know about this?

Some people have you (or your brother Farina)
for breakfast, drown you in milk, shower you
with cinnamon's rusty rain, dredge you
with a grainy web of sugar.

(108)

Obviously, adult African Americans like the equally maligned "Mammy" *do* "know about this." During the time of the original "Our Gang" short movie series—the post-Depression thirties and the wartime forties—and during the pre–Civil Rights movement ethos of *The Little Rascals,* they lacked the social power to combat the unkempt image of Buckwheat's tresses, even as they were aware of how "African ways" have included the orderly, hygienically sound art of braiding for centuries: "Buckwheat, I honor you / and what was explained as / African ways. // What did they know / of the comfort of a flour sack, / those who designed your costume, / seeking a match / for the discomfort assumed / you felt wearing your skin?" (108). Perhaps Moss honors "Buckwheat's" appealing personality, his *lack* of "discomfort" about the "skin" that others perceive him to be "wearing," which may undermine, if only partially, the visual/auditory caricature that has been foisted on him.[7]

"Birmingham Brown's Turn," the longest poem in *Small Congregations,* impressively demonstrates Moss's ability to take hold of fatuous pop culture depictions of African Americans (and also, in this case, Asians) and to ring rhetorically powerful changes on these denigrations. Moss's rhetorical play in this and numerous other poems stands (or moves) solidly within the African-American literary, musical, and general verbal tradition of "signifyin(g)." Noting that "scholars . . . have often taken [a] part" of the multivalent concept of signifying "as its whole,"[8] Henry Louis Gates Jr. in *The Signifying Monkey: A Theory of Afro-American Literary Criticism* demonstrates that among the forms of signifying can be found equivalents of what in the European tradition are termed irony, synecdoche, metonymy, hyperbole, litotes, metaphor, and metalepsis (87). For Gates, the "importance" of the "signifying monkey tales," a potent set of examples of signifying, lies "in their repeated stress on the sheer materiality, and the willful play, of the signifier itself"; such "play" is socially motivated, embodying "chiastic fantasies of reversals of power relationships" (59).

In general, African-American signifying involves parody and/or pastiche, both of which are to be found in "Birmingham Brown's Turn." Originally published in *Rainbow Remnants in Rock Bottom Ghetto*

Sky (1991), the poem consists of forty tercets and a concluding quatrain.[9] Perhaps the tercets call attention to the presence of a racial trio
of white, yellow, and black rather than the usual binary opposition.
The character mentioned in Moss's title, played by Mantan Moreland in numerous Charlie Chan films of the forties, is the African-
American driver of Chan, the extremely clever but stereotypically
rendered Chinese detective from Hawaii created by novelist Earl Derr
Biggers and featured in numerous films from 1926 to 1981.[10]

Moss wishes to give Birmingham Brown a "turn" in the sense of
a "chance" (to exceed the limitations of his cinematically stultifying
visibility) and also give this figure a troping or signifying. Even as
the poet's speaker begins by acknowledging the comic absurdity—
heightened by purposefully awkward enjambments—of how the character is visually and thematically situated, she zanily reframes some
of these negatives as features of the sublime:

> I know how ridiculous this could seem, the
> moon as one of Birmingham Brown's pop eyes when
> he's admiring Charlie Chan as living
>
> icon, but I can't stop seeing the magic, even
> as Birmingham drives Charlie around
> in a car black as Birmingham, black as
>
> compliment, emulation, and adoration. Ridiculous
> were it not wonderful, Birmingham's enormous
> feel for the night, moving in it
>
> like something made for it, made
> of it; the city, every city, wearing
> his face at night, his smile a
>
> handy lantern.
>
> (103)

This passage confirms Gates's emphasis on the centrality of complex figuration in African-American signifying. Along with rueful
irony in this passage's flights of hyperbole, I cannot help but find "up-
lifting" pleasure in the opening simile. Brown's shadowlike "worship"
of Charlie Chan is transformed into a traditionally exalted figure of
sublime illumination, even as it causes part of the driver's face to
be "detached" from the rest of it. Indeed, linking Mantan Moreland
as a player of stereotyped characters with two forerunners who had

previously played Chan's sidekick, Stepin Fetchit and Willie Best,[11] Donald Bogle asserts that "no other actor could widen his eyes like Moreland" or "manage his trick of running without actually moving at all" and that Moreland brought "demented energy" to his role as Chan's "dubiously reliable chauffeur" (74). The performance of false visibility is so masterfully absurd and excessive that it may foil the racist viewer's attempt to confuse it with accurate representation.

The speaker appreciates the powerful "chiarascuro" effect of Birmingham's visual appearance in an alluring urban setting, even as she puns on his first name's connection with the city in Alabama where, years later, white supremacists killed African-American children by bombing their church. The contrast between the "whites" of his eyes and teeth and the darkness of his skin and the night allow "black" to be a "beautiful" element in a lovely composition. Acknowledging that "Birmingham is supposed / to be insult, a debit not credit // to his race" (104)—and thus ironically recycling the cliche of white condescension and pseudopraise to "acceptable" blacks—the speaker refuses to go along with the "surface" observation.

When Moss reverses the hierarchy and makes the servant a "leading man," his enhanced status is based on his assumed intimacy with the mysterious "night," which "he glides through . . . as though // in a coach; it sure pampers him, opens / itself so that walking towards you / he disappears before reaching you" (104). Recalling Ellison's notion of African-American "invisibility," Moss identifies this eerie sense of visual "evaporation" with the character's access to a rich experience unavailable to those who view (and may disrespect) him: " . . . the // night, a woman dark, passionate, heavy with / her love, pulls him into her secret / chambers, won't give anyone a chance at // taste" (104).

Close to the poem's midpoint, Moss's speaker begins mouthing stereotypes about Asians, performing a kind of signifying that Gates, borrowing the narrative theory of Bakhtin, calls "double-voiced discourse." In this form of parody, "one speech act determines the internal structure of another, the second effecting the voice of the first by absence, by difference" (111). Moss's speaker spews forth many ridiculous generalizations in a short space in a sequence almost as unpredictable and disjointed as that of a typical John Ashbery poem. While one voice seems to take the stereotypes as givens, the "different" voice sometimes enters into the former's by alluding openly to the suspect functions of the absurd generalizations. For the bigoted voice, it goes without saying that a white actor, the Russian Peter Ustinov, *should* play the movie's major Chinese character, as white actors like Warner Oland and Sidney Toller—along with two Japanese and, apparently, one Korean actor—had done in all previous Chan films.[12] (Ustinov appeared in the last of these films, *Charlie Chan and the Curse of the Dragon Queen* [1981], directed by Clive Donner.) Eugene Franklin Wong, while acknowledging the relatively "sympathetic portrayal" of Chan in the movies, observes that "the institutional exclusion of the Chinese accounts for Chan's 'never having been portrayed by a Chinese actor' " and points out the "racist cosmetology" that marred the portrayal.[13]

The poem's bigoted voice finds the "cosmetology" downright reasonable: "the beard stuck on Ustinov . . . seems // appropriate for his purpose: / effigy, caricature" (105). Far be it from her to question the justice of this "purpose." Next, mentioning "that broken English / tripping out his mouth appropriately // in bound footsteps," she offers a quirky comparison between the pidgin and another demeaning stricture that a racist would associate perpetually with the "essence" of Chinese culture. To her, it is not worth mentioning that Ustinov, his predecessors in the role, and linguistic caricature in the film-texts have contributed to Asian (and Asian American) false visibility by excluding the possibility that Chinese actors and other cultural producers can construct their own self-representations. Instead, she defends the "appropriateness" of whatever accoutrements are needed to "make" the Russian-born actor "Chinese," since he labors under so many experiential "disadvantages":

> Now how would it look
> for Charlie Chan not to be recognizably
> Chinese especially when Ustinov cannot
>
> draw from his rickshaw infancy, his
> ideographic preschool scribbles, his
> chopstick crutches to help him eat
>
> moo goo gai pan, his first words, before
> even *mamasan* or *papasan* or is that
> Japanese?
>
> (195)

Listing what Ustinov has missed, the speaker makes several thoughtless assumptions based on cultural clichés. Since a "Chinese" "infancy" in the first half of the twentieth century might take place in a variety of divergent locations and socioeconomic contexts, how likely would it be for a baby to ride in a "rickshaw"? In a Hollywood film, perhaps. Also, "moo goo gai pan" would not appear on a growing Chinese boy's plate nor would the words form on his lips, unless his family happens to be dining in an *American* Chinese restaurant that has adapted its cuisine to *non*-Chinese American tastes. The speaker suspects that *san* is a term of respect in Japanese—at least avoiding the usual racist trap of saying that all things Asian are the same—but she blithely grafts English slang onto the Japanese suffix, as though English is the Ur-language that other cultures appropriate and thus "contaminate."

Next, during a marvelously strained bit of signifying that turns "the beard stuck on Ustinov" (and its relation to the rest of his face) into a jungle during the Vietnam War, "the Russian / stubble poking through to ferret out / Viet Cong, Viet anything" (105), the speaker feebly attempts to manage distinctions among Vietnamese, "Hmong women," Cambodians, and even Polynesians. However, the effort is promptly exhausted with the signal-cliche of dismissal that Nixon's Vice President Spiro Agnew applied to U.S. slums: "As for the rest, // see one, you've seen them all, hovering / above the number one son like a mist / to cool his face, so hot // under the makeup that upsets, tilts / his eyes. Appropriately. Asian eyes / being the claim to fame. And silk" (105–6). After the typical synecdoche of "eyes" as visual key to representation of the Asian "other," the speaker produces a flurry of further absurd stereotyping, including the racist metonymy linking Chinese American immigrants and the laundry business[14] and an outrageous conjecture grossly impugning Chinese hygiene: "You can bet that Charlie can take you / to the cleaners; isn't he Chinese? / Don't they boil the clothes and the // rice in the same woks?" (106). She also tosses the vicious association between the features of Mongolians and those of the mentally retarded into the perverse stew of absurdities: "Isn't this / the year of the horse, the broken, / tamed stallion? Of the Mongoloid / Idiot? Of Peking sitting duck?"

Finally, however, the second voice in this "double-voiced discourse" appears, relieving tension generated by this stupidity: "That's / what Charlie said, that's all he can say, / cliche after cliche, stereotype after stereotype" (106). "Charlie," no human being, is a degraded, degrading trope, material evidence of a failure of imagination and perception. The passage recalls lines on "Jim Crow" in Moss's "Interpretation of a Poem by Frost": "With the grass covered, black and white are the only options, / polarity is the only reality" (116).[15] A loaded, fanciful conceit comparing "railroad tracks" with the visual configuration of the sleeping Chan and "his Geisha," the quintessential trope of the objectified, Japanese exotic "other," enables the two parts of the double-voiced discourse to seem to converge: "even when he's alone sleeping parallel with / his geisha (he says no matter what she really is), / together they're models for the railroad tracks, // just straighten the cross's horizontal arm, / lengthen both to infinity, crucify the same" (106). (Generally, Chan is portrayed as being eager to solve mysteries in order to get back to his wife in Hawaii.) The position of the sleepers, identified as retrospective "models" and vulnerable to the displacement of "crucifixion," is designed to remind us of a nineteenth-century "model" of exploitation: the use of Chinese laborers to build the monumental Central Pacific Railroad, followed by a narrowing of their socioeconomic opportunity that was later codified as the Asian Exclusion Act of 1882.[16]

Moss's second voice, uneasily continuing to cohabit with the first, insists that, despite the avalanches of racist "stereotype after stereotype," the misrepresented do not wither, but struggle to realize their dreams of personal fulfilment and self-validation:

> For they can move in and out of shadows cast
>
> when a Hiroshima girl's thousand cranes
> fly by the sun; their silhouettes
> are exclamation marks. We turn it all around
>
> and still dare to dream of it, digging to China,
> going through the center of the earth's meaning
> and potential to *earn,* to *deserve* passage there;
>
> through the center and cleansed.
>
> (106–7)

The presence of the first voice within the second is signaled not only by the awkwardly trope-laden allusion to the impact of the first atomic bomb on Hiroshima but by the appropriation of the old, absurd figure of "American" adventurism. It is as though even the native Chinese are "digging to China," which stands for a deeply desired experiential threshold rather than a geographical location. In the poem's carnivalesque ethos, unsavory connotations of the ego-centered conquest of "otherness" cannot be entirely extricated from the sincere expression of the desire to affirm one's dignity through merit, to be "cleansed" of demeaning caricature and other unjust treatment, even if there may be no way of making this sincerity visible that can withstand the possibility of caricature. (Note Moss's witty transformation of the cliche "earning potential" to "potential to *earn* . . . passage there.") The speaker further characterizes this desire with a ludicrous, "Orientalizing" fantasy, supplemented by a Western religious allusion out of left field: "wanting / that moment that worms complete their evolution / into egg rolls and dandruff is recycled into bait // that entices some junk boat occupants / to take us in because they're the ones / who walk on water all the time" (107).

Nevertheless, for the marginalized, part of the process of "cleansing" is to tell off the representatives of coercive authority. To realize the good fortune of delivering such a gesture may seem a random occurrence, like the message in the cookie received in an American Chinese restaurant that Moss parodies: "*To hell with Peter,* that's what Birmingham's / fortune cookie said; either one, Ustinov / or Jesus' right-hand man" (107). By cursing the "organization man" rather than Jesus himself—through the typical signifying vehicle of communication through a third party, the "anonymously" written fortune[17]—Moss's speaker indirectly tweaks the institution of Catholicism. Most importantly, she alludes to the accretion of oppressive images and concepts in processes of cultural transmission. The concluding quatrain may imply a danger in the loss of cultural specificity that stems from the collapsing of major distinctions, even as it holds promise that a common denominator, the desire for "salvation," can break down hierarchies and assuage some conflict among disparate groups: "Going there, we notice how Jesus / can become Confucius without a hitch / and can keep his parables if he wishes. / We all keep salvation" (107). The possessive "his" is fruitfully ambiguous here: is Jesus keeping his own parables or appropriating Confucius's parables when he "turns into" the Chinese life-philosopher?

Not only can would-be colonizers dress up their religion in the terms of "the other" in order to convert the latter and use that leverage to rob them of self-determination, but the sentimental erasure of differences in general promotes a smug ignorance that fosters racism. Amid its many ironies, "Birmingham Brown's Turn" may "keep" the concept of "salvation" from the buffoonish stereotypical figuration of such cultural texts as the Chan movies. Perhaps its closure maintains the hope that space can be cleared for the pursuit of analytic/perceptual specificity, rather than facile visual representations, so that divergent groups can interact with an awareness of common spiritual desires *and* a respect for differences between "Jesus," "Confucius," and other figures.

As Robert McDowell, a major proponent of "the New Formalism," states in a mixed review of *Small Congregations,* Moss's poetry is frequently preoccupied with "religious," as well as "historical and personal landscapes."[18] Quoting "One for All Newborns" (156), the poem that Moss chose to conclude *Small Congregations,* McDowell views the poet's "religious attitude [as] that of the wisecracking, elder daughter assessing a lovable yet grumpy father who is 'watching the kids through a window, eager to be proud / of his creation, looking for signs of spring' " (159). At times, as McDowell states, Moss's "faith" appears "reassuringly traditional, consist[ing] of belief in sin, guilt, and penance," but most of Moss's poems that treat religion do not exhibit this kind of faith. More often, Moss examines how dominant Euro-American religious institutions have constituted the visibility of people of color, especially those of African descent, in such mystifying and unjust ways that the idea about the "father's" eagerness to take pride in his *entire* "creation" is easily misplaced. Perceiving that many Moss poems include an "indictment of conditions that impede economic and social progress" and seek "to blow the whistle on hypocrisy," McDowell does not place Moss's "wisecracking" about God in the context of that "indictment."

In "The Adversary," first published in *At Redbones,* Old Testament lore is viewed as allegorical fodder for the justification of racist representations. The poem's deployment of the figures of God and Satan signifies "wickedly" and concisely upon such redoubtable (and sententious) revisions of the Old Testament as Milton's *Paradise Lost* and Blake's own signifying on Milton in *The Marriage of Heaven and Hell* and elsewhere. Moss dares to portray God as a rather narcissistic exploiter and Satan as a scapegoat:

> I could understand God's keeping Satan
> to himself; you don't share
> your best thing, your private stock, personal
> ego stroker, but God let the devil loose,
> he says. Satan didn't just make up his mind
> to leave, disgusted by the chauvinism
> among other things. Let him loose
> then hunted him down and bid us praise
> the staging. The devilish contract
> gets Satan second-banana high and
> dismissed by jungle terminology.

The Joe Johnson against the Great White Hope
of a God.

(25)

When Moss's troping identifies "the contract" that God draws up
as "devilish" and the deity's "staging" of the division as more pernicious than Satan's actions, and when it indicates that the "devil" has
patiently borne the "chauvinism" rampant in a hierarchical heaven,
she is not merely aiming to vex "good Christian folk." Using an
allusion to the troubling visibility of race in early-twentieth-century
U.S. heavyweight boxing, Moss draws an analogy between Eurocentric
representations of racial conflict in the U.S. and the God/Satan
struggle. The composite figure of Jack Johnson and Joe Louis is
delightfully outrageous, because the public personae of the first and
second African-American heavyweight champions could not have
been more divergent.

A major contender for eight years before being allowed to cross
"the color line" and fight for the title, Jack Johnson was repeatedly
singled out for persecution by government agencies and the boxing
and entertainment communities and was reviled by the white press,
because, in biographer Randy Roberts's words, "as a rebellious black
man he threatened America's social order."[19] Johnson bedded and
married white women, drove cars recklessly, eventually dying in an
auto crash, relished playing the dandy, and trounced such "Great
White Hopes" as Jim Jeffries. On the other hand, biographer Chris
Mead states that, from the beginning, Joe Louis's managers sought
to "dissociate Louis from the memory of Jack Johnson" by spreading
an "'official' image of Louis's character"—as a fighter who stayed
away from white women, avoided alcohol, "never gloat[ed] over a
fallen opponent," and kept "a 'dead pan' in front of the camera"—
"that strongly influenced public perceptions of Louis for the rest of
his career."[20] Temperamentally very different from Johnson, Louis
abided by this image.[21]

Ironically, Moss's composite figure *is* appropriate. Before Louis's
deeply appreciated, self-sacrificing gestures of support for the U.S.
participation in World War II made him an almost universally beloved
figure, numerous sportswriters routinely praised Louis's opponents,
including the Nazi-affiliated Max Schmeling (in their first fight),
downplayed Louis's skills and triumphs, peppered any positive depiction of his boxing and physical appearance with egregious racist
images of bestial attributes, and made endless references to his lazi-

ness, stupidity, and voracious appetite. In the 1930s Jack Dempsey even called for a "White Hope" crusade.[22]

Moss's term "top bananas," with its metonymic relationship to monkeys and the phallus exemplifying a demeaning "jungle terminology," is at once an epithet of distinction and debasement that reflects sportswriters' and others' racist representations of Johnson, Louis, and other African Americans. The racists ignore the "primitive," "jungle" attitude of their own desire to find a "Great White Hope" who will "destroy" a black champion. In the larger social sphere of the fighters' eras and in the realm of Christian theology that Moss is interpreting, the contest is rigged against African Americans as a group and Satan respectively: "The problem: God's need for adversary, / worthy opponent, for just short of equal" (25). Satan and African Americans—the latter having a long history of winning gold medals in the Olympic 100 meters—are thus assigned the role of "runner-up, sprinter / in the next lane who could have grabbed the gold / if he could have afforded its blinding him." Hurled from heaven, Satan is subject to "what rains down, / the heavenly sewage and trash, the blame / for holy wars, rescue rages. For every drop of blood. / For whatever will not be blessed, the unchosen" (25). Especially during times, like the eighties, when fears of economic scarcity run rampant, "unchosen" black Americans are scapegoated for the ills of U.S. society by those whites who refuse to explore how the institution of slavery, the terms of Reconstruction, and other elements in a chain of historical causation have practically guaranteed staggering obstacles in daily living for a multitude of African Americans over numerous generations.

As "The Adversary" moves to a close, Moss continues to use her central analogy to elucidate the ramifications of scapegoating, the victims' reactions to it, and the dominant group's "readings" of these responses: "In heaven Satan was a minority in a neighborhood / where everyone else was saint. Crosses burned and / his car, house, clothes, wings; all / his possessions. And the burning and reburning / of memories establishes hell" (25–26). The speaker reverses the traditional view that the greatest sin of Satan, whose "authority" is "denied him / by a nose, a longer, pointier Caucasian nose," is defiance of the deity's will; such defiance is actually a remarkable subservience to the master: "Where's the gratitude for Satan who is there / for God no matter what; Satan / who is the original Uncle Tom" (26). Moss's signifying tomfoolery stresses that Satan's displays of defiance are self-destructively *obedient* to God, because he allows the latter to make him visible as a sign of ultimate Evil so that God can be defined as an ultimate embodiment of Good. Without the adversary's cooperative negativity, his willingness to be used as a foil, God would probably seem less benevolent and less powerful to those faithful caught in the middle.

The use of the "Uncle Tom" epithet stresses that defenders of institutional racism exploit an African American like Jack Johnson who reacts defiantly to having "authority denied him / by [prej-udice's] nose" as much as they exploit one who unquestioningly serves the status quo. (Joe Louis, neither an "Uncle Tom" nor an activist, tempered an apparent acceptance of U.S. social conditions with behind-the-scenes challenging of antiblack discrimination.)[23] Able to ignore their own group's pattern of despicable behavior, white supremacists thrive on visible examples of "evil," which they link to a racial "nature" or "essence," that they "need" to banish or obliterate. From this perspective, bigots "should" be "grateful" for the confirmation of their false sense of superiority. However, they need to repress this awareness in order to remain die-hard racists, lest they see that this self-satisfaction does not stem from their own virtue and abilities but from the appearance and actions of the objects of scorn.

"The Lynching," which originally appeared in *Rainbow Remnants*, takes the literal fact of such white supremacist terrorism as cross- and person-burning and traces the roots of its justification in Christian theological discourse. (One might view the poet's use of quatrains as an allusion to the bisected planks of the cross, or, perhaps more fancifully, as the meeting of the holy trinity and the devil.) Wyn Craig Wade argues that Christian fundamentalism's "most critical impact on our social and political history was that, without it, the Ku Klux Klan could never have enrolled the fantastic numbers nor have gained the remarkable power it wielded between 1922 and 1925."[24] Having "realized that Klansmen and fundamentalists shared . . . an intolerance for ways of life different from their own, a frustration with postwar change, and a passionate commitment to restoring things as they used to be," the Imperial Kleagle, then a chief Klan officer, spear-headed the highly successfully movement to "enlist" fundamentalist ministers' "support for the Klan" (170) which, when secured, enabled the Klan's ranks to swell. "A former preacher himself," the Klan's Imperial Wizard instituted "Klan oaths, and other ceremonies" which "were essentially religious rites, complete with prayers and hymns" (169) including frequent references to the imperative of absolute faith in Jesus Christ and of militance against "the anti-Christ forces of Satan" (440).[25]

The Klansmen depicted in "The Lynching" are obsessed with "black" skin and associate its visual presence with absolute sin. According to Frantz Fanon, writing in 1952, this visual/conceptual linkage has been central to European psychopathology: "*In Europe, the black man is the symbol of Evil.* The torturer is the black man, Satan is black, one talks of shadows, when one is dirty one is black— whether one is thinking of physical dirtiness or moral dirtiness."[26] To purge themselves of insomnia—restlessness in the "dark"—the poem's Klansmen rationalize that they can purge black people of *visible* properties of their original fallen condition, as well as their lives, if they baptize them in flames: "They should have slept, would have / but had to fight the darkness, had / to build a fire and bathe a man in / flames. No // other soap's as good when / the dirt is on the skin" (109). The Klansmen consider those "black since / birth" to be "burnt by birth. His father / is not in heaven. No parent // of atrocity is in heaven."

The speaker, child and apologist of the homicidal pyromaniac, expresses the lynchers' lack of spiritual illumination yet implies the existence of their menacing emotional "heat": "We are white like / incandescence // yet lack light" (109). (The Latin root *candere* signifies "to be white.") However, s/he sees the solution as the use of a black man as a "candle." The speaker's father, first compared to the Jesus of the apocalypse as he "baptizes by fire as Jesus will," is then figured as the third member of the trinity: "Becomes a holy ghost when / he dons his sheet, a clerical collar // out of control." According to Wade, "Klansman and their wives" often regarded wearing the robes as 'a holy experience' " (183), as if an illusory benediction could blanket the unholy uses of this ghostly secrecy. The fiction of a divine imperative justifies psychotically "out of control" behavior. Amid this bombast, the speaker notices the sheet's material resemblance to the "warp // of miscegenation," the supreme dread (and perhaps deeply buried desire) of many white supremacists: "fifty percent cotton, dixie, confederate / and fifty percent polyester, man-made, man- / ipulated, unnatural, mulatto fiber."

The child of the murderer is suddenly transfixed by the bizarre vision of the dead African American "hung as if / just his washed shirt, the parts / of him most capable of sin removed. // Charred, his flesh is bark, his body / a trunk. No sign of roots" (109–10). The reference to castration as a removal of the capacity to sin reflects Fanon's point about how European racism turns the "essence" of "the Negro" "into a penis" (170), as in the obsession with miscegenation. "For the majority of white men," he asserts, "the Negro represents the sexual instinct (in its raw state). The Negro is the incarnation of a genital potency beyond all moralities and prohibitions" (177). However, the speaker's description of the vision of death is so horrifying that it may provoke a dawning of conscience, a sense of the stark gap in the father's worldview: "This is the life after / death coming if God is an invention as were // slaves" (110). When the institution of slavery and its justifications are seen as "an invention," and that lynching is an ultimately dehumanizing act, the existence of God is also questioned. The speaker seems to inherit the insomnia of which the father has allegedly purged himself through the act of lynching: "So I spend the night, his thin moon-begot / shadow as mattress; something smoldering / keeps me warm. Patches of skin fall onto me / in places I didn't know needed mending" (110). One can object to how s/he is exploiting his/her father's murder victim—for example, the illusion of the "shadow" functioning as "mattress," the "warmth" generated by "smoldering," and the "patches of skin" that serve as a trope for the child's spiritual (and perhaps political) "mending"—but this is surely a preferable response to the possibility that the speaker might resolve to carry on the lynchers' genocidal practice.

In "For Hagar," identifiable either as an extremely long-lined poem or perhaps a prose-poem and collected in *Last Chance for the Tarzan Holler,* Moss ironically retells the story of Hagar to underscore how racial hierarchy is inscribed in the text of Genesis. The Egyptian Hagar is identified as "the first surrogate mother, a maid, who was alluring anyway and needed little persuading (she'd made goo-goo eyes at Abram before) was offered to her mistress's husband as his concubine so that the mistress could have a product of her husband's bloodline, the bloodline that mattered" (32). Hagar's "inter-racial child, the famous call-him-Ishmael," though "Abram's firstborn"—and hence, according to Jewish patriarchal law, "the heir supreme"—suffers, like his mother, from the problematic visibility of his racial status and the set of double standards that "God" sanctions in the process of a racialized sexual politics akin to what would, millenia later, transpire in the "new world": Ishmael, though presented with "some sort of affirming" (if not *affirmative*) "action," a kind of lesser blessing by the deity, is

> not the one that God wants as beneficiary of His covenant; no, that has been reserved for a second child that God permits the ninety-year-old Sarah to have (He changes her name and changes Abram's to "Abraham,"

exalting them above past infidelity; it wasn't us, they can say, but Sarai and Abram who cheated), child of more certain ethnicity, pure-bred, not one of those mulatto bastards of many new-world masters (32).

As in "Birmingham Brown's Turn," the second voice (the demotic, the profanely secular) in Moss's "double-voiced discourse" "cohabits" intimately with the first (the sacred "Word"), and the pristine authority of that "Word" is tarnished by the presence of egocentrism and ethnocentrism. Wanting "no rival for her son Isaac," especially not "Ishmael, with that Egyptian glowing within him, his adolescence about to burst forth, oiled black panther," who "makes the celibate feel foolish,

> Sarah . . . says to Abraham matter-of-factly: *Cast out this slave woman with her son; for the son of this slave woman shall not be heir with my son Isaac.*

> God has no problem with this (!) so tells A. to follow his wife's orders, reassuring him that Ishmael will be blessed. Ordained Hagar is given bread and water, exhausted in short order in the wilderness of Beersheba where she abandons Ishmael so death can be a real father to him. What's wrong with these boys saying *our father,* Hagar wonders. Just in time, because Hagar's about to invent the NAACP and the Supreme Court, God reveals to her a well of exceptional water that empowers Ishmael with a dream of becoming one of Egypt's finest, expert with the bow and with his Egyptian wife that Hagar selects, and they all live as well as can be expected ever after in Paran as servants

> of the Lord (33).

When the "separate but *un*equal" doctrine prompts Hagar to perceive the need for a primordial version of "the NAACP and the Supreme Court"—that is, a court that enjoys "supreme" jurisdiction in human, not divine terms—the deity supports Sarah's desire for dominance in worldly affairs and reinforces the notion of the Jews' supremacy over others by intervening in a way that diffuses Hagar's burgeoning activism. His magical "water" presents the illusion of a "separate but equal structure." Of course, from rival claims of theological entitlement and land-rights, Jewish-Arab relations would come to embody a series of bitter, devastating struggles.

Another poem in *Last Chance for the Tarzan Holler,* "Crystals," presents a chilling narrative that demonstrates the severe consequences for women (especially African-American women) of the ways in the white patriarchal medical institution has used their visibility against them. The poem begins with the clincal analysis of a painful vaginal condition:

> In 1845 Dr. James Marion Sims had seen it many times,
> vesico-vaginal fistula, abnormal passageway
> between bladder and vagina through which urine leaks
> almost constantly if the fistula is large
>
> as it tends to become after those pregnancies
> not quite a year apart in Anarcha and her slave
> friends Lucy, Betsey. *If you can just fix this*
> the girl said, probably pregnant again, her vulva inflamed,
> her thighs caked with urinary salts; from the beginning
> he saw his future in those crystals.
>
> (34)

The minute specificity of Dr. Sims's scrutiny of Anarcha's genital region—linked with his "crystalline" sense of personal destiny—causes his flawed perception of her as a human being, one, in fact, who has probably already endured a good deal of unwanted male invasiveness: "Through the vulva was the way most tried to access her / yet they did not come close" (34). Knowing that "society women sometimes had this too," the doctor pursued "his future" by using Anarcha with deadening repetition as a passive object of experimentation. The speaker and reader's horror about what is being narrated strains against the mouthing of the affectless discourse of "objective" reportage, relieved only slightly by ominous allusions and understated evaluative comments:

> He tried to help Anarcha first, drawing on what
> he was inventing: frontier ingenuity and gynecology,
> and operated thirty times, using a pewter teaspoon
> that he reshaped, bent and hammered for each surgery,
> no sterilant but spit, while she watched; it became
> his famous duck-bill speculum too large and sharp
> to be respectful, yet it let him look.
>
> Such excoriation, such stretching of the vaginal walls, tunnel
> into room; such remembrance of Jericho, prophecy of Berlin
> when his mind was to have been on her comfort and healing. . . .
>
> Using
> a half dollar he formed the wire suture that closed

Anarcha's fistula on the thirtieth, it bears repeating, thirtieth attempt.

(34)

In the first strophe of the passage above, the language of the visual is central. The "famous duck-bill speculum," a trope for the rapacious phallus of patriarchal authority in a medical context, is both an instrument of kinesthetic penetration and the ability *to see*. A "speculum" is a mirror that gives rise to *speculation* from a safe (aesthetic) distance from the perceived. In addition, Anarcha is forced to see, thirty times, what is being done to her; she must perceive how another person drastically limits and disfigures her visibility. In this "frontier gynecology," *spec*ulation that makes the woman a *spect*acle is more important than being "re*spect*ful" of Anarcha or "helping" her overcome the "anarchy" in her womb, because this visual activity may lead to information. The beneficiaries of the new information are to be the "society women," who can afford to make Sims's name: "successful," Sims "went gloved and shaven to help ladies / on whom white cloths were draped; divinity / on the table to indulge his tastefulness" (35). Dr. Sims's "mind" cannot be on Anarcha's "comfort and healing" because he is intent on conquest; as "field" of inquiry, Anarcha is, in large measure, the object to be conquered. The reference to Berlin links the medical invasion with the outrageously sadistic experimental procedures performed on Jews by doctors like Joseph Mengele in Nazi Germany.

Not only did Anarcha suffer the pain and indignity of thirty operations, but these procedures produced permanent consequences. Dr. Sims had left indelible imprints on her body, her daily life, and on her place in U.S. history:

For the rest of her life she slept in the Sims position:
on her left side, right knee brought to her chest; she, so long,
four years, on his table came to find it comfortable, came to find
no other way to lose herself, relieve her mind,
ignore Sims' rising glory, his bragging in the journals
that he had seen the fistula *as no man had ever seen it before.*
Now they all can.

Anarcha who still does not know anesthesia except
for her willed loss of awareness went on peeing as she'd
always done, just not so frequently and in reduced

volume, hardly enough for a tea cup, but whenever
necessary, the doctor poked, prodded, practiced. . . .

It should be noted
that Anarcha's fistula closed well,
sealed in infection, scarred
thickly

as if his hand remained.

(35)

If Dr. Sims's butcheries, source of Anarcha's torment far more than
her original physical complaints, ironically constitute a trigger for her
slight relief from the havoc that he wrecked, it merely underscores
the brutal fact that she has been forced to become *habituated* to
abuse. Not only does "infection" place a permanent "seal" on her, but
as Moss's simile—which cannot be called "heavy-handed" because
its crude force is entirely apt—demonstrates, the "hand" of white
male patriarchal power "remains" in and upon her, indicating its
possession of the body and destiny of the African-American female
slave. Sims thoroughly ignores his many failures in the "case" of
Anarcha; he sees (and boastfully articulates) only his success at *seeing*
and thus gaining power over women through "accessing" what was
previously "secret" or invisible about them. As the brief sentence,
"Now they all can," announces, his perceptual "victory" is shared with
all men who wish to enjoy the domination of those who are differently
raced and gendered.

John Yau, born in 1950 in Massachusetts, is the author of nine
books of poetry, beginning with *Crossing Canal Street* (1976) and,
most recently, *Forbidden Entries* (1996).[27] He has also published a
novel, a book of short stories, and six books of criticism about contemporary visual art, and he has edited an anthology of fiction.
Various critics read him exclusively (and, I believe, wrongly) as a
junior member of what might be termed the John Ashbery wing of
the New York School of Poetry. Yau studied with Ashbery, a fellow
art critic who selected his collection *Corpse and Mirror* (1983) for
the National Poetry Series.[28] As John Gery observes, Yau's work of
the late seventies and early eighties does bear strong comparison
with Ashbery, since it often focuses "on the space between experience and thought, between observation and interpretation, a space
that wavers even as he isolates it."[29] His poetry of the last fifteen

or so years, however, includes various stylistic strategies that bear scant resemblance to Ashbery's work. More importantly, Yau's frequent engagement in serious play with the discourse of race marks a significant difference from Ashbery, as well as other New York School poets.

In an interview with Eileen Tabios, the Chinese American Yau, whose "father's mother was English, but claimed to be French," expresses an interest "in identity but not the fixity of identity," and he raises the problem that "multicultural issues sometimes want to fix identity but that's against multiculturality."[30] Thus, in keeping with the features of his own multiple identity and his aesthetic investigations of various traditions and countertraditions, he seeks to understand the *hybrid* character of identity-formations. As Yau puts it in a 1988 article on the Afro-Chinese-Cuban painter Wilfredo Lam, marginalized by American art institutions who cast him as a mere imitator of Picasso,

> The bind every hybrid American artist must deal with is this: Should he or she investigate the constantly changing polymorphous conditions affecting identity, tradition, and reality? Or should he or she choose to assimilate into the mainstream art world by focusing on the approved aesthetic issues? Instead of assimilating, Lam infiltrated the aesthetic rules governing the pictorial conventions of "the exploiters." He became, as he says, "a Trojan horse."[31]

Yau has displayed a keen interest in the representation of race since the beginning of his career. Nearly all of the poems in *Crossing Canal Street,* which antedate Yau's contact with Ashbery, elliptically question the visibility of denizens of New York's Chinatown. Take, for example, the interplay between visual representation and psychological reticence, between a "servant's" accommodation and a subtle hint of refusal, in "The Waiter":

> Smooth hairless face of the waiter:
> beneath rows of fluorescent lights
> the skin is shiny. The eyes,
> almond petals, black drops of oil
> glistening in each do not betray
> what he is thinking.
> Balancing trays on his shoulder
> with one hand, cordial,
> almost friendly, making "small talk,"
> he is paid to watch you eat,

bring the food, refill the water
& tea:

> as the flowers speak
> in their fragrance, color, bending
> in the breeze

> we do not blossom
> we do not blossom for you.

(unpaginated)

As this passage exemplifies, the poetry of *Crossing Canal Street* gains its lyrical energy predominantly from a visual emphasis; the work seems close to early-twentieth-century U.S. Imagism and its succcessor Objectivism, both of which draw on the accomplishments of Chinese poets like Li Po and Tu Fu. In an interview with Edward Foster, Yau recalls that he was especially drawn to Ezra Pound's "Cathay" poems and that, "at a certain point," he found that his "poems were so dependent on the visual image that [he] wanted to react against that," since "it felt like a habit or a dependency," and so he strived to "undermine [his] own tendency or habit with the visual."[32] In the mid-seventies, Yau learned about techniques of linguistic substitution and other defamiliarizing procedures directly from Harry Mathews, a founding member of the French literary (and mathematical) group OULIPO,[33] as well as Ashbery; he began to explore various experimental modes and has been doing so ever since. In his interview with Tabios, Yau speaks of the value of arbitrary "constraints," which "help prevent you from repeating yourself" and enable the writer "to break . . . habits" (383). "Because whatever sense [he has] would have limited the poem," Yau uses "words [he] wouldn't ordinarily use, say, from science and biology books, as well as from the newspaper or the dictionary." Furthermore, "constraints . . . break apart the notion of bounded ego or 'I' " (384), which Yau considers coercive.

In his work of the last two decades, Yau's experimentation has enabled him to concoct intriguing collages, fractured narratives, and modulations from surrealist transport and irony to abstraction. Also, he often concentrates intensely on the material properties and processes of language, including the way particular signifiers, not permanently bound to particular signifieds, continually slip and slide to new contextualizations. Especially considering the attention to racial "hybridity" to which I have alluded, this experimental drive does not reflect a merely aesthetic predilection, nor does it make

Yau a Language Poet pursuing a decidedly marxist exploration of textuality.[34] In *The United States of Jasper Johns* (1996), Yau probes the reasons for Johns's use of flags and maps in his early work in a way that reflects the poet's own philosophical and social concerns:

> The connection between the flag and the map goes to the heart of Johns' work, which is his recognition not only that the individual lives in a world of uninterrupted change but that society, which is the collective expression of individuals, repeatedly denies this fact. If reality, . . . the world we inhabit, is continually reformulating itself, then how does one both recognize and accept a process which eventually subsumes us all? How can the individual be true to change and entropy, which is the stuff of life, rather than uphold the social ideas of stasis and its concomitant illusion that any one of us can exist outside time and chaos?"[35]

Dominant social constructions of race are, in a sense, "flags" and "maps" that "uphold . . . social ideas of stasis" and deny individual and group change. Stating that Yau "writes especially to interrogate the rituals that foster social cohesion and position subjects within a culture," Priscilla Wald, who cogently analyzes various prose-poems and poems in which the problematics of Chinese American experience are raised, emphasizes how the "ever-changing tale" emblematic of his poetry as a whole "challenges the symbolic process that stabilizes experience; the world becomes less knowable, less predictable."[36]

In "No One Ever Tried to Kiss Anna May Wong," a poem in *Radiant Silhouette: New and Selected Work, 1974–1988* (1989),[37] Yau concisely addresses how U.S. cinema raises a false "flag" of Chinese American visibility and how a particular object of such (mis)representation responds. Yau has mentioned: "The poem's title and some of the lines" (about violence done to the actress's characters) "came from a remark Wong made after she stopped acting in film. As I remember, the remark was 'I've been stabbed, beaten, etc., but I've never been kissed on screen.'"[38] Yau adds that the "reason is miscegenation laws." The title may also suggest the fact that the Los Angeles-born Anna May Wong, who made her screen debut at twelve as an extra in *Red Lantern* (1919) and played an "evil" slave girl in *The Thief of Baghdad* (1924), predominantly played "villainnesses" in the last phase of her career, the late thirties and early forties. In *Shanghai Express* (1932), her character, Hui Fei, is raped by the film's villain, the Eurasian warlord Chang and later avenges herself by stabbing him to death.[39] Thus, she is depicted as both vulnerable and too dangerous for white males to try to kiss. Furthermore, as James Parrish and William

Leonard state, "Hollywood film-makers held to the tenet that players of particular ethnic backgrounds"—including Asian—"could not be stars in the accepted sense," and Wong "was forced to accept the dictates of the studio system, and only provide exotic atmosphere for other players' vehicles."[40]

Gina Marchetti believes that the *Shanghai Express* character of Anna May Wong, who in real life never married, exhibits another dark stereotype: that of the "predatory," castrating lesbian. Of the encounter of Hui Fei and the European Shanghai Lilly, played by Marlene Dietrich, in a compartment on the *Shanghai Express*, she says: "Ambivalently presented as captives or as spiders ready to lure others into their web, they both functional as tokens of the potential dangers as well as the possible forbidden pleasures associated with their sexuality. When the 'respectable' passengers refuse to share a compartment with Hui Fei, Lilly, finding a kindred spirit moves in."[41] The fact that "Lilly pulls down the shade, keeping the camera at a distance," suggests an "illicit" relationship, one which is ironically displaced once and for all when Hui Fei kills Chang, thus enabling Lilly to reunite with a male lover named Doc. While the scene of Yau's poem is also a train, it is a European train, perhaps alluding to Wong's leaving the U.S. in disgust "with Hollywood's treatment of her"[42] to find better opportunities in Germany and England in 1928. The poem's language does not give away the gender of its speaker; the "I" who sits next to the Anna May Wong figure could be a male figure like the poet, Dietrich's Lilly, or perhaps Dietrich herself:

> She's trying to find a way to turn her cup
> upside down, while sequestered on a train
> from Dublin to Vienna. Every angle
> glistens from behind a celluloid scrim.
> She's wearing a crescent scarf
> and chilly snake high smile:
> others claim she's all skin and eyes.
> No longer lashed to this oily chatter
> I enter her compartment.
>
> > She's languishing
> on a ledge, annoyed at all the times
> she's been told to be scratched, kicked,
> slapped, bitten, stabbed, poisoned, and shot.
> Lightning flickers between the frames.

On the seat beside me I find a circle
smaller than one left by a wet apple.

(187)

Though "sequestered" on the movie set, Anna May Wong is vulnerable to excessive exposure. Turning "her cup / upside down" to
protect herself from too much scrutiny proves difficult, because the
camera can exploit every "glistening" angle and reduce the actress to
a simplification of ethnic difference ("all skin and eyes"), as though
the individuality of her "crescent scarf / and chilly snake high smile"
did not exist. The speaker asserts an ability to extricate him/herself
from the "oily chatter" of racist compartmentalization and to "enter"
not only Wong's traveling area but the compartment of her psychic responses to being represented as someone worthy of violent treatment.
Of course, s/he may be deluded; Wong's protest may be part of the
original drama and not a subversion of it. However, the "lightning"
that "flickers between the frames" seems to signify the energy within
the actress "on a ledge"—out on a limb—that manifests the potential
to exceed the control of the film auteur's fiction-making apparatus. It
may also represent the "celluloid's" inadvertent admission of its own
materiality, its failure to convey unmediated narrative "presence."

Priscilla Wald offers the plausible assertion that "desire finds its
own voice in the poem, in which the speaker shares his uninterpreted
discovery of a wet spot with the reader. He will not repeat culture's
speaking for the subject, but instead presents the sign of her desire,
hitherto erased" (152). Aside from my lack of certainty that the
speaker is male, I believe that it is not clear whether the trope of the
small "circle" is authentically outside cinematic control or whether it
has been planted by the movie-makers as the visible "voice" of Anna
May Wong's desire. The poem's presentational economy and the dramatic flair of the concluding image leave open the possibility that the
poet, who might wish to enable his speaker to step into the fiction and
then, along with the "compartmentalized" actress, effectively observe
and critique it from the outside, knows that "celluloid" authority can
coopt visual tropes pointing to transgression of its reifications.

The successive sections of Yau's ongoing long poem, "Genghis
Chan: Private Eye," have appeared in *Radiant Silhouette, Edificio Sayonara* (1992), and *Forbidden Entries*.[43] The sections in *Forbidden Entries*
appear in "Hollywood Asians," part III of the book, alongside five
short prose-poems about Peter Lorre, whom Yau identifies in his
interview with Tabios as the "Austrian actor who plays a Japanese

detective in the Mr. Moto series" and "in at least one role . . . was feminized" (385). In these prose-poems, Yau imagines that Lorre would experience "anger . . . because he's trapped in his roles." Of course, such anger could hardly compare to that of Chinese at the spectacle of their misrepresentation in the Charlie Chan series. The title "Genghis Chan: Private Eye" collapses the fictitious Charlie Chan with the Mongolian conqueror Genghis Khan, who has long been marshaled to support the notion of Asian barbarity and, in that sense, is as much a "Hollywood Asian" as mild-mannered private eye Charlie Chan. Speaking of anti-Asian stereotyping in American literature, Elaine H. Kim observes, "When the Asian is heartless and treacherous, the Anglo is shown indirectly as imbued with integrity and humanity; when the Asian is a cheerful and docile inferior, he projects the Anglo's benevolence and importance" (4). Since "Genghis Chan" merges these opposing representations, Yau's title initiates a comic "dysfunctioning" of the usual effects of racist visual constructions. (So far, in the twenty-eight sections of this poem-in-progress, there are numerous references to Charlie Chan and seemingly very few allusions to Genghis Khan.)

The poem's first section (in *Radiant Silhouette*) begins with an ominous, bizarrely surreal flirtation between the "private eye" ("I") and a woman (whose race cannot be identified) or an image of a woman:

> I was floating through a cross section
> with my dusty wine glass, when she entered,
> a shivering bundle of shredded starlight.
> You don't need words to tell a story,
> a gesture will do. These days,
> We're all parasites looking for a body
> to cling to. I'm nothing more
> than riffraff splendor drifting past the runway.
> I always keep a supply of lamprey lipstick around,
> just in case.
> > She laughed,
> a slashed melody of small shrugs.
> It had been raining in her left eye.

> (189)

Speaking on a metalevel that is never scripted into the actual Chan movies, what I take to be the celluloid figure of "Charlie" as a mediated visual "presence" verbalizes the concept that he is not a solid

entity, but a "floating" signifier that is designed to permeate socially constituted boundaries. To sell the entertainment product,
his makers must gauge the "cross section" of public attitudes. Predictably, the detective meets another stereotype, the trope of female
vulnerability and luminosity. Yau emphasizes the violence done to
women's visibility through adjectives like "shivering" and "slashed."
The speaker's cynical reference to a pervasive parasitism—foreign to
Charlie Chan's wholesome proverbs—implicates writers, producers,
directors, actors, the Hollywood studio, and audiences. Alluding to
his ingenuity at using common objects as props of detection, which
(in this revised context) might double as odd seduction devices, Yau's
stereotype knows that, at the same time, his represented prowess is
"splendid" and his caricatured image is "riffraff."

As the flirtation or business talk continues, the woman offers a dark
mood: "dervish bleakness and glistened sediment" (189). Yau's Chan
closes the section by underscoring the (often clunky) artificiality of
cinematic constructions: "It was late / and we were getting jammed
in deep. / I was on the other side, staring at / the snow covered moon
pasted above the park. / A foul lump started making promises in my
voice." The characters are "jammed" in a straightjacket of cliché and
not any authentic sense of erotic inevitability. The "foul lump" of the
endlessly reiterable narrative formulas acts as a ventriloquist manip-
ulating the (living) dummy to "promise" to assist in the confirmation
of racist expectations.

The pidgin English of Charlie Chan's aphorisms blunts the impact of his brilliant functioning as a "private eye" and makes him
a "rusted pundit" (192). The five single-lined stanzas of section VI
poignantly and ironically comment on such mutilation of Asian
American "presence":

> I am just another particle cloud gliding across the screen
>
> A swamp chanter doodling on the margins of the abyss
>
> I prefer rat back flames to diplomatic curls
>
> I am the owner of one pockmarked tongue
>
> I park it on the hedge between sure bets and bad business.
>
> (194)

Any detective must wade through a "swamp" of details to crack
a case, but Charlie Chan's own English "song" is rendered murky.

Even if one of the marginalized persons works directly and effectively for those at the center, his "abysmal" and fragmented ("particle") status confines him to marginal "doodling." The third line above exemplifies Yau's ability to elude precise readability without recourse to incoherence. The opposition of "flames" to "diplomatic curls" may suggest a preference for experiential intensity over the kind of obsequious behavior that Chan must practice in the presence of his frequently racist employers; however, the adjectival use of the nouns "rat" and "back" as modifiers of "flames" derails any neat interpretation. Since the back of a rat does not emit fire, I am led to read "rat back" as a transformation of "rat pack"; perhaps this indicates that the Chinese American Chan longs for the kind of centrality and respect accorded the (real) African American Sammy Davis Jr. in his collaborations with Frank Sinatra and Dean Martin. Hedging his bets, the Chan figure "parks" his speech-effects on a "hedge," not even as comfortable as a ledge, between an incoherence that would prevent the solution of crimes and a fluency in standard English that would be "bad" for the "business" of midcentury Hollywood. It is important to note that Yau's perfect grammar in all sections of "Genghis Chan" that are not written deliberately in fragments overrides the representation of Chan as someone with a "pockmarked tongue."

In the first section of "Genghis Chan" included in *Edificio Sayonara*, section VIII, the speaker's focus on *in/visibility* plays on the notion of an "original" detective and his "copy," the movies' Chan:

> I plugged in the new image fertilizer
> and complained to my audible copy
>
> We did tour the best spots
> trying to attract basic signs of pity
>
> touched a disaster every now and then
> and remained ridiculous and understaffed
>
> Now I am clamped to the desk
> unravelling thought's stunted projectiles.
>
> (73)

The first line recalls the words "Private Eye" in the poem's title, which not only "means" a detective but probably reflects Yau's understanding that he is perceived solely as an aesthetic investigator of the visual—an art critic and experimental poet—whose discourse is hermetic, and not as a social critic. More generally, the "original"

Chinese American's complaint to the laughable "copy" constructed by European-American pop culture is that the latter renders actual Asians "inaudible" (and, implicitly, invisible) by usurping their discursive space in U.S. culture. If "original" and "copy" alike are reduced to the demeaning task of putting themselves on display ("touring") to seek "pity" rather than equality, an "original" Chinese American, unlike any of the non-Chinese actors who play Chan, receives no financial remuneration from the humiliating display. The verb "touched" in the third couplet is suggestively ambiguous: It could refer to encounters with discrimination or to the notion that characters like Charlie Chan are able to prevent "a disaster now and then" for the socially powerful by influencing ("touching") the situation through their interpretive prowess. As Elaine Kim ironically puts it, the "clever Chinese detective solves mysteries for the benefit of his ethical white clients and colleagues" (4). The clients' "ethics" do not extend to the point where they can remove the "ridicule" attached to Chan, who lacks the cultural capital for "staff" to do his bidding in pursuit of a more acceptable reputation.

Yau's "image fertilizer" is a machine that produces counterridicule based on strategies of disjunction and recontextualizing ("mulching") of the dross of anti-Asian absurdities from pop culture. "Clamped to the desk" of cultural reflection, the scholarly "private eye"/poet can "unravel" the "stunted" thinking that has been hurled at Asian Americans and, in so doing, he may diminish the impact of these "projectiles." Yau's parody is especially fertile when he renders pronouns like "you" unaccountable to determinate antecedents, as in the second half of section 8:

> Had I been as visible as a chameleon
> I would have crossed my eyes
>
> so as to look more like you
> than your silver reflection
>
> I would have hummed to the statue
> inside your black eyes and black tongue
>
> I would have memorized its song.
>
> (73)

The speaker pretends to seek communion with what Eugene Wong calls "racist cosmetology," the "inaudible copy's" "essential" reification—beyond even the "silver reflection" of celluloid. Thus, as Moss does in "Birmingham Brown's Turn," Yau mocks the fetishistic attention to a caricature of Asian eyes. Of course, the fantastic identification is unattainable because degraded cultural representations have made actual Chinese Americans seem not even "as visible as a chameleon." However, a form of self-referentiality further ironizes this negation: Creative writers of any race possess the resource of personae that can enable them to displace their individual "identities," socially constructed by oppressive others, with as many imaginative possibilities as the trope of the "chameleon" evokes.

In other sections of "Genghis Chan" in *Edificio Sayonara*, Yau reflects how Charlie Chan, as a low-level employee of the culture industry (corporation) is burdened by a general psychic containment well beyond the natural restraint expected of private eyes. The "I" in section XI seems to represent a Charlie Chan transposed into Yau's unbuttoned, surreal idiom:

> I patrol the mattress stained windows
> twiddle down hours
>
> until the next shifter releases me
> from my solemn valves
>
> A service examiner of bodies
> pumped into the last lanes of alley grass
>
> I keep my head in my lap
> and train small turtles to cry
>
> I am a piece of cake
> stacked against the company wall.
>
>   (76)

The Chan figure is stuck in the reifying structures of representation ("valves") of his scripted identity and social functioning—which confine him to "solemn" subservience ("head in . . . lap") amid a succession of slurs, yet which are anything but solemn to consumers of racist imagery. He is waiting for a recontextualizing "shifter" like Yau to use "shifty" (pronominal and tropological) linguistic or pictorial means to "release" him from such irksome banalities. Despite his ability to outsmart shifty criminals and crack criminal duplicities, he cannot resist the fictional straightjacket that the exploitative "company" places on him. Yau depicts the detective as a kind of coroner examining corpses of those in "the last" rather than the fast "lanes";

he "services" bodies like cars for clues of who placed them in the "alley" or "grass." The freshening of clichés indicates that Chan's "superiors" in the corporate hierarchy consider him easy ("a piece of cake") to manage, as he is "up against the wall." Similarly, in the next section, a corporate stamp of dubious "approval," coupled with the deletion of Chan's humanity, is parodied through one of Yau's zany substitutions for the commonplace: "I receive my certificate / to practice being humus" (77).

If the "private eye" is a vehicle for the illumination of "truth," caricature binds its "owner" to the grotesque in this circus of in/visibility: "I too am a yellow lamp / bolted to the elephant sky" (77). Several other sections of the poem in *Edificio Sayonara* utilize reiterations of "yellow" to mouth and mock the nasty visual identification of race through an absurdly simplifying naming of skin tone:

> My new yellow name
> was ladled over
>
> your installment plan.
> (79)

> Watching a yellow moonlit
> race of bold potatoes.
> (80)

> I stuffed bullet boxes
> with yellow jelly snacks.
> (82)

> Cast a cold
> and dirty style
>
> on every yellow leaf
> of lassitude.
> (84)

Problematic names can be distributed ("ladled") like soup to encourage uncritical moviegoers to "pay" again and again for the dubious investments of Hollywood moguls. The absurdity of seeking entertainment in a "race" among "potatoes" (thrown by children or "racing" to a boil?) resembles the ridiculous practice of viewing the common racial identity of many individuals as proof of their homogeneity in many ways; this perspective "boils" people as if they were potatoes. The transformation of "ballot boxes" and "yellow belly" to phrases that are, respectively, more sinister and sillier demonstrates how the poet's playful verbal "stuffing" of multiple contexts can diffuse the psychic violence of racist categorizing. Parodying W. B. Yeats's epitaph and proclamation of aesthetic distance by substituting "style" for "eye" after the words "cast a cold . . . ," Yau valorizes the play of signification over merely visual representation. "Style" is "dirty" because it embraces the impurities of the sociolect and transforms Asian American weariness of discriminatory images into "leaves" (pages) of active contestation.

The two tercets of section XIII take aim at the ignorant equation of Chinese Americans with the laundry business:

> It's hard to keep pretending
> you're a dusty chink
> in a hall of yellow linen
>
> You begin believing
> you're just another handkerchief
> wiping away the laundresses' tears.

(78)

"Hard" as it is for Chinese Americans, Charlie Chan is frozen in a situation where he must pretend to be the stereotype exemplified by the racist shortening of the word "Chinese"; furthermore, as a private eye, he must painstakingly utilize "chinks" in walls and character armor to make his discoveries as he rummages through "halls" for "dirty laundry." Rather than identifying with his function of helping whites, Chan begins to see himself as an object in the context of mourning: somehow, despite the contribution of his image to the mistreatment of Chinese Americans, he must comfort "laundresses" who despair of the permanence of their socioeconomic marginalization.

Forbidden Entries includes sections XXI to XXVIII of "Genghis Chan: Private Eye." Section XXI presents an intriguing jumble of Chan's acquiescence and resistance to his cinematic situation:

> I am a hat softener
> in the trade confession
>
> a belly down carpet stamp
> Jerks are my toys

I spray them
with my battering ham

over easy side order
flies to grow

Slime covers us tall
Flags flow meaner.

(92)

If Charlie Chan "softens" the "hard(ened) hats" of criminals through the "trade" of extracting "confessions," he also finds it necessary to get his "belly down" on the "carpet" to make discoveries. He gets himself dirty while his employers remain unsoiled, and he allows himself to be "stamped" by their base perceptions. Unlike the unfailingly courteous, understated Chan of the movies, Yau's speaker is able, at least for a moment, to play the "ham," to brag about how he "toys" with some wrongdoers ("jerks"), displays a comic, phallic mastery over them, to "cook" and "serve" them to his bosses, but then he appreciates the notion that such "fast food" entertainment as Chan movies encourages a distasteful form of narrative development ("flies to grow"). The "slime" and "meanness" of externally imposed constructions of identity ("flags," as in Jasper Johns's painted critique) grow "meaner," however much they are open to change ("flow").

In section XXII, Yau thrice emphasizes the elusive doubleness of his use of the Chan character:

Aquarium night steers
two intersected occupants:

(a motel I and the one
inside its vowel remnant)

toward a library of ledges
Stack doodle know-how

and lake metal shivers
A frigid stare card

I or my tongue
am the lizard

who bakes
your last animal residue

A tropical fossil haze
in an empty

farmhouse suit. . . .

I or the one

curled around
my voice

celebrate the humid glow
of another radius

burning the staircase of
its insect logic.

(94–95)

The convoluted layering of tropes in the opening couplets indicates the difficulties of representation and the elusiveness of "presence": visibility is problematic inside the atmosphere of an "aquarium
night." The figure of a "motel I," who can never seem to be "at home,"
"intersects" with whatever material, spirit, or absence exists inside its
fragmentary linguistic trace, the "vowel" "I." The scene of textuality
is a "library of ledges" because it comprises a complex "between,"
a perhaps illegible nexus of interstices that refuses to produce solid
"identity," even as others use "a frigid stare card" to invade individuals'
boundaries.

Can Yau, the real Chinese American investigator of cultural regularities, speak in the poem from his own critical perspective, and,
when he is exercising signs of his own "identity"—"I" and "tongue"
(metonymy for his "voice")—do the mediating effects of these signs
displace his power to form intentions, to act as the "lizard" who
configures ("bakes") cultural waste ("animal residue") so that its
insidious effects can be recognized and resisted? Is it possible that the
character Charlie Chan, as constituted by his "inventors," occupies or
"contaminates" this discursive space of the poet's "voice" by encircling
("curling around") it and, thus, dilutes critical potential? It makes a
great deal of difference which figure is "celebrating" the "light" of "de-
creation" to be produced in "another" space or context. On the one
hand, Chan's work to undermine the "staircase," the minute "logic" of
criminal escape from detection merely preserves the narrative "logic"
of his subservience to those who refuse to consider him or his people
their equals. On the other hand, linguistic energy ('burning") might

demystify the process of elevation ("stairs") of white racist cultural "logic," which sports a perspective no more capacious than that of an "insect."

Section XXIII, parenthetically subtitled "Haiku Logbook" and divided into thirty tercets, presents diverse "materials" discovered by the "private eye" during his investigations. Whether they enable him to solve mysteries of whether they spawn further conundrums is a moot point, but the deranging of cliches continues apace: "Feed him his lights / Poke down wallet sniffer / Probe hoisted tar dispute" (96). One "clue," "Empty star on a valley sheet" (96), may allude to the fact that Charlie Chan could not earn a "star" on Hollywood Boulevard; mainstream history ensures his marginality. In various "Haiku," such as 29, truncated ambiguous syntax and elusive language make it all but impossible to gather the clues into a cause-effect pattern: "Bank clobber miss lap / Spotted race crack lasher / Earned his graft" (100). Among many possible questions, the interpreter may ask: Does the U.S. economic system "clobber" an individual or group, or does someone "clobber" the "bank" during a holdup, or who has the mishap of missing a "lap" of a "race" "spotted" by a procedural flaw? Which ethnic group or competition is "spotted," "cracked," or "lashed," and by whom or what? Instead of learning his craft, how has the undetermined "lasher / Earned his graft," how does that relate to "race," and what is the private eye going to do about any of this?

The last five sections of the poem in *Forbidden Entries* consist of groups of couplets with two monosyllabic words in each line. Using a good deal of rhyme, off-rhyme, assonance, and homonymic play, these extremely concise, unpunctuated utterances exaggeratedly mimic a stereotypical forties or fifties (Hollywood) rendition of "Chinese" speech in English. Section XXIV reads:

Grab some
Grub sum

Sub gum
machine stun

Treat pork
pig feet

On floor
all fours

Train cow
chow lane

Dice splayed
trade spice

Make fist
first steps.
                    (102)

For the bigotedly ignorant, "some" Chinese food "treats" like "sub-gum," "pig feet," and chow mein (as opposed to Yau's "chow lane") comprise the "sum" of Chinese cultural accomplishment. Such individuals may happily "grab some" "chow" in a Chinese restaurant and wolf it down as quickly as a "machine" gun does it work. Who is down on "all fours" "on [the] floor" is not determined, but the couplet may indicate a general posture of debasement for those who misrepresent the Chinese and for the representation itself. The section's closure follows a rhymed chiasmus pointing to the two ways that the racist imagination sees Chinese in the U.S. making money—one somewhat respectable, the other not—with a frisson of emergent revolt (the "first step" of making a "fist") against the very kind of stultifying depiction being parodied. Against the "Duck walk / talk muck" (103) of Charlie Chan and similar creations, the "Sly jive / Yell high" (106) of Yau's playful, surreal, collagistic, counternarrative fragments offer fertile desedimentations of Chinese American visibility in popular culture. As he puts it in "Peter Lorre Dreams He Is the Third Reincarnation of a Geisha," crowding a host of cultural clichés in a handful of sentences:

> First I was delicate, a white peony, then I was a shiny
> delicatessen, something to snuffle over and return. Our leader
> said I was climbing the ladder of cultural evolution. I took
> mincing steps, I bowed and shuffled quietly across the
> rosewood floor, a prized worm. But I didn't mince words,
> they weren't mine to abuse. My teeth are straight and black in
> the proper manner. My thighs are long jade mirrors catching
> the moon's passage from one myth to another, a striped tiger
> unfurling its blurred banner. Why do you shun me? One of
> us inhabits a sad drama, the other entertains noisy guests.
> Don't squawk to me about nobility or honor.
>   (81)

Born at the beginning of the Kennedy presidency, Denise Duhamel reached maturity as a poet in the Reagan-Bush era, a perplexing time for U.S. feminists, and this fact has strongly influenced both the style and substance of her feminist poetry and its speculations on women's visibility. In *Backlash: The Undeclared War against American Women* (1991), Susan Faludi documents how reactionary forces, discrediting feminist ideology in the U.S. mainstream, did much to erode the gains that women made in the seventies. She indicates how men—especially working-class ones—blamed the loss of earning power and employment on a new influx of women workers and not on such "remote or intangible" factors as "leveraged buyouts that larded up debt and spat out jobs; . . . the 1987 Black Monday stock market crash, a shift to offshore manufacturing and office automation; a loss of union power; the massive Reagan spending cuts for the poor and tax breaks for the rich; a minimum wage that placed a family of four at the poverty level; the impossible cost of housing."[44] According to Faludi, "economic pains most often took a disproportionate toll on women, not men" (67), but, outside of feminist circles, this perception was not widely circulated.

An obvious cultural manifestation of this eighties "backlash" can be found in increasing mainstream legitimation of the "New Right" crusade against women's control of their reproductive processes and on behalf of patriarchal "family values." Less obvious is the plethora of seemingly reasonable antifeminist discourse deployed by *non-*Reaganites. Faludi demonstrates how the "men's movement" led by such figures as Warren Farrell and poet Robert Bly, "neofeminists" like Sylvia Ann Hewlett, the post–*Feminine Mystique* Betty Friedan, and pop posychologists like Toni Grant reinforce "backlash" ideology. Furthermore, according to Faludi, the mass media, deploying "sympathetic and even progressive-sounding" language, "cosmeticized the scowling face of antifeminism while blackening the feminist eye" (77). The press coined "terms" like "'the man shortage,' 'the biological clock,' 'the mommy track' and 'postfeminism'" and attributed women's dissatisfaction with their recent accomplishments to "feminism's achievements, not society's resistance to all these partial achievements." These examples of women's distorted visibility received ample confirmation from the plots and characterization of numerous TV sit-coms, including the *Cosby Show, Full House, Family Man,* and *Blossom.*[45]

In such a social climate, it is difficult for "protest" literature to reach media-blitzed minds. Citing attitudes presented in eighties "entertainment and advertising," Faludi notes: "To make a fuss about sexual injustice is more than unfeminine; it is now uncool. Feminist anger . . . is dismissed breezily—not because it lacks substance but because it lacks 'style' " (72). Denise Duhamel's response to this predicament is to write poetry that manifests "style" and powerful implications of anger. In an unpublished interview that I conducted in 1995, she stresses that "humor" can "draw in people who might otherwise feel excluded, or worse, who might otherwise dismiss a message (in my case, feminism) completely."[46] The humor in Duhamel's poetry is an integral (but not a dominant) part of a set of aesthetic strategies that allow feminist critique to be heard above the din of backlash. Duhamel's strategies include varieties of irony, hyperbolic fantasy mixed with the mundane, surrealistic uses of simile, "thick" description of individual and interpersonal experience, and surprising narrative juxtapositions. The poet provides the readers with an aesthetic environment in which they may arrive at their own cultural analyses without the annoyances and distractions of overt didacticism.

Duhamel, a poet of French-Canadian descent, is the author of five full-length collections of poetry: *Smile!* (1993), *The Woman with Two Vaginas* (1995), which consists of poetic adaptations of Eskimo (especially Inuit) myths, *Girl Soldier* (1996), *Kinky* (1997), a group of witty, incisive de/reconstructions of the Barbie doll, and *The Star Spangled Banner* (1999).[47] Duhamel's work appeared in the 1993, 1994, and 1998 editions of *The Best American Poetry*.

"Bulimia," perhaps the strongest poem in *Smile!*, problematizes the socially constructed visibility of the female body as an "object" by examining the consequences of the woman's internalization of some of the values that objectify her. In her comment for *The Best American Poetry 1994*, Duhamel notes that she "gathered stories of binges and purges from several women and one man" and "interwove" them, along with her "own struggles with the disease . . . into the one character who wanted to speak—and also . . . not speak— in 'Bulimia.' "[48] Calling "a bulimic episode . . . probably one of the most private and shameful of human experiences," one understandably blocked from consciousness, Duhamel seeks in the poem "to capture . . . the bulimic who is aware of her bulimia in scientific and psychological ways, the bulimic who has read up on her madness and still can't stop" (221). The poet's choice of third-person narrator enables "the bulimic" to view herself "as an outsider."

The female bulimic's shame may actually be intensified by the reading that makes her perceive herself as a bulimic "in scientific and psychological ways." In *Unbearable Weight: Feminism, Western Culture, and the Body,* Susan Bordo argues that scientific and mainstream psychological discourses on eating disorders reinforce female oppression by concentrating solely on individual "psychopathology" and ignoring powerful social influences on women's thinking and behavior. A contemporary woman who suffers from eating disorders, Bordo maintains, reflects culture's "ubiquitous and thoroughly routine grip . . . on the female body."[49] Concurring with Faludi's analysis of backlash, Bordo notes that "this situation has gotten worse . . . in the culture of the eighties" (66). The speaker in "Bulimia"—lacking a thorough, conscious understanding of these insights but, thanks to the author's ideological distance from the first-person posing as third-person narrator, inadvertently embodying them for the reader—lacks the chance to unburden herself of some shame by "sharing" it with its cultural sources.

Bordo perceives bulimia in women as an embodiment of "the unstable double bind of consumer capitalism." Hence, for her, bulimia is an extreme version of externally stimulated collisions of desire and shame that most American women of the eighties experienced:

> Conditioned to lose control at the mere sight of desirable products, we can master our desires only by creating rigid defenses against them. The slender body codes the tantalizing idea of a well-managed self in which all is kept in in order despite the contradictions of consumer culture. . . . [B]ulimia precisely and explicitly expresses the extreme development of the hunger for unrestrained consumption (exhibited in the bulimic's uncontrollable food binges) existing in unstable tension alongside the requirement that we sober up, "clean up our act," get back in firm control on Monday morning (the necessity for purge—exhibited in the bulimic's vomiting, compulsive exercising, and laxative purges).
>
> (201)

In "Bulimia's" opening strophe, Duhamel foregrounds the binary oppositions that inform Bordo's discussion: consumption/elimination, release/control, and—within notions of control—inside/outside. Before doing so, however, the speaker presents a desire that consumer culture either tries to displace or submerge when it elicits craving for commodities:

> A kiss has nothing to do with sex,
> she thinks. Not really. That engulfing, that trying to take
> all of another in for nourishment, to become one with her, to become

part of her cells. The way she must have had everything she wanted
in the womb, without asking.

(13)

Identifying "a kiss" with nourishment and the quest for a safe, nonhierarchical merging of two individuals (figured as an idealization of
pregnancy from the child's standpoint), the speaker wishes to "quar-
antine" it from its usual associations with "sex," since the latter for
this heterosexual American woman is bound up with forms of release
that signify a dangerous loss of autonomy, including her consent to
her own status as "object." The goal of such a union challenges the
either/or logic of the opposition, release/control, and thus suggests
a positive alternative to patriarchal values. Unfortunately, by the
poem's sixth line, a recollection of an auditory similarity between
osculation and intercourse "contaminates" the speaker's associative
drift, and notions of wholesome nourishment and egalitarian "merging" do not resurface:

>   Without words,
> kisses have barely the slurp sound of a man entering a woman
> or sliding back out—neither movement with even the warning of a
>   bark.
> The Greek word "buli," animal hunger.
> Petting, those kisses are called, or sometimes necking.
> She read this advice in a sex manual once: "Take the man's penis,
> slowly at first, like you are licking melting ice cream
> from the rim of a cone." But the gagging, the choke—
> a hot gulp of tea, a small chicken bone, a wad of gum grown too big.
> That wasn't mentioned. It's about what happens in her mouth
> past her teeth, where there is no more control, like a waterfall—
> or it being too late when the whole wedding cake is gone.

(13)

Humorously and grimly, Duhamel's citation of the sex manual's
simile displaces the equation of kissing and nourishment with an
equation of sex and the filling (not satisfaction) of a hunger without nourishment. Implicit comparisons of a woman's actual experience of fellatio with that of bulimic binges and purges graphically
signify parallel losses of personal control in the areas of sexuality and food consumption. These losses point to the coercive impact of larger social forces that dictate how women are supposed
to be seen and to see their actual and "ideal" selves. Suggesting
the resistance of the poem's material to "bite-size" formal

packaging, the extremely long, enjambed lines that characterize this passage and "Bulimia" as a whole do not evince a Whitmanian confidence; their frantic movement mimics the bulimic's inability, despite elaborately contrived efforts, to exert substantial control over her life.

In eighties' dessert commercials, Bordo asserts, "food is construct- ed as a sexual object of desire, and eating is legitimated as much more than a purely nutritive activity" (112). However, women are directed by the ads and by patriarchal culture to see desire as a problem to be managed: "Women are permitted such gratification from food only in measured doses." As Duhamel puts it in "Tulip," a poem in *The Star Spangled Banner,* "This is what the fashion magazine said: / if you must eat pasta, you should never eat more / than a tulip-sized amount, your meat never bigger / than a deck of cards" (46). Bordo notes that, according to Western masculinist mythology, "women's sexual appetites," which are linked with hunger for food and which undermine the masculinist value of female passivity, "must be curtailed and controlled, because they threaten to deplete and consume the body and soul of the male" (116–17).

This fantasy bears no resemblance to the desire of Duhamel's bu- limic "to become one" with another person, not to deplete her/him. However, a barrage of cultural advertising stemming from this misog- ynistic misperception influences the bulimic to abandon any realistic striving for a healthful approximation of this ideal. Embarking on another binge, she does not choose any random object of desire but a major traditional "Good Housekeeping Seal of Approval" for the adult woman, the wedding cake:

>   She's eating
> slowly at first, tonguing icing from the plastic groom's feet, the hem
> of the bride's gown, and those toothpick points that kept them
> rooted in pastry. She cuts the top tier into squares,
> reception-like. (The thrill she knew of a wedding this past June,
> stealing the white dessert into her purse, sucking
> the sugary blue gel from a napkin one piece was wrapped in.
> She was swallowing paper on her lone car ride home,
> through a red light, on her way to another nap
> from which she hoped a prince's kiss would wake her.)
>
> The second tier in her hands, by fistfuls, desperate
> as the Third World child she saw on tv last week, taking in gruel.
> Her head, light like her stomach is pumped up with air.

She can't stop. She puckers up to the sticky crumbs under her nails.
Then there are the engraved Valentine candies;
CRAZY, DREAM GIRL, ACT NOW, YOU'RE HOT. She rips open the
    bag,
devouring as many messages as she can at once.
They all taste like chalk. She rocks back and forth.

(13)

Duhamel's precise rendering of the movement from a languorous oral eroticism to frenzied gorging—with acute attention to every relevant detail and irony—enables the nonbulimic reader to imagine concretely how debilitating the psychophysiology of desperation can be. The "many messages" the bulimic "devour[s] at once" include the notion that a woman's sole road to positive visibility in her culture and, hence, self-esteem is a successful entrance into the "scene" of traditional marriage. "Valentine candies' " literal "chalkiness" is due both to their poor quality as confections and the binger's speed of ingestion; the eating disorder ironically deprives the bulimic of the pleasures of taste. On a figurative level, the puerile, limited, limiting cultural "messages" are unsavory "junk food." Despite obvious objections, the risky simile comparing the bulimic's desperation with that of a malnourished "Third World child" depicted on TV makes sense: used as "material" for news media, both are represented as objects of "pity" whose sufferings somehow "transcend" sociopolitical contexts.

The last two strophes of "Bulimia" send messages about the bulimic that go in intriguingly different directions. Reinforcing the association of heterosexual sex with the danger of gendered power relations, the agony of vomiting is described in sexual terms: "Her back jerks and arches the way it might / if she were moving her body to meet a man's during intercourse. / She wipes what has sprayed back to her chest, / her throat as raw as a rape that's happened to someone else" (14). In line with Duhamel's comment for *The Best American Poetry 1994* about bulimics' shame about their affliction and Bordo's observations that male-dominant cultures influence women to feel anxious about food-cravings,[50] desperation caused by the binge/purge routine is compounded by the dread of its discovery and the mental strain of concealing actions ironically intended to enhance the woman's visibility: the bulimic "orders" a wedding cake "from a different bakery this time, so no one / will remember her past visits and catch on" (13). At the poem's end, the speaker reports that the bulimic, after crushing "the cake box into a plastic garbage bag," "leaves to dispose it, not in the trashcan downstairs, / but in a dumpster way on the other side of town" (14).

Ironically, Duhamel's character is resourceful in developing strategies for "managing" aspects of bulimia and its in/visibility:

> She's learned it's best to wait ten minutes
> to make herself throw up. Digestion begins at this point,
> but the food hasn't gotten very far. As ingenious as the first
> few times she would consciously masturbate, making note of where
> her fingers felt best, she devises a way to vomit
> that only hurts for a second.
>
> She takes off her sweatshirt and drapes it over a towel rack.
> Then she pokes a Q-Tip on her soft pallet. Keeping in mind
> the diagram in her voice class, the cross section
> of the mouth showing each part's different function,
> the pallet—hidden and secret as a clitoris.
> The teacher's mentioning of its vulnerability, split-second
> and nonchalant like a doctor and his tongue depressor.

(14)

The impressive management skills and creative thinking that the bulimic currently uses for psychological and physical depletion could be harnessed in ways that would increase her own and other women's empowerment, but she vainly chases the illusion of instant gratification of appetite and a stulitifying form of prescribed visibility—the latter exemplified by the uproariously parodied "protagonist" of Duhamel's *Kinky*, Barbie.[51] As the winking reportage in the opening lines of "Bicentennial Barbie" informs us, the doll's visibility as an object of consumption grants her a social significance no less grand or absurd than Coca-Cola's:

> Because she is the most popular doll
> of the twentieth century, Barbie
> is buried in a time capsule in Philadelphia
> on July 4, 1976. She is scrunched between an empty Kentucky
> Fried Chicken bucket and a full Coca-Cola can.
> She's become a cultural icon, and now she has to pay
> the price.

(34)

By suggesting that Barbie, a figure of *impossible* proportions, is a prototype for human models who themselves represent extremely unusual body types, Duhamel in "The Limited Edition Platinum Barbie" incisively illustrates how the fashion industry contributes to women's immense insecurity about their appearance: "Now here she is, a real fashion illustration, / finally a model whose legs truly make up / more than half her height / . . . . Less demanding than Diana Ross / or Cher, Barbie has fewer flaws to hide" (46). The poet captures a misogynistic rage for the material and psychic diminution of women:

> No plastic surgery scars, no
> temper tantrums when Mackie's bugle beads
> don't hang just right. Calvin Klein
> won't design certain styles
> for any women larger than size eight.
> He "doesn't do upholstery" is the way
> he likes to put it. So imagine Bob Mackie's thrill
> of picking up this wisp of a model,
> Barbie weighing less than a quart of milk.
>
> (46)

Not surprisingly, "Barbie," who "like Miss America, never went gray" (63), also turns out to be the quintessential model for preening contestants in Atlantic City like "Miss Arizona," who "roller-skates to 'Amazing Grace,' / and Miss Pennsylvania," who "thanks God for her kidney transplant." As they mouth general pieties about current social issues and relatively uncontroversial partial solutions, these women in "Miss America 1990" disclose the "unnatural" things that they have done to overcome their own physical "deformities" in the quest for a "perfection" sanctioned by contemporary patriarchy, and the narrator offers another irony through her own mouthing of an uncritical acceptance of the entire proceedings:

> How lucky and right for them to be here—smiling, as they remind us
> about unfortunate discrimination against the hearing impaired,
> that it's so important for our youth to say no to drugs.
> If we only recycled our bottles and cans, why
> the world would be perfect, and they're here to prove it.
> They're like cupcakes on a plate just for us,
> like pheasants under the glass of our TV screens.
> The "girls" have sliced off what they don't need—
> extra fat on their noses, lumps jiggling
> along their thighs. And they've pumped up
> what they could use "just a tad" more of—
> there's breast surgery and hairspray.
>
> (62)

The visibility of these smiling candidates—archly characterized with a simile ("cupcakes") long used by sexist men to confirm women's "cute," subordinate status—is about as socially nutritious for American women (and men) as actual "cupcakes" or the "Valentine candies" in "Bulimia."

In a review of Evelyn Lau's fiction, Duhamel considers another problematic aspect of the discourse of women's visibility, effects of feminist representations of women's physical victimization. Noting Lau's numerous "descriptions of brutal sex," Duhamel praises her efforts "not to eroticize the violent" and "to capture the depression and rage of her female characters so that the sex in these books is not particularly sexy."[52] "The Raping of the Sun," one of the poems derived from Inuit tales in *The Woman with Two Vaginas*,[53] confronts this issue and the difficulty of anticipating the neutralization of feminists' resistance to antifemale violence. The poem features a young rape victim's attempt at a self-fortifying expression of her rage. After the first of two rapes in the dark of a "dance house," during which her attacker's identity could not be discerned, the girl devises a strategy to ensure that the "pleasure" of dancing would not be "taken" from her": "so the next night she returned to the dance house / with soot on her hands" in order to "dirty / her attacker's back" (37) if he struck again. After the second rape,

> the girl saw her palm prints on her brother's parka.
> She cried, "Such things are unheard of!"
> Her body still felt the ache of his presence
> as she took a sharp knife and cut off both her breasts.
> She flung them into his hands, screaming,
> "You seem to have a taste for my body—Eat these!"
> He held her bleeding breasts, in shock.

(37)

In her horrifying self-mutilation, the girl claims the role of victim through a visible gesture of ethical self-empowerment, and she offers her brother a tangible "gift" of guilt. How high a cost in pain should be paid for the moral high ground? The linking of victimization and identity may be so thorough as to block a vital component of identity based on agency (in this case, active resistance). Furthermore, oppressive forces might respond to the demand for ethical accountability by asserting their "right" to behave abusively to those "naturally" constituted as victims. In the narrative, "No one is sure if the brother meant to apologize / or simply attack his sister again"

(37). At the poem's end, "a wind . . . lifted" the siblings "high into the sky," the girl assuming the status of the sun and the boy that of the moon. The sister uses her light to do "all she can / to alleviate the dangers of the dark," while "she stays as far away as possible / from her brother, the cold dim moon." This security system, dependent on a fantastic deus ex machina, obviously cannot bring about a substantial shift in power relations in the actual world.

Sometimes the discourse of women's visibility in contemporary society focuses, not on their victimization or on presumed "aptness" for a subordinate status, but on their newly attained power in domains previously closed to them. In the title-poem of *Girl Soldier*, which is subtitled "(looking at Palphot Herzlia's photograph *Girl Soldier of the Israel Defense Force*)" and yet does not feature details that limit the poet's concern to Israeli gender politics, Duhamel trains her skeptical lens on this phenomenon. (The poet has told me that she attaches no pejorative connotation to the word "girl" when it is used to describe a child or a young woman.)

Duhamel's poem appeared a few years after the Persian Gulf War, which, as Major General Jeanne Holm asserts, "refueled a long-simmering debate over just what should be the outer limits, if any, of their roles in the armed forces."[54] According to Holm, "Of the 540,000 Americans who served in Operation Desert Storm, nearly 41,000 were women. . . . It was the largest wartime deployment of American military women in history" (xiii). "On land, at sea, and in the air," the women "piloted and crewed jet planes and helicopters over the battle area, refueled fighters in mid-air, . . . and loaded laser-guided bombs on F-117 Stealths for raids on targets in Baghdad. They directed Patriot missiles, drove trucks, ran enemy prisoner of war facilities, . . . and guarded bases." The Gulf War destroyed the myths that "*military women are protected from exposure to combat*" and that "*women would not be able to perform in the pressure of the combat environment*" (462).

Since Holm documents the long history of the patriarchal U.S. military establishment's efforts to marginalize women in all branches of the service, a feminist might conclude that women's proven record of accomplishment and valor during the Gulf War—made eminently *visible* by CNN and the mass media in general—could break down sexist stereotyping and establish women's right and ability to perform in this and many other spheres of endeavor once reserved for men. Nevertheless, Holm documents the postwar resistance in Congress and the military to women's expanded participation as well as new-found support (473–509). Duhamel's poem raises the possibility that patriarchal forces may attempt to coopt and hence domesticate the image of the "girl soldier." First, the poet discloses the juxtaposition of the girl's new role with signs of traditional femininity:

> The girl soldier wears lipstick,
> wisps of hair falling from her bun,
> her eyelashes as long and dark as spider legs.
> She undoes her top buttons, not really enough
> to show cleavage, but her army insists
> on a sprig of collarbone
> as a reminder that she is dainty.
> She holds her gun like a hair dryer
> or a kitchen appliance she loves
> but, until recently, has taken for granted.
> The ocean waves crash behind her—
> the enemy boats glistening in the sun
> along with her hat-pin and the metal crowns
> on the lapels of her jacket.
>
>   (16)

This contemporary focus on appearance resembles how, according to Holm, U.S. recruiters in various branches during the fifties and sixties were directed to find the most "attractive" women possible (142–43, 145, 179, 181–83). Even "the indocrination programs more closely resembled ladies' finishing schools than military programs," because "subjects designed to enhance femininity and women's proper role in the military were emphasized" (181).

Whether or not the "lipstick" or the "wisps of hair" escaping "from her bun" are Duhamel's soldier's idea, the army's insistence "on a sprig of collarbone" as a trope of adherance to a feminine norm diminishes the impact of her possession of "male" firepower and the "glistening" danger of "enemy ships" in the background. The simile linking "her gun" and "a hair dryer" demonstrates how masculinist perceptual maneuvering reduces the gravity of lethal violence to the "triviality" of the domestic sphere when a female soldier is the object of representation. While a man's weapon could "naturally" stand for the powerful phallus, the gun in a woman's hands is merely "handy"; it enables her to clean up the mess (enemy soldiers) more efficiently than a lesser weapon.

However, the attempted domestication of the girl soldier is not tidy enough; subversive potential cannot be swept away: a gun is a gun is a gun. The soldier's femininity coexists uneasily with the murderous potential of her mastery of a technology that could undo alleged biological disparities in physical power between the two genders. Nevertheless, in creating a dramatic juxtaposition of women's internalization of (or surface complicity with) patriarchal constraints and the potential activation of feminist anger and determination to effect change, Duhamel indicates how the former keeps the latter under wraps:

> She is proud to be part of the Defense Force
> is the lie the picture is telling,
> as blatant as the old lie that all women love to iron
> or live in the suburbs
> as long as they have the right products.
> How big these falsehoods are, how many seas they span.
> If there have to be girl soldiers at all,
> shouldn't they fight for girl things?
> To get them out of girl ghettos,
> to shed them of their pink collar jobs
> and the hoods that hide their faces
> in so many places of the world?
> To get a girl's perspective of religions?
> To overthrow offices and put girls
> in charge of governments?
> But girls have been brainwashed they're safest
> using their oppression as protection.

(16)

Rather than finding progress in differences between the image of the girl soldier and depictions of fifties and sixties American middle-class women who spew cheer about technologically facilitated suburban domesticity, Duhamel's simile insists upon a deep kinship in the two ads' underlying ideological messages. Frozen in a photo, the girl soldier, a device for the recruitment of other girl soldiers, advertises the illusion of gender equality while patriarchal standards remain largely unchallenged. Through rhetorical questions, the poet's speaker briefly imagines a literal militarization of feminist political activity in place of a common figurative militancy—for example, that of the New York art scene's "Guerilla Girls"—but then returns to the notion of women's internalization of patriarchal images as a prime reason for the fact that many do not actively embrace a feminist agenda. Even when the speaker disputes the masculinist drivel that "girls" without male assistance would "be naked and squashy, just ready for soup," her rhetoric is problematic:

> But when they're reminded
> this is not true, girls feel a deep strength
> that has something to do with the earth.
> Vaginas from all countries make peace—
> the root of the word literally meaning sheath,
> a resting place for men and their swords.
>
> (17)

While "girls" might "feel a deep strength" by embracing vague essentialist affirmations of their gender's "special" connection or identification with nature, that same logic is a staple of "backlash" rhetoric that justifies the assignment of child care as their fundamental task. Also, Duhamel's speaker does not posit how their feeling and the accompanying thoughts can translate into a concrete, collective "fight for girl things." If etymology points to the significance of "vaginas" as instruments of peace through their "taming" of heterosexual men's battle-lust, as in Aristophanes' *Lysistrata,* such an objectifying view of women's peace-making is extremely limiting. Perhaps, however, the poet irreverently deploys "vaginas" as a synecdoche for women in the act of developing political strategies for the displacement of violent masculinist impulses through structures of peaceful interaction. Rather than proposing hasty solutions to the impasse embodied by the girl soldier's image, Duhamel offers a sense of unease in the poem's closure; hence, she cautions feminists to guard against infiltration of "backlash" rhetoric into their own emerging discourses and visual representations of social transformation.

Presenting intriguing depictions of the appropriation of opposite gender roles, a number of poems in *The Woman with Two Vaginas*[55] illustrate Judith Butler's contention in *Gender Trouble* that "gender ought not to be construed as a stable identity or locus of agency from which various acts follow; rather, gender is an identity tenuously constituted in time, instituted in an exterior space through *a stylized repetition of acts*" (140). Because the *public* "action of gender requires a performance that is *repeated,*" that "is at once a reenactment and reexperiencing of a set of meanings already socially established," however "natural" the "action" appears to many, this "performance" effectively aims to maintain "gender within its binary frame—an aim that cannot be attributed to a subject, but, rather, must be understood to found and consolidate the subject." Thus, after an accident "deflates" the prime visual sign of the character's male identity in "Vagina," a poem taken from an East Greenland Inuit tale, the man's conscious striving to be visible as a traditional woman does not have to be judged "unnatural," but can be viewed as a utilization of what Butler calls "the rules governing signification" of gender which "not only restrict, but enable the assertion of alternative domains of cultural intelligibility" (145). "*Within* the practices of repetitive signifying," the "emasculated" man is permitted to enact "a subversion of identity":

> One day a fisherman's penis got tangled up in his harpoon line.
> The fisherman was never really good at catching seals
> and as both prey and hunter tugged and hauled in opposite directions,
> the man felt all the strength gush out of his penis.
> He was relieved, if the truth be known.
> He went home and dressed up like a woman.
> He called himself Vagina and announced he was in need of a husband.
>
> (10)

Since the fisherman's masculinity ebbs because he has botched a central male activity that he had never mastered or enjoyed, his "relief" is understandable. Previously, the thorough social conditioning that made him visible as a male discouraged him from questioning the traditional gender-"performance" that he was commanded to "repeat." However, incurring his mother's anger and her threat to "kick" her/him "out of the house / if he didn't again dress like a man and go out on the hunt," Vagina uses "magic"—which, unlike today's surgery, is not quite powerful enough to make his male genitals disappear and replace them with female ones—intended to silence societal rejection of his performative reversal and to articulate an essential humanness beyond limiting perceptions of gender: "Vagina knew a little magic, so she stripped the skin from her body / until she was just a skeleton. Her mother dropped dead in fright" (10). Resuming the effort to "behave more and more like a woman," not only fretting "with her hair" but going so far as to make "cuts at her groin" once a month "so she could bleed," Vagina squarely faces the difficulty of establishing a sanctioned "heterosexual" relationship:

> Vagina was still having trouble getting a husband
> when a neighbor agreed to loan hers. When Vagina
> removed her dress, the neighbor's husband
> noticed her penis and called Vagina a madman.

Again, Vagina removed her skin as if to prove deep down
there was no difference between women and men
and their skeletons. Instead of consenting to have sex,
the man was so frightened he fell dead, like Vagina's mother, on the
    spot.

(10)

"Deep down," the fisherperson has caught the recognition that,
regardless of anatomical distinctions, a human being could com-
petently perform many "oppositely" gendered actions through an
understanding and careful copying of what "s/he" has observed.
"Beneath the skin" and prior to the imprint of social imperatives,
each human mind is "no different" from others in the sense that
anatomy and cerebral wiring do not preordain specifications of the
"clothing" of gender-identity that an individual will necessarily appropriate. Stripping away deceptive "flesh" to reveal the bare bones
of polymorphous potential, this insight administers a lethal shock to
the systems of those rigorously schooled (and strongly) invested in
the inevitability and naturalness of the strict separation of the sexes'
characteristics.

When Vagina adopts an orphan, he eventually judges "her" a good
"mother." Although he "had seen Vagina pissing / while standing
up" and "accused his mother of being a man" (10), the boy learns
to cherish "her" self-sacrificing devotion to him. When "she" turned
into "a skeleton again," he was not frightened but "ran his fingers /
over his mother's eyeball sockets and ribs. He drew a circle around
her pelvis and laughed" (11). This "circle" may signify, not only a
vagina, but a zero or a playful bracketing of the concept of biological
sex. "Forced to use stronger magic," Vagina then "reached into her
chest / and pulled out her entrails. 'There,' she exclaimed, / 'do
you still insist on having some blubber?' " This sacrifice stands in for
the image of the traditional mother's selfless service, as well as the
nourishment that any biological mother internally and naturally gives
her child. Unfortunately, in this case, Vagina's precious gift is stolen
by "some dogs" who "burst their way into the igloo," and when she
chases the dogs, she suffers a greater loss:

But before she could catch up, the biggest dog had eaten her
    heart.
And everyone knows a person is nothing without that.
Slowly Vagina wasted away as the orphan watched.
The orphan buried his mother beneath a pile of stones,

loving her in spite of her magic and foolish penis.
Loving his dead mother in spite of her skeleton games,
the orphan went to search for seals and whales and blubber on his
    own.

                                                                    (11)

In another context, the "dogs" might represent negative environ-
mental forces that could threaten the security of any family's private
space; here, they seem to be enraged masculinists determined to
punish the former fisherman's self-styled transformation with ultimate severity. Consuming "her heart," "the biggest dog" is devouring
Vagina's fundamental desire to nurture. Although Vagina's resistance
to patriarchal norms has been cut down by the poem's coda, the
orphan's ability to see and love "her" as a "mother" despite the visual
incongruity of "her" penis indicates some measure of triumph.

Nevertheless, the example of the martyred Vagina's individual
ability to throw off constraints of "her" masculinity and to perform
gender as s/he wishes has limited value for the feminist rethinking of
the social construction of gender. While Butler valorizes "subversive
laughter" occasioned by "the pastiche-effect of parodic practices in
which the original, the authentic, and the real are themselves constituted as effects" (146) and perceives these "strategies of subversive
repetition" as enabling "local possibilities of intervention through
participating in . . . practices of repetition that constitute identity
and, therefore, present the immanent possibility of contesting them"
(147), Vagina's gestures subvert their own parodic potential. Her determination to assume the role of traditional, self-sacrificing "woman"
tacitly endorses a grotesquely oppressive form of female visibility.

Having been unable to establish a homosexual relationship mas-
querading as a heterosexual marriage, s/he must forego the task
of becoming a minimally competent fisherperson (or of asserting
the right to hunt) and, thus, can only satisfy "her son's" request for
"blubber" by splitting open her own body. Vagina's acceptance of
traditional prescriptions about how the visibility of a performer of
gender should be constituted provides no room for any person to
develop—simultaneously—various competences conventionally associated with each sex, gain access to a range of opportunities, and
benefit from structures of interdependence that make self-sacrifice
unnecessary.

Like "Vagina," "My Grandmother Is My Husband" inadequately
challenges patriarchal deployments of the binary opposition, man/

woman. "Left alone with" her "only grandmother," the poem's young female speaker states that the rest of the family never returned, but "luckily," the old woman possessed a "magical" ability to become a "male" provider:

> With a few words and a trance, she could turn herself
> into a man. Her seal-bone penis
> was always full of pleasure, her blubber-balls
> were always warm. And being a man, she was able
> to get food without as much danger. Her vagina
> transformed into a mighty sled. She created
> a team of dogs from her own lice. I spent my days
> hidden in the hut, sewing animal skins and singing.
> Grandmother always returned by evening,
> sometimes with a ptarmigan, his dead feathered feet
> stiff in the cold. I learned how to cook
> all kinds of soup. This went on for many days of dark
> and light, many years and changes in my body.
> Sometimes I feared my handsome grandmother's death
> and wondered if I'd be able to hunt for myself.
> How could I sleep without her curled into me?
>
> (53)

Rather than having changed sexes, the resourceful grandmother seems to have mastered a typical male role to avert her shrunken family's starvation. Her "penis" is a culture-specific dildo, and her scrota are made of "blubber." The appearance of maleness and not an actual male body, as well as hunting skills and a knack for disguising advanced age, enables her "to get food without as much danger." The utilitarian surrealism of the vaginal "sled" can be read as a trope for the necessity of displacing her femininity in order to make it and her newly adopted masculinity useful in a time of crisis. Interestingly, the granddaughter continues to use the terms "she," "her," and "grandmother" to denote her benefactor while simultaneously calling her "a man" and her "husband." The speaker's sociolinguistic training does not permit her to deploy a vocabulary of hermaphroditism (which would be inaccurate) or "butch" and "femme" lesbianism (much less lesbian incest), or one that characterizes her grandmother solely as a woman who dares to exercise human abilities conventionally, but wrongly, coded as male. Later, the granddaughter even puts forth the magic fiction that her partner's "child filled [her] belly." Although alternative gender/sexual arrangements are implicitly represented, their full social implications are obscured, undermined, or not quite rendered comprehensible.

When a man whose "penis" and "wrinkled testicles" are "real skin and blood" finds the speaker at home alone and learns about her unique "marriage," he forcefully asserts his privilege to restore the patriarchal order of things: "I kicked as he threw me over his shoulder, / promising he would make me a happier wife" (53). Somehow, though her new "husband" has taken her away, she knows how her grandmother reacts to the loss of her "wife" after returning "that evening as usual": "She cried out my name / over and over, looking for boiling water, some proof / that I was coming back. She saw no point / in hunting or eating anything else." Lack of community, even a community of two, undoes the perceived need for a visible performance of gender roles and even gender identification: "She saw no point / in being a man any more. She undid / her magic spell—man or woman, it's all the same / when a person dies alone." Whereas the undoing of all such constraints might constitute a movement toward the end of sexism and abundant possibility for any individual, here it marks a psychological end of the road.

In my introductory chapter, a citation from Audre Lorde raises the issue of European-Americans' tendency to render women of color invisible, and this is surely an obstacle to feminist collectivity. While Duhamel includes critiques of racism in such poems in *Smile!* as "What Happened This Week" (37–38) and "Stories from the Body" (40–41) and, in *Girl Soldier,* "How to Help Children through Wartime" (18), she never *explicitly* interrogates white feminist exclusions and omissions. However, several poems in *Kinky* which *overtly* depict commodity capitalist culture's racist cooptation of multiculturalism can be interestingly reframed as implicit critical articulations of a complicity between the moves of Mattel's masterminds and those of some white feminist leaders. "Oriental Barbie," for example, speaks of an expunging of specificity in the representation of Asians:[56]

> She could be from Japan, Hong Kong, China,
> the Philippines, Vietnam, Thailand, or Korea.
> The little girl who plays with her can decide.
> The south, the north, a nebulous
> province. It's all the same, according to Mattel, who says
> this Barbie still has "round eyes,"
> but "a smaller mouth and a smaller bust"
> than her U.S. sister. Girls, like some grown men,

like variety, as long as it's pretty, as long
as there's long hair to play with.

(19)

These lines may remind us that some white feminist community-builders and cultural theorists "like" a kind of "variety" (in their constituency and interpretive objects respectively) that does not turn out to be too various but is based on broad generalizations about "others"—for example, Asian culture and Asian women. While paying lipservice to demands for pluralist inclusivity, such individuals continue making their own experience and subject-position the standard for the representation of all women. As in the case of "the little girl who plays with" the "Oriental Barbie," the privileged European-American feminist "can decide" what fiction to impose upon "Oriental" women during her intellectual "play." Of course, feminist community would be infinitely better served if she were to engage in a respectful dialogue with a complex heterogeneity of *self*-representations by women "from Japan, Hong Kong, China, / the Philippines, Vietnam, Thailand, . . . Korea," and elsewhere.

In "Black Barbie History," a poem that offers the remarkable observation that each Barbie doll has a "waist not much thicker than her neck" (20), the presumption of "whiteness"—amid claims about the accomplishment of "diversity"—as paradigm for female humanity is even more obvious than in "Oriental Barbie": "Black Barbies look exactly like White Barbies. / Identical molds, not unlike uniform squares / of Nestles' Dark and Alpine White chocolate bars" (20). "White Barbie's tiny hands, flexed feet, and slight nose" even appear on a "doll . . . supposed to resemble" a real African American, "the actress Diahann Carroll."

As in other poems in *Kinky,* Duhamel uses plastic surgery as a trope for women's submission to the violence of patriarchal disfiguration. Here, it might also offer a warning about the negative consequences that would ensue if a version of U.S. feminist community largely defined by Eurocentric standards valorizing women's "uniformity" were to prevail over the challenges of feminists of color like Lorde, Moss, and Gloria Anzaldúa: "Today, the same plastic surgery / used on Black Barbie can smooth those ethnic features / in all of us. We can all look the same, as we jump / into a vat of anesthesia and knives" (20). Through her ironic mouthing of this "commercial," Duhamel suggests that the effort to destroy dynamic differences in the interest of feminist collectivity would not only "dull" "sisterhood" but could boomerang in such a way that such differences would drastically fragment the community: "So let's bring our check books, our intolerable foibles, our fat selves. / There'll be no more competition when we emerge, identical / and redone, only dulled sisterhood and numbed love." Never assuming that she can posit a visibility for women that will somehow overthrow male dominance, Duhamel in her poetry consistently challenges every form of patriarchal or "redone" visibility, whether homogenizing or crudely differentiating, that threatens to disable possibilities for the elucidation and attainment of feminism's widest-ranging emancipatory aims.

2

The Effacement, (Re-)tracing, and Reconstruction of History: Carolyn Forché, Joseph Lease, Martín Espada, and Gloria Anzaldúa

IN THE INTRODUCTION TO HER ANTHOLOGY *AGAINST FORGETTING, Twentieth-Century Poetry of Witness* (1993), which she calls "the result of a thirteen-year effort to understand the impress of extremity on the poetic imagination,"[1] Carolyn Forché discusses features of a "poetry of witness," a concept which had guided her own poetics for close to two decades, and which informs her representation and contestation of the erasure of aspects of twentieth-century history in her long poem *The Angel of History* (1994).[2] Marking "a resistance to false attempts at unification," this poetry "speaks for what might, with less than crippling irony be called 'the party of humanity' " (46). It constitutes "a rejection of unwarranted pain inflicted on some humans by others, of illegitimate domination." For Forché, the poetry of witness embodies a "resistance to terror" that "makes the world habitable" and an "insistent memory" that "renders life possible in communal situations."

Born precisely at midcentury, Forché has long struggled productively with the question of what forms her own "poetry of witness" should take. When Stanley Kunitz chose her first book, *Gathering the Tribes* (1976), for the Yale Series of Younger Poets, her poetic witness was not focused on "the insistent memory" of repressive violence. The poems feature general (not very "political") evocations of the erasure of "tribal" history and attempts at psychic compensation for such losses, and, as the title indicates, the effort to represent and bring into alignment nurturing communities.[3] In his introduction, Kunitz right cites "kinship" as "the theme that preoccupies" the young

94

Forché. Speaking of her "passionate and tribal" imagination and her predilection for "narrative . . . leavened by meditation," Kunitz states: "She remembers her childhood in rural Michigan, evokes her Slovak ancestors, immerses herself in the American Indian culture of the Southwest, explores the mysteries of flesh, tries to understand the bonds of family, race, and sex."[4]

Not long after *Gathering the Tribes* appeared, Forché's exposure to conditions of harrowing extremity and egregious social injustice in El Salvador, coupled with her growing awareness of the moral bankruptcy of "a controversial American policy of support to a government deemed responsible for the systematized slaughter of its" numerous "political opponents,"[5] propelled her toward writing a politically engaged journalism and poems of witness that bear little, if any thematic resemblance to her earlier poetry. In the essay "El Salvador: An Aide Mémoire" (1981), she reports: "Between 1978 and 1981 I traveled between the United States and Salvador, writing reports on the war waiting to happen, drawing blueprints of prisons from memory, naming the dead."[6]

"In Salvador, 1978–80" is the first of three sections of Forché's second book of poems, *The Country between Us,* which won the Lamont Prize for 1981.[7] (The book's third section consists of the five-page poem "Ourselves or Nothing," which addresses the poet's close friend, the social critic and activist Terrence Des Pres, and includes passages about El Salvador. In "Reunion," the second section, there are poems about Forché's experience of foreign travel, about the influence of the Vietnam War on herself, her peers, and her entire generation, and about memories of childhood.) As Mary S. Strine states of a particular poem in "El Salvador, 1978–80," the entire section of *The Country between Us* can be "understood as a response to or argument against the dominant 'official' text" about U.S. involvement in El Salvador "by the U.S. State Department and most of the American press."[8]

The most widely cited and anthologized of Forché's texts, "The Colonel," a paragraph-long prose-poem dated "May 1978," is a powerful indictment of the Carter administration's failure to fulfill its "human rights" policy with respect to the situation in El Salvador. In an interview with Bill Moyers, Forché states that Salvadoran military officers, like the colonel in the prose-poem, thinking that she might be "working for the U.S. government," sought her out and voiced their anger at "the human rights policy of President Carter"; they considered the U.S. "hypocritical in its relation to them: they were still getting support, but they were embarrassed because they were being insulted internationally about their human rights behavior."[9] Because the prose-poem articulates a political context that was equally relevant *after* the late 1979 establishment of the "moderate" Salvadoran government and the departure of Carter from the White House, it stands also as a critique of the Reagan administration's foreign policy.

The prose-poem opens with a gesture affirming Forché's witness-status, "What you have heard is true. I was in his house," and moves to the depiction of a serene domestic scene, which is jarred at various points by the presence of tools of a death squad leader's trade: "a pistol on the cushion" and "broken bottles . . . embedded in the walls around the house to scoop the kneecaps from a man's legs or cut his hands to lace" (16). Thus, unspeakable violence bankrolls domestic tranquility. Midway through "The Colonel," after "some talk . . . of how difficult it had become to govern," the colonel's self-dramatization begins, and, building on the ominous images that preceded it, shoves domesticity into the background once and for all:

> The parrot said hello on the terrace. The colonel told it to shut up, and pushed himself from the table. My friend said to me with his eyes: say nothing. The colonel returned with a sack used to bring groceries home. He spilled many human ears on the table. They were like dried peach halves. There is no other way to say this. He took one of them in his hands, shook it in our faces, dropped it into a water glass. It came alive there. I am tired of fooling around he said. As for the rights of anyone, tell your people they can go fuck themselves. He swept the ears to the floor and held the last of his wine in the air. Something for your poetry, no? he said. Some of the ears on the floor caught this scrap of his voice. Some of the ears on the floor were pressed to the ground. (16)

The colonel believes that the Carter administration's relative *lack* of interest in ending human rights violations in El Salvador, due to its overriding concern with the containment of "communist" influence, has much greater force than its public complaints or North American "people's" protests. Therefore, he can afford to tell them off without fear of serious retaliation. Feigning a godlike power through his gross parody of baptism and resurrection, the colonel flaunts his ability to deliver a death-sentence and to employ the physical remnants of that sentence as objects of his whim to represent his will's superiority to any moral imperative. The raising of the wine glass adds a finishing touch to the gruesome parody of Christian sacrament.

When the colonel dares Forché to cite his performance in her poetry, he implies that it would make a titillating spectacle. Knowing that she must bear witness, the poet must also dissociate the telling from an apolitical sensationalism.[10] Forché was probably concerned that the aesthetic aptness of the simile visually linking the severed ears and "dried peach halves," could—as she puts it in "El Salvador: An Aide Mémoire"—end up "poeticizing horror" and have a similar effect as "the photographic image that might render starvation visually appealing" (257).[11] On the other hand, a close approximation of accuracy is required for the vital tasks of witness and censure to succeed, and so the poet accompanies the image with a grim assertion of its necessity.

Forché manages to weaken the social force of the colonel's drama by including his challenge for her to depict it in writing. Thus, she underscores the notion that, however locally omnipotent he currently seems, the colonel depends on others to represent his (and his group's) actions to foreign powers influencing the range of his own domination. The poet further stymies the colonel's aims by repeating his fiction of making the ears regain "life," but with an important difference: she displaces the simile of "dried peach halves," the sign of remnants of human life as commodities, with a metaphor that "cures" them of their death-induced deafness and lends them sufficient existence to hear (and judge) the murderer's "scrap" of language. The prose-poem's final sentence may suggest living ears listening for a menacingly close explosion, a violence that the colonel and his ilk have initiated and sustained.

For several years after the publication of *The Country between Us*, Forché experienced writer's block while undergoing an epistemological shift that would lead her away from the kind of "poetry of witness" in *The Country between Us* to a new kind, one that directly confronts the issue of the erasure of history. In a December 1987 interview with David Montenegro, held roughly a year-and-a-half after she began writing *The Angel of History* (1994), Forché expresses her realization that, "as one moves farther from events" like the German Holocaust and the bombing of Hiroshima and Nagasaki, "they become more apparently complex"; "to say *one* thing," a "reductive" and "exclusive" gesture, is now "impossible."[12] As Forché tells Montenegro, her "discovery" of the starting point of *The Angel of History* came after five years of writing numerous "fragments and notes," when she "realized that" the accumulation "constituted the beginning of [her] new work," something distinct from "the poem [she] had written in the past"

(64–65). Instead of deploying "the fictional, first-person voice" of *The Country between Us,* in which "the self" coercively "derives its authority from its privilege over "the 'other,' whether . . . the implied reader" or the poem's addressee, Forché's new poetry of witness would "question this voice, or . . . permit a dialogue of selves, or at least . . . render the artifice apparent," thus "questioning the idea of closure" and, hence, "linearity" (64).

In the opening paragraph of the "Notes" of *The Angel of History,* Forché declares: "the first-person, free-verse, lyric-narrative poem of my earlier years has given way to a work which has desired its own bodying forth: polyphonic, broken, haunted, and in ruins, with no possibility of restoration" (81). Forché's comments about differences between the poetics of *The Country between Us* and *The Angel of History* resemble Language Poet Lyn Hejinian's distinction in "The Rejection of Closure," a 1985 essay/discussion with other Language Poets, between the "closed text," "one in which all the elements of the work are directed toward a single reading of the work"[13] and "the open text," which, "invites participation, rejects the authority of the writer over the reader and thus, by analogy, the authority implicit in other (social, economic, and cultural) hierarchies," and "speaks for writing that is generative rather than directive," so that "ideas and meanings are permitted to evolve" from a reader/writer "collaboration" (272). While, in the discussion section of the article, at least three of the fourteen other Language Poets take exception to the rigidity of the binary opposition, open/closed (286–91), Hejinian's cautiously promulgated valorization of texts that writers have intended to leave extremely "open" over ones that seem more "closed" (because of authorial choices) is a justification for the high degree of disjunctiveness in Language writing. Hejinian asks, "Can form make chaos (i.e., raw material, unorganized information, uncertainty, incompleteness, vastness) articulate without depriving it of its potency, its generativity?" and "Can form . . . actually generate the potency of uncertainty, incompleteness, vastness, etc.?"; answering affirmatively, she calls these aims "the function of form in art" and asserts "that form is not a fixture but an activity" (275).

Of course, some readers might argue that they do not wish to "collaborate" with Language authors who relinquish "authority" by supplying scant "traditional" devices of coherence; they might find in this "generativity" the "closure" of undifferentiated chaos. I would surmise that, since Forché is concerned with bearing witness in *The*

Angel of History, she cannot afford to develop the kind of poetic form that features the extreme "openness" of much (not all) writing known as Language Poetry. Therefore, she must strive for form that can be situated somewhere between Language writing's disjunctiveness and the relatively closed structures of *The Country between Us.* This long poem does not turn "raw material, unorganized information, un-certainty, incompleteness" into false certainty, illusory completeness, and information organized in such a way that other possibilities are often excluded. However, it *does* organize raw material with some degree of coherence and somewhat reduce uncertainty and incom-pleteness through the articulation of historical detail and implied political perspectives on it, even as it fulfills Hejinian's dictum of generating "the potency of uncertainty, incompleteness, vastness" through carefully placed disjunctions, stylistic ellipses.

The poem's epigraph, which traces the source for its title from Wal-ter Benjamin's "Theses on the Philosophy of History," part IX, brings the problem of "chaos" to the fore. Benjamin's "angel of history," whose "face is turned toward the past," does not "perceive a chain of events," but "one single catastrophe which keeps piling wreckage and hurls it in front of his feet."[14] Although he "would like to stay, awaken the dead, and make whole what has been smashed," the angel—whose inspiration Benjamin attributes to a Paul Klee painting[15]—must contend with the "storm . . . blowing in from Paradise" that is violently "caught in his wings"; this "storm irresistibly propels him into the future to which his back is turned, while the pile of debris before him grows skyward." Pointing to numerous examples of excruciating suffering and unspeakable destruction in the twentieth century, most of *The Angel of History*'s collaged fragments can be said to comprise "a single catastrophe," a unity of negations, and yet "the storm" of further agonies prevents the resolution of many innumerable gaps in perception and understanding—caused by displacements and destructions—and the *disparateness* of juxtaposed fragments into a unity of perception.

In the first unnumbered part of the opening title-section of *The Angel of History,* a new mother, perhaps the poet herself, contemplates her position in the world as witness of innocence/awareness of secu-rity/danger. Forché's free verse, dominated by extremely long lines full of caesuras but punctuated by several short and medium-lengthed ones, is typical of the poem as a whole:[16] "There are times when the child seems delicate, as if he had not yet crossed into the world. / When French was the secret music of the street, the cafe, the train, my own receded and became intimacy and sleep" (3). While Forché cherishes her son's temporary period of prelinguistic innocence of the social, this tenderness and her desire to protect him coexists with her heightened sense of vulnerability to large, antagonistic political forces.[17] Remembering her fleeting "April in Paris" and comparing it to the unsettling movement into worldliness that will soon happen to her son, who now can only "question" her "with his hands," the speaker mourns the loss of "intimate" French and rues its displacement by "the language of propaganda," which spurs her to forge a self-"explanation" in more liberatory terms. Even as she would embrace images of aesthetic luster, her historical perspective questions the lyricism: "Years later, on the boat from Beirut, or before the boat, an hour before, helicopters lifting a white veil of sea. / A woman broken into many women" (3). She evokes the turmoil that has repeatedly occurred in Beirut, the uses of helicopters in war, and the tropological significance of veils in women's oppression.

In the next part of the title-section, the "polyphonic, broken" qualities of collage assert themselves more intensely. Contemplation of the erasure and painful reconstruction of histories of oppression emerges. Forché describes and cites Ellie, "a German Jew who had spent the war years hiding in barns in Europe, making her way from farm to farm" and who was her hospital roommate for a week after the birth of the poet's son (Montenegro 66): "In the night-vaulted corridors of the Hotel-Dieu, a sleepless woman pushes her stretcher / along the corridors of the past. *Bonjour, Madame. Je m'appelle Ellie*" (4). Ellie remembers "autumns" in which "the fields were deliberately burned by a fire so harmless children ran through it / making up a sort of game. / Women beat the flames with brooms and blankets, so the fires were said to be *under control.*"

The burning marks the actualized desire of a group, probably Nazi leaders, to dominate nature and other human beings and to consolidate its power by suppressing vexed historical memory: "Children . . . were forbidden to ask about the years before they were born," and false assurance signals veiled destruction: "yet everything was said to be *under control* / with the single phrase *death traffic*"(4). This "population transfer" constitutes the realization of genocide as a guarantee of Aryan cultural and economic ascendancy. On the next page, Forché evokes traces of "forty-four children . . . hidden successfully for a year in view of the mountains" in Izieu before they "were taken to Auschwitz in Poland singing *Vous n'aurez pas L'Alsace et la Lorraine*" (5).

As fragments of her narrative accumulate, we find that Ellie, who, "afflicted with" eczemous "scales," sits "at the edge of / her bed, peeling her skin from her arm as if it were an opera glove" (7), "lifting tissues of herself from herself" (13), has been subject to various crushing displacements due to the social significance of her Jewish ethnicity. With repeated geographical displacement comes a loss of physical and psychological security, her sons' death during periods of flight and hiding—"Barn to barn in the haylight, field to cellar. Winter took one of her sons, and her own attempt to silence him, the other"—the death of her husband, *"a soldier against the Nazis . . . of cholera"* (8) after World War II, a permanent separation from the rest of her family, presumed dead, massive alienation from sources of cultural solace, and a loss of religious faith. For Ellie, belief in God's "insanity" is logical: *"Le Dieu est en feu. A psychopath. . . . // It isn't normal for a mother to outlive her children. / It isn't normal that my sons should be dead"* (7).

Ellie has undergone a series of horrors that seems to exemplify the angel's sense of history as a piling of "wreckage," but Forché is careful, later, to say: "How can one confuse that much destruction with one woman's painful life?" (20). Lacking Judaism's consolations, Ellie experiences the brutal irony of her cultural deracination when trying to resist succumbing to unbearable sadness: *"I am Jewish. Do you understand? Alone in a small room on the third floor, always alone. / To remain sane, I sing librettos to myself, German lullabies, can you imagine?"* (7).

The "arbitrary system" of "language" (9) is variously exposed as a barrier, a sign of displacement, and an instrument of social control. The notion that "one must go no further than the sign NO ADMIT-TANCE" saddens the poet in the hospital, especially because she is quarantined from her newborn son and husband (10, 13). Language, for the powerful, can involve self-immunization from criticism: *"And admittance, what does it mean? That they are not going to blame themselves for anything"* (9). For political exiles, the efficacy of words is particularly questionable: *"there is nothing between the word and those who are not, who do not reviennent."*

"The Notebook of Uprising," part II of *The Angel of History*, consists of twenty-eight short sections of fragments that evoke and contemplate the severities of Czechoslovakian history ranging from the Nazi invasion to the Soviet crackdown in 1968 and the economic difficulties of the 1980s. In the first section, Forché's grandmother Anna stands as a figure of survival against great odds: "Anna said we were all to be sent: Poles, Romanians, Gypsies. / So she drew her finger across her throat" (25). Section XVIII recounts how Forché and her companions "find" another Czech relative, her aunt Ana Borovska—who was persecuted by the Nazis for involvement in an effort "to shelter and protect Czechoslovakian Jewry during World War Two" and "later helped to resist the Communist regime, resulting in her internal exile" by Stalin[18]—"in a block of worker housing flats on a small *namesti* [square] bordering a ditch near one of the places where / Hitler could have been stopped." The poet cites Ana bearing witness to the erasure of human lives with an immediacy belying the temporal gap of half a century. The language that paper (on which the poem is preserved) accepts points to horrors that words cannot encompass: "A language even paper would refuse, / bell music rolling down the cold roofs, / their footsteps disappearing as they walked" (42).

In "The Notebook of Uprising," Forché seeks to locate the "disappearing" of history's "footsteps." Brutal erasures of Czech life and culture are made to rise up out of obscurity, though the concept of "notebook" suggests the provisional character of these findings. Wherever possible, the poet hopes to recuperate even the barest traces of what destructive forces had wanted to obliterate. The retrieval of "a few invisible souvenirs" might include "words spoken by coals in a tile oven, / empty iron benches wrapped in snow" (25). The witness's desire to retrieve important memories is severely tested by a lifetime's accretion of detail and the seemingly arbitrary triggering of (relatively useless) associations: "This is close, and passing time brings it no closer: the years, the cities moving beside a train. // What comes back? That Majetka could fold his ears up and stick them inside his head. / That the women of his village pissed standing up" (32).

Luckily, "erasure" does not constitute an absolute absence; the survival of traces is possible: "This is a map drawn from memory of the specular itinerary of exile. // An erasure of everything destroyed yet left intact" (43). Normally, one thinks of "exile's" trajectory as an emptying of images from the mirror ("speculum"). However, because one may find traces while visiting actual scenes of erasure and hear verbal reconstructions of direct witnesses' memories, the residue left "intact" by erasure permits at least the imagining of a desired presence. In Section XX, Forché observes that "the ordinary world" has been "taken . . . to mean: bootprints in clay, / the persistence of tracked field. // What was here before imperfectly erased / and memory a reliquary in a wall of silence" (44). Totalitarian ideologues cannot possibly plough over all of the "tracks" in every historical "field"; the terrain is too vast. Even if traces of remembrance enabled by imperfect erasure cannot assuage the sting of loss or raise "a banner completely fashioned of hope" (33), they can, almost ritualistically, honor what has been lost by expanding or deepening an approximate awareness of historical events: "As if a cemetery were a field of doors" (27).

There is no assurance, however, that any door will stay open. In this "Notebook's" second section, the poet depicts a mesmerizing process of sudden illumination (literally, within erasure), enabled by her grandmother, that bespeaks the fragility of a moment of powerful remembrance:

> Anna stands in a ring of thawed snow, stirring a trash fire in an iron
>   drum until her face flares, shriveled and intent, and sparks rise in
>   the night along with pages of burning
>   ash from the week's papers,
>   one peeling away from the rest,
> an ashen page framed in brilliance.
>
> For a moment, the words are visible, even though fire has destroyed
>   them, so transparent has the page become.
> The sparks from this fire hiss out among the stars and in thirty years
>   appear as tracer rounds.
>
> *They didn't want you to know the past. They were hoping in this way you*
>   *could escape it.*
>
> (26)

However different in tone and imagery from the poetry of *The Country between Us,* the degree of narrative and imagistic coherence in this passage is not far from that of the earlier book, and it marks Forché's distance from Language Poetry. Nevertheless, this passage is a coherent representation of a coherence that cannot sustain itself. Although Anna, the dazzled witness, would want the significance of the illuminated language to endure in her consciousness, the memory probably grows dim or dormant until, much later, it acquires an uncontrollably different energy in a different context. This section's concluding line points to another reason for the difficulties that the poetic archeologist has in recuperating traces. Choosing not to pass on the darkest aspects of what they know, unlike Anna, well-meaning elders who have experienced extremity wish to protect the young from the psychological torment of ancestral history. However, Forché's image of the delayed appearance of "tracer rounds" suggests that children cannot be protected from the pressures of history, which "insists upon" an inevitable return of the repressed knowledge in some alien, threatening form.

Some traces of political violence in "The Notebook of Uprising" are nearly as shocking as those in "The Colonel" and similar poems in *The Country between Us*. Take, for example, section IV's description of devastation in a rural village, in which we learn of "crows descending on a child to pull hair for their nests" (28). In other traces, implications of the sudden interruption of quotidian routine and customary priorities underscore the sense of insupportable brutality: "In the leather valise, a Dominican habit, altar linens, soap, the clothing of a railway conductor wrapped in *Rude Pravo* / Moth-winged curtains, a blizzard of moths from a trunk's maw, piano and corpse dust, gold attic shafts of spirit" (38). Amid the emptiness of "*Important*" boxes, the "corpse dust," and writing on the calendar and in the diary—as in another entry in the next section pointing to an approaching death or flight into exile: "There is a diary open to the words *cannot remain here*" (39)—the poet employs the conceit, "gold attic shafts of spirit," to maintain that politically motivated murder cannot expunge the presence of past spiritual energy from an otherwise blighted scene.

In brief details of her visits to prison camps, the poet presents glimmers of a history of heroic resistance to totalitarianism during the second World War. She mentions children determined to hold on to normal forms of imaginative play while imprisoned, then offers signs of natural growth—"flowers growing on the roofs of the cell blocks, the low-bricked grass-roofed prisons, / the *au revoir* of the tunnels" (37)—suggesting a possibility of renewal. These images refer to "the prison and transit camp Terezinstadt," where surrealist poet and French resistance activist Robert Desnos, whose English *Selected Poems* she and William Kulik translated,[19] died "two days after the camp was liberated by Russian troops" ("Notes," 82). Forché and her companions pay tribute to Desnos's heroism and imagine a scene in which the material presence of his poetic language continues to take a life-enhancing stand: "We picked forget-me-nots and left them where he died. / Somewhere here, somewhere with his name carved into a wall, are the words, *into your sun-blessed life*" (34).

Another exemplar of resistance in "The Notebook of Uprising" is Jan Palach, "the young student who immolated himself in 1968 in protest of the Soviet and Warsaw Pact invasion of Czechoslovakia" ("Notes," 82) and who had been elegized memorably in David Shapiro's "A Man Holding an Acoustic Panel."[20] In section XIII

Forché notes the juxtaposition of the site (and diminished com-
memoration) of Palach's act of self-sacrifice with signs of economic
privation typical of Soviet "satellites" before, during, and after the
unraveling of the Soviet state: "A two-hour queue for pears, a waxen
hill of spent tapers where Jan Palach immolated himself. / Meat lines,
bridge lights in the Vltava" (37). Section XXVIII, which concludes
part II, begins with another juxtaposition involving Palach, this time
with a contemporary gesture of protest: "They've made a shrine in
hissing rain to Jan Palach near where four men are starving themselves to death" (52).

Consisting of ten sections, each about a page long and divided
into one to four strophes, "The Recording Angel," part III of *The
Angel of History,* has a less fragmentary appearance than the first two
parts. However, as before, frequent disjunctions keep any semblance
of overall narrative continuity in abeyance. In *The Best American Poetry
1991,* Forché states of "The Recording Angel": "The title refers to the
Metatron, the prince of the Seraphim charged with the welfare and
sustenance of human life."[21] Since some human beings are intent
on depriving others of "welfare," the "angel," like Benjamin's, may
be guiding the world to survive two World Wars, but cannot fulfill
its "charge" in the case of many people. Instead, the angel primarily
"records" instances of its inability to sustain lives.

In the first section, a woman, "alone" with "memory" "where once
hundreds of thousands lived," testifies to the nightmare of war turning "normal" romantic love into a phantom surreality: "Doves, or
rather their wings, heard above the roof and the linens floating /
Above a comic wedding in which corpses exchange vows. A grand
funeral celebration / Everyone has died at once" (55). In a situation
where numerous violent deaths are almost a daily occurrence, the
hallucination acts as a kind of realistic image. Recollection of the
"one face" in the crowd and the prewar cityscape, along with contemplation of the contemporary ruins, affords the tragic sense of "*had
it not been for this*" lining "up behind *if it weren't for that* / Until the
past is something of a regiment." The speaker would like to imagine
"the river" as a "recording angel" who can transform the shattered
present into the coherent past, "As if, in reflecting the ruins, the river
were filming what their city had been."

"The Recording Angel" is filled with fragments and mininarratives
that demonstrate how social upheavals and acts of cruelty engender
dehumanizing abuse. The violent mockery of various, treasured life
processes does not end with death: "The dead girl" in section IX "was

thought to be with child / Until it was discovered that her belly had already been cut open / And a man's head placed where the child would have been" (63). Section III's speaker accidently discovers photographs of a woman who "had been wounded by so many man, abused by them / From behind in a silk yukata" (57). "Standing on her toes in [the] silk yukata, her arms raised / Wearing a girl's white socks and near her feet a vase of calla lillies / Otherwise she wore nothing" and, in one photo, "her long hair . . . gathered into a white towel / Or tied back not to interfere," the woman assumes a calm, stylized pose that promotes the fallacy of a woman's consent to male domination and her willing embrace of her role in its aesthetic representation. This hideous sham is a psychological reiteration of the physical abuse.

Perhaps to indicate disorienting contradictions, fragmentary narratives and images of brutality in "The Recording Angel" sometimes give way to tender images of a child wondrously exploring "earth," which is figured as "a school . . . . for desires, small but beautifully done / The earth is wrapped in weather, and the weather in risen words" (58). These moments are always shadowed by "the defenselessness for which there is no cure," as Forché puts it in the tenth section, only to add, "But it is a matter of shared history, or, as it were, we lived the same lie / Why lie? Why not life, as you intended?" (65). There is no answer, but the question keeps open the hope that "life," the value of egalitarian community, can significantly challenge "the lie's" apparent control over "shared history."

In part IV there are three short poems. "Elegy," a poem concerned with the Nazi Holocaust, cites fragments from Claude Lanzmann's 1985 film *Shoah* that "revolt against silence with a bit of speaking" (69). Simone de Beauvoir observes in her preface to the published text of *Shoah* that "the Nazis' great concern was to obliterate all traces," yet since "they could not wipe out all the memories, . . . Lanzmann has succeeded in ferreting out all the horrible realities hidden beneath camouflage, like young forests and fresh grass."[22] In a section of the film text on the Sobibor death camp, a train-worker there remembers that, after the Nazis "liquidate[d] the camp, . . . they planted pines that were three or four years old, to camouflage all the traces" (10). For the poet of "Elegy," the redeployment of traces enables her to lament the injustice of the victims' irrevocable absence and to honor their deepest desires: "The page is a charred field where the dead would have written / We went on" (69). Fragments of testimony from Holocaust survivors in *Shoah* ("Notes," 83) themselves demonstrate how incriminating traces were "wiped out" or "camouflaged":

> "When things were ready, they poured on fuel and touched off the fire.
> They waited for a high wind. It was very fine, that powdered bone.
> It was put into sacks, and when there were enough, we went to a bridge on the Narew River."
>
> And even less explicit phrases survived:
> "To make charcoal.
> For laundry irons."
>
> (69)

The first strophe above combines the testimony of Motke Zaidl and Itzhak Dugin about Sobibor (15) and that of Simon Srebnik about Chelmo (102). These Jewish survivors were forced to assist the Nazis in disposing the traces of the latter's genocidal activity.[23] Since in the Jewish religion, the deceased must be buried underground, cremation is a further desecration of the victims. Details about the "fineness" of "that powdered bone," the transfer of the human remains into "sacks," and the reference to quantification as a criterion for the next phase of operations possess a horrifying accuracy. At the end of the strophe, although Forché does not complete Simon Srebnik's actual sentence or add his next two— ". . . and dumped the powder. The current carried it off. It drifted downstream" (15)—it is obvious that the bridge is not a point of transition to the repose of urns but the place where *un*ceremonious submerging of traces occurs. In the second strophe, "even less explicit phrases" are responses to Simon Srebnik's question to his Nazi captors about the purpose of the ovens, which he helped build. The Nazis are telling the truth, but they are not saying that the material for household items comes from parts of their victims' corpses.

To represent those traces in *Shoah*, the survivors felt as though they were "living through something again one could not live through again" (69). Another individual who bravely faces such a task appears in Forché's "The Garden Shukkei-en," which bears the name of "an ornamental garden in Hiroshima" that "has been restored" ("Notes," 83). The poem's unnamed woman, who was in Hiroshima when the atomic blast hit, "has always been afraid to come here" (70), knowing that aspects of the scene would trigger unendurable memories. She evokes a crisis of such magnitude that there is no time for a normal awareness of crushing loss: "It is the river she most / remembers, the living / and the dead both crying for help. // A world that allowed neither tears nor lamentation" (70). Even a lovely natural object can be saturated with appalling associations: "I don't like this particular red flower because / it reminds me of a woman's brain crushed under a roof" (71). Any sign of disfiguration, however accidental, also summons agonizing recollections. The woman's depiction of her burns recalls Ellie's suffering from eczema: "She strokes a burnt trunk wrapped in straw: / I was weak and my skin hung from my fingertips like cloth // Do you think for a moment we were human beings to them?" (70).

Organized primarily in couplets and single-lined stanzas, the poem emphasizes both the difficulty of *and* the urgent need for dialogue between the Japanese *hibakusha* (fire-bombing victim) and a citizen of the country responsible for the bombing: "Do Americans think of us?" (71). Although the woman wonders whether her language's precision makes it too "difficult to understand," both she and her listener know that the most precise language is inadequate to the task of representation: "If you want, I'll tell you, but nothing I say will be enough." For this survivor, the approximate restoration of Shukkei-en's garden and other destroyed cultural assets in Hiroshima signifies the severity and enormity of an absence that the recent presence of simulacra cannot fill: "Where this lake is, there was a lake, / where these black pine grow, there grew black pine. // Where there is no teahouse I see a wooden teahouse / and the corpses of those who slept in it" (70).

On the other hand, the *hibakusha*, who "have not, all these years, felt what you call happiness," find it necessary to use these imperfect simulacra, "at times, with good fortune" to "experience something close. / As our life resembles life, and this garden the garden. / And in the silence surrounding what happened to us // it is the bell to awaken God that we've heard ringing" (71). Perhaps utilizing the Judeo-Christian reference to "God" as a cultural translation for her American listener, the *hibakusha* confronts the egregious disparity between a destruction so violent that it seems as though it should awaken protective forces in nature and the relative silence about the bombing's effects on its victims.

"The Testimony of Light" stresses the absolute disorientation inflicted on Hiroshima's *hibakusha*. Robert Jay Lifton speaks of "a widespread sense that life and death were out of phase with one another, no longer properly distinguishable—which lent an aura of weirdness and unreality to the entire city."[24] Forché's "Testimony" describes the ghoulish impression of irradiation's unnatural light in the land of the rising sun: "Outside everything visible and invisible a blazing maple. / Daybreak: a seam at the curve of the world. The trousered legs of the women shimmered. / They held their arms in front of them like ghosts" (72). "Ghostly" auditory reminders of destruction deepen the sense of "unreality": "The coal bones of the house clinked in a kimono of smoke." Evidence of annihilation must be gathered where a form of sustenance should be placed, and infants are left unnaturally to fend for themselves: "With bones put into rice bowls. / While the baby crawled over its dead mother seeking milk."

To characterize the crushing derangement of normal experience, Forché borrows a phrase used by *hibakusha*: "Muga-muchu: without self, without center. Thrown up in the sky by a wind." The phrase, states Lifton, "suggests an obliteration of the boundaries of self" resulting in part from the victims' "complete or near nakedness (partly because of clothes blown off by the blast and partly through being caught in an early-morning state of undress), various injuries and forms of bleeding," and other, similar factors (26). The poem's closure expresses doubts that the *hibakusha,* who may be subject to radiation-induced cancer and a slow, agonizing movement toward death, can recover a "center": "The way back is lost, the one obsession. / The worst is over. / The worst is yet to come" (72). If the Hiroshima explosion, caused by a far less potent bomb than current versions, is "the worst," then a new "worst" is conceivable, even after the "Cold War's" end.

The three highly disjunctive "Book Codes" of part V resist periphrasis more thoroughly than preceding parts. While "Book Codes: I," "a fragmented citational text from Ludwig Wittgenstein" ("Notes," 84) evincing the flavor of his pursuit of ordinary language functions, displays a "voice" resigned to the use of an imperfectly measuring and mirroring medium as the instrument of witness, "Book Codes: II" and "III" point to a fragmentary awareness of the diminishment of narrative plenitude and efficacy that informs the entire book. In the second "Book Code," which nevertheless concludes with a simple invitation to the work of mourning ("whoever can cry should come here"), dislocation is the syntactical and thematic norm: "the sign of the cross on an invisible face with the calm of a butcher / as if it bore witness to some truth / with whom every connection had been severed" (76).

The second-hand witness in "Book Codes: III" is caught in a per-spectival and experiential "box" hampering her account's reliability; despite empathy, she cannot "enter" the victims' unimaginable suf-ferings. As elsewhere in the book, scattered traces of ruin must stand as testimony in place of "substantial," coherent stories. The abject image of "bone [become] black with flies again hatching in ruins" (77) serves as a reminder of the notion that some insects would be the sole survivors of a nuclear explosion. Congruently, the poem's closure, while reiterating difficulties of witness, alludes to a sign of the inaugural realization of technology's most monstrous promise: "given the task of painting wounds / through the darkened town as though it had been light // at the moment of the birth of this cloud." It is likely that many of the notes that were eventually collaged into this long poem were written during the mid-eighties, during the last gasp of President Reagan's acerbic anti-Soviet rhetoric, and prior to *glasnost,* when numerous members of the U.S. antinuclear movement were deeply concerned that the president was bringing the superpowers close to a nuclear showdown. Thus, it is reasonable to contextualize references in this section, as well as in "The Garden Shukkei-in" and "The Testimony of Light," to weapons of mass destruction in World War II as a warning to those living during the Cold War to be vigilant about trying to prevent history from repeating itself. Since the poem was published in 1994, such a warning would apply to possibilities of nuclear violence generated by ethnic war in the regions of former Soviet satellites.

The Angel of History's concluding quotation from a parable of Paul Valéry[25] at first posits the fiction of an ultimate "book code": "The angel handed me a book, saying, 'It contains everything that you could possibly wish to know. / And he disappeared" (78). When "scholars translated" the book from its "unknown character," both their "versions" and "the very senses of their own readings" clashed. Is Forché citing this uncannily "poststructuralist" trope to underscore the concept that the irreducible conflict of interpretations dissolves the dream of objective epistemological unity or intersubjective con-sensus? The concluding sentence of the passage lifted from Valéry supplies an aura of great ambiguity: finally, "it seemed to" the speaker "that the book melted, until it could no longer be distinguished from this world that is about us."

The trope of the "melting book" may reflect the thematic force of the erasure of history to which the fragmentary form of *The Angel of History* continually points; it may be another instance of the poetic witness's resistance to illusory totalization. On the other hand, this figure can be taken to indicate a mysterious unification of signifier and signified. According to this viewpoint, if the book "becomes" the world, it does not really "disappear"; it becomes a transparent vehicle for perfect representation of a world lacerated by war. Even if the interpreters mentioned earlier cannot agree with one another, the persona of the passage asserts faith in a transcendence of mediation. The clash of the two readings I have identified itself calls this transparency into question, but it at least foregrounds the dynamic of two desires that animate *The Angel of History*: the impulse to be faithful to an enduring fragmentation and ruin caused by twentieth-century wars and the longing for a recuperative understanding of these horrors that will effect a healing.

Language Poets like Lyn Hejinian denounce any sense that poetry can or should ignore history and be said to evince "eternal" values. As much of their prose indicates, as well as the interpretations of critics who valorize their work, these writers are interested in and adept at historicizing how they, the contemporaries with whom they differ, and their literary influences are situated in cultural and social contexts. To cite only one example, Susan Howe's collagistic poetry is filled with the shards of American history. In their theory and practice, Language writers insist that a questioning of narrative, as Forché would hold, is necessary in avoiding the falsification of history. However, many of them go farther than questioning narrative structures: the example of their work suggests that a predominantly *antinarrative* drift is a precondition for experimental poetry.

Joseph Lease, author of *Human Rights* (1998),[26] has been hailed by such writers as Donald Revell and Forrest Gander as a poet whose experimental impetus is especially salient when and because he revitalizes narrative modes (*and* learns from the Language Poets' antinarrative stance).[27] Lease's poetic experimentation, especially in his long sequences, features elegant "leaping" among various aesthetics and developing collagistic juxtapositions that build brief narratives and articulate social critique. His poetry combines evocative storytelling, imagism, irony, transformative (even visionary) language, and self-reflexive discursivity to strive for a fullness of the representation of history that accounts for the actualities of effacement.

Lease's 1997 essay, "A Study in 'counter-dependence': Language Poetry as 'collective voice,' "[28] suggests how his own inclusive, experimental poetics is informed and enabled by a particular openness to the deployment of what he calls "the representative 'I.' " Lease argues that the Language poetics that evolved in the seventies and eighties—and one should add, in fairness, that nineties articulations of such poetics are often considerably more nuanced in their critiques of other modes—attacked the "idealized" stance of "American poetic nonconformity" (1). The Language Poets were marking their critical distance from a "reliance on the culturally representative lyric 'I' who denounces America in the name of America" (1) found in the "postromantic oppositional" poetry of Allen Ginsberg, Amiri Baraka, Adrienne Rich, Charles Olson, and others associated with sixties social movements like the mobilization against the Vietnam War. Citing the prose of Bruce Andrews, Barrett Watten, Ron Silliman, and others, Lease states that in "exploding the lyric 'I' " Language Poets sought "to resist [the] American cultural symbology" of the "representative American self" as "a kind of advertisement for individualism as the cultural logic of late capitalism" (7–8).

According to Lease, poets who use "the lyric 'I' " do not have to promote individualistic thinking: "The American tradition of introspection in lyric is never, from Whitman on, 'merely personal' but *representative*—personal and political"; therefore, he considers "the lyric 'I' . . . the ground for the critique of romanticism and materialism in American culture, whether that critique takes the form of protest, storytelling, allegory, or politicized textuality—exploding the lyric "I." (25–26). For him, the vital "dialectic in American lyric poetry"—already present in the work of Whitman, Melville, and other nineteenth-century writers—"depends on both the explosive doubts, lacks, and gaps that animate intrasubjectivity and the faith that makes intersubjectivity representable" (29–30). Thus, the "representative I" need not drown out other voices; it need not assume the posture of an "imperial self."[29] Its engagement with the problematics of the social can and should be rigorously self-critical. Facing problems of political representation, Lease's poems meditate on intersubjectivity, the limits of the self, and the demands of the collective. His lyric "I" invites, invokes, and probes community.

Although *Human Rights* includes powerful short lyrics like "Michael Kohlhass," a critique of German idealist fanaticism, "Essay on Addiction," "Hammer," "Petition," and the "Language"-influenced " 'Footloose Radish . . . ,' " Lease's particular uses of the "representative 'I' " are most evident and given fullest play in his various longer poems, five of which can be found in *Human Rights*. "Slivovitz," the concluding poem in the book, explores the vexed task of representing the

Jewish Holocaust—especially for Jewish-Americans like Lease (born in 1960 in Chicago) who are substantially removed in time from the event. The poet confronts the overwhelming *erasure* of Jewish history embodied by the Nazi regime's literal erasure of six million Jewish lives, as well as the knowledge that many U.S. Jews themselves have avoided a serious encounter with the Holocaust's implications. In doing so, Lease meditates on how the effacement of history can be avoided and combated. His self-conscious questioning of poetic language and structure serves this end.

The need for such a meditation should be understood in the context of three decades of astounding instances of revisionism that Deborah Lipstadt has studied in *Denying the Holocaust: The Growing Assault on Truth and Memory* (1993). As Lipstadt argues, "extremists" who insist that the Holocaust was a fabrication have helped produce "a situation whereby added latitude may be given" in the "center" of the general cultural marketplace "to ideas that would once have been summarily dismissed as historically fallacious."[30] Recent German historical revisionists like Hellmut Diwald and Ernst Nolte try to blur "the boundaries between fact and fiction and between persecuted and persecutor"; invoking relativism, they dilute their recognition of the existence of the Holocaust by saying that "the Nazis were only trying to defend themselves against their enemies," that "most Jews died of starvation and disease," that "the Jews' behavior brought" extermination "on them," that the Holocaust was similar to "an array of other conflagrations in which innocents were massacred," and that "we 'only' hear about the Holocaust" since the Jews currently exert such great "power" (215).

Amid such distortions, Lease explores the roles of the representative "I" and narrative—and how poetry can help prevent further Holocausts. Immediately sensuous, "Slivovitz" approaches directly the act of writing, conditions of history, and social poetry. As Lease has put it, "the poem's structure embodies a ritual process, making absent experience vividly present, even as historical distance and loss are probed."[31]. The post-Holocaust gothic language of "Slivovitz" underscores the necessity of myth for any collective elegy—along with the awareness that history's erasures have exploded myth. In a review of *Human Rights,* Larissa Szporluk declares: "It's almost as if he were trying to will a flood on the visible world, recreate a state of the beginning of things, undo the damage of this century, . . . with the psychic forces that align themselves with every genesis."[32]

Speaking of the desire "to separate ourselves from" the "horror" of the Holocaust, "and with most caution, out of respect for those who survived," David Shapiro, to whom "Slivovitz" is dedicated, affirms the importance of speaking "for those . . . who were without speech: children thrown into the ovens. For those without speech, there must be an attempt to speak."[33] Shapiro grapples with Theodor Adorno's famous negation of poetry after Auschwitz. Calling "the Holocaust . . . the proper name for events that subvert language and myth," he denies that "poetry becomes impossible after the Holocaust" but states instead that "myth and its language and corruptions become dubious if not unbearable. Yet we know reality is unbearable without the consolations of metaphor and myth" (458).

"Slivovitz" asks how U.S. Jews in the nineties can face their historical situation—how they can confront their own experience and identity without parody. The struggle is dramatic in language, in lyric structure, in primal metaphors. The poem's first section is a dance of parody and contradiction; the second is a kind of Hades, in which the poem finds and goes to the dead to bring reality back to life and to awaken contrast and the courage to perceive contradiction; the third deploys a visionary political storytelling in which the narrator psychologically enters and sees situations that were inaccessible to him in the first part. Leaving parody behind, this final section reaches identification.

In the poem's opening lines, Lease confronts the notion that the Holocaust has subverted "language and myth," and the obstacles facing the representative "I":

> The sun we see
> 　　　　is not the real sun.
>
> 　　　　The dead will not give back water,
> they cut my face,
>
> have what they want.
> 　　　　A pane of glass
>
> 　　　　between you and what you touch:
> write "Holocaust"—
>
> try to imagine night
> 　　　　thoughts of survivors
>
> 　　　　in the suburbs of Chicago.
> By now they have grandchildren

I have no right to picture.
    The real sun, deceived,

    stolen from the sky,
put to death.

(57)

Imagining that the "sun" has lost the authority it had before the Holocaust, this representative of late-twentieth-century Jews born roughly a generation after World War II ended indicates how this deception or "eclipse" has drained civilization. Awareness of what "the dead" have suffered "defaces" the speaker; of course, "the dead" refuse the responsibility of restoring the "water" of vitality to the living. Lease's image of the dead's contentment, though somewhat consoling in the sense that it reflects the survival of the Jewish people, despite the Holocaust, is chilling when one realizes that death has rendered the victims unable to desire anything—they literally *want* nothing.

The trope of mediation, "a pane of glass," demonstrates that "you" (which represents both the earlier, problematic "we" and "I" and the reader) are prevented from "grasping" the profound significances of the Holocaust, not only because of what historical archeology cannot recuperate, but because of layers of distorted narrative. These distortions arise, not only from revisionists but even from well-meaning historians and other cultural storytellers who, in Lawrence L. Langer's terms, "persist in weaving elaborate fantasies about the dignity of dying under or living through such miserable circumstances" in an effort to "alleviate the harshest truths of the Holocaust."[34]

To "write 'Holocaust'" is not to know the "essence" of what one has written, not only because the Jew in his thirties has never known a world before the event, as the survivors have, but because the word itself, which the poet grew up using, has a Greek derivation signifying "burning" of the "whole" that lacks the particularly Jewish resonance of *shoah*. The speaker says that he has no right to "picture" the "grandchildren" of the survivors, as they embody a continuity that is proof of survival and he, because of circumstance, does not. The annihilation of the six million is figured as a deception, theft, and murder of the natural order ("the sun") itself; thus, the speaker entertains the thought that nature as it currently manifests itself is a degraded simulation.

A witty rewriting of Ecclesiastes' most celebrated negation, which further evokes Adorno's proscription, conveys the impact of the Holocaust on his daily experience: "Nothing new about being alive, / nothing fancy" (57). The speaker doubts whether he can take himself and experience seriously; he measures his fortune, stature, aspirations, and troubles against the impossibly monumental scale and standard of the suffering of death camp victims and survivors: "If we met at a party, / for example, I // could not look at you / and tell you about being alone . . . // in the split second— / *after* we were introduced // and *before* someone else / arrived to take you away—" (57–58). Deploying a comic self-consciousness, Lease has the speaker end the long sentence by refusing to do what he is obviously doing; the poet's self-reflexiveness is a kind of metadrama: "And I will not, I *refuse* / to sit at the counter // of Dunkin' Donuts / on Boylston street late at night // writing in this notebook" (58). Concurrent poetic impulses toward witness and the cultural work of negation create a tension that animates the poem: "Parody, the redemption // we deserve." Roughly half a century after the loss of a large portion of his entire group, Lease's task is to imagine language that could connect an individual and collective despair amid history's cruelty. Knowing that he cannot recover the pre-Holocaust (tantamount to a prelapsarian) Jewish experience, the speaker refuses to settle for "parody." He is poised between impossibility and necessity. In precise, soulful language, "Slivovitz" must proceed by contradiction, enacting what it also recognizes as sublime, inexpressible:

> When was the sun
>
>   the real sun? I listen and wait
>   (sometimes I want to be
>
>
>   helpless) for knowledge
>   that will not fall. If the dead spoke to me
>
>   after all this time
>   I would lose my voice
>
>   and have to keep
>   singing of Zion,
>
>   waiting for the dead.
>   Parody, the redemption

we deserve. A sun faltering
was the last thing I saw.

(58)

Like Forché in *The Angel of History*, Lease embodies history's violent ruptures in images and knows that he cannot know "when" or if "the sun" could ever be described as more "real" than at other times. Waiting for unassailable "knowledge," he has no hope—confronted by the enormity of Jewish loss—that his patience will bear fruit. On the contrary, he senses that the necessary miracle of a full, direct reception of the dead's exigent voices will overwhelm his own. The poet's song is the measure of his waiting. At the end of the section, the speaker displaces the opposition between "real" and "false" sun and marks "a sun faltering" as a "final" perception that enables the opening of a "ritual" process in the next two sections.

In the prose-poetry of the second section of "Slivovitz," which opens with the haunting invocation "*He doubted whether he knew anyone and he could not awaken the dead he needed*" (59), Lease tests possibilities for a "representative 'I' " through a provocative juxtaposition of a narrative from his personal ancestral history and one relating his current experience. He "awakens" the story of a catastrophe in the life of his grandfather as a step on the path of consciousness of the Holocaust:

A bottle of Slivovitz on the kitchen table. Alter never drank on a weekday, at midday. Not his fault—a boy died, a boy fell off Alter's bus—he climbed on the rear ledge for a ride, for fun, then fell under an oncoming car. Alter didn't know the boy was there until he fell off—everyone heard the impact. My father, a seven or eight year old boy, watched his father, ashamed, in shock. (59)

Although his role in the tragedy of the thrill-seeking boy's death is a matter of contiguity, the bus driver is as much "ashamed" as "in shock." The brief story's placement in the poem implies that the victims of the *Shoah* were "in the wrong place at the wrong time." In response to contemporary anti-Semitic ravings and pockets of Jewish self-hatred, it needs to be underlined that various strands of social factors that led to the lethal scapegoating of Jews in Germany in the 1930s cannot be traced to some essential "nature" of Jews— a collective "original sin" or archetypal victim-status—or, for that matter, of Germans. Moreover, Lease evokes the emotions of U.S. Jews who escaped the Holocaust by virtue of accident, at once distancing *and* connecting American Jews and victims of the *Shoah*.

In the second narrative of section II, the world of the pre-Holocaust, relatively unassimilated Jew gives way to the postmodern landscape of the post-Holocaust Jew:

> Sixty-eight years after that accident, I'm in a mall. Watches with gorgeous faces, displayed in threes in windows. Laughing teenagers. The Clinique counter full of mauve oils and creams and bright blue astringent. I want to kiss between Donna's breasts. I wish we could slip into that storage room. Wearing the charcoal gray sweater she gave me, I think, This world is not real. And I think, My father liked the shirt I bought him.
>
> No one here is wealthy, but everyone here is shopping: couples walk arm in arm and talk quietly and smile and shop for gifts and household things. No one is yelling here, or haggling. This place does not smell like Coney Island in 1924: there is no ritual slaughter in this mall, no chickens are being killed in the sacred way. (59)

Lease depicts the scene of late-twentieth-century American pleasures with an acute imagistic specificity, a quality typical of his work, and with a blend of tenderness and irony. The juxtaposition of Alter's experience with his grandson's, and the reader's awareness of the overarching context of the Holocaust, intensifies the fragility of the calm pleasure that the latter narrative exemplifies. We are reminded that, before Hitler rose to power in January 1933, many Jews felt at home in Germany. Saul Friedlander notes that Jews, who in 1933 comprised less than "1 percent of Germany's overall population" were visible because of "their relative importance in . . . business and finance, journalism and cultural activities, medicine and the law," as well as "liberal and left-wing politics."[35] The Jews' "striving for advancement and acceptance" in the face of "social discrimination" was "interpreted as Jewish subversion and domination," thus exacerbating "hostility and rejection" (77).

Larissa Szporluk speaks of how, along with an "awareness of horror, human horror, as evidenced by the Holocaust" and "the inevitable injustices of a modern capitalist society," Lease exhibits a "unique power" to summon "the entire history of trust . . . how to trust the dead, who owe the living nothing; trust the fable, which clings to the subconscious, toyingly; trust recovery, which is never complete" (14). In juxtaposing the retracing of his grandfather's experience with his own, Lease proceeds by contradiction: he bridges the split between past and present by, first, invoking it. With the weight of history in mind, Lease can balance the unreality and reality of his given social context, and he recognizes its positive functions while never losing sight of its incompleteness. He can bask in the warmth of the neutral-toned sweater that his lover had given him and suddenly realize that "this world is not real." The sexual frisson near the "storage room" and the thought about the gift to his father represent a tranquility that affords temporary protection and respite from the unbearable erasures of the *Shoah* and from the future's uncertainty.

The first part of section III, which begins with the epigraph, "*tomorrow belongs to me . . .*" (60) [36], ominously suggestive of fascist arrogance, responds to Ernst Ludwig Kirchner's painting *Self-Portrait as a Soldier,* in which Kirchner depicts "himself standing in his studio, wearing his military uniform and raising the bloody stump of his severed hand" ("Notes," 63). Lease's couplets create a neoclassical motion through which the act of retracing history permits distance and interruption to open gradually into identification and understanding:

> When his hand exploded
>   it kept dripping
>
>   and they liked that,
> they said it was a good one.
>
> What have you got left?
>   Smiles crash in the little details,
>
>   such as trying to dab up
> the shreds of your hand
>
> from a bus seat.
>   From the back of the bus
>
>   a voice piped up,
> "Abandon every hope,
>
> ye who enter."
>   It was Kirchner,
>
>   some haunted German
> guy seeing through war-
>
> coated eyes, another Messiah.

(60)

Declaring that Kirchner "saw himself in the true tradition of German art, *even had the bold idea of reviving* [it]," Wolf Dieter-Dube cites the self-portrait's "symbolic stump" as an indication of the impact of "conscription for military service" during World War I on this romantic, nationalist aesthete: "This violation by military force, having to wear a uniform, that symbol of the death of individuality, he found quite unbearable. . . . In 1915"—the year the painting was done—"while still undergoing training, Kirchner suffered a complete mental and physical breakdown."[37] By 1917, the artist, whose mental troubles persisted until his suicide twenty-one years later, had settled in Switzerland, and he never returned to his native land. Thus, having striven for aesthetic means to promote a German nationalism that honors individuality, Kirchner found himself emotionally mutilated by a nationalism heading in the opposite direction, toward the fascism of the Third Reich, which tried to erase difference.

While the "eyes" of the would-be aesthetic "messiah," whose name was to appear on the Nazis' list of "degenerate artists," have been "coated" by World War I, Lease utilizes the allusion to his self-portrait as a sign of the disfiguring psychopolitical effects of Nazism on its adherents and its victims. The audience who find titillating entertainment, and not social critique, in the display of mutilation evoke German citizens who watched and approved of Hitler's ascent. They ask for further "thrills." I am reminded of the lurid fascination that Nazi scientists displayed in cutting off the body parts of Jews in concentration camps and reattaching them in strange places. Moreover, Kirchner's *Self-Portrait* triggers and echoes the poem's movement through parody to identification.

The bus is taking its German Jewish passengers to death camps; the "haunted" artist's echo of Dante's *Inferno,* embedded in the gruesome self-portrait, sings of this imminent hell. (The phrase, "from the back of the bus," alludes to Southern U.S. buses, almost twenty years later, as a locus of Civil Rights protest.) Next, Lease moves to an image of concentration camp destruction that indicates the representative "I" living simultaneously with a wedding and the gas ovens": "Smoke from human bodies // drifts above the canopy. / The audience is laughing // at you. It's your wedding / and you just said, 'death camp' " (60). Here, the "canopy" may signify the roof of a bus going to the camps, the top of a Nazi crematorium, and the canopy (*chuppah*) under which a traditional Jewish wedding occurs. The reader and the representative "I" must each confront the terror of the laughter and its horrific referent. Unlike the post–World War I German audience enjoying the "comedy" of Kirchner's painting, the wedding audience must be laughing in horror at the potential simultaneity of joy and abject misery in consciousness.

In the next (penultimate) part of "Slivovitz," the poet articulates how Jews who have opened themselves to the Holocaust's implications might struggle with the specter of such overwhelming despondency, what literary critic Jahan Ramazani, following Freud, would call an extreme form of "melancholic" (as opposed to "normal") mourning.[38] In the opening couplets of this part, disjunction is a sign of liminality; a boundary is crossed: "The earth has a beard. / A shadow blew the windows open. // Follow the boot tread / on my face. // We were on foot, / traveled by night" (61). The earth's covering ("beard") suggests the ancient wisdom that one who has contact with it may be able to tap. The "shadow's" synesthetic effect of opening the barrier ("windows") between the young nineties Jew and a fuller awareness of the Holocaust indicates the power of death in shaping sociohistorical imagination. This is a response to the "pane of glass / between you and what you touch" in the poem's opening section. Difficulties of looking through that open window are prodigious, and "the boot tread" of linguistic marks appear on the face of a notebook page, as marks of psychological turmoil can be said to register on the poet's actual face. Traveling "on foot"—the variable measure of free-verse—by the "night" of uncertainty and imaginative effort with like-minded readers, the poet seeks to establish solidarity with the brutally silenced. In saying, "I wish I had tried / to answer her arrogant questions," he may refer to questions about the "aura" of the "gaze" of those, like the corpses in the sea in Coleridge's "The Rime of the Ancient Mariner,"[39] who "sleep in an open grave," since they were deprived of the minimal dignity of funeral rites and burial. This effacement leaves vexing questions "open."

Mindful of the presence of "fringe" groups, including neo-Nazis, in the U.S., the recently united Germany, in former Soviet satellites, and elsewhere, the speaker urges himself and the Jews of his generation—despite limits to capacities for empathy—to be vigilant about the possible return of persecution: "You don't know the value / of love, but don't // let yourself be eaten" (61). Also, the unsettling reference to the Christian Eucharist reminds us that the old diatribe against Jews as unrepentant killers of the (ironically Jewish) Jesus has long served as a justification for anti-Jewish violence.[40] Expression of the will to survive is informed by the realization that death "stands above" existence and acts as a "guide" for the "journey": "Death

inherits / the mountains. Death knows the land better than you."
These are not wholly negative observations; they sanction a bracing
awareness. The first couplet of this part returns at the end, and
the reader can perceive more fully how "a shadow" can create an
"opening."

At the beginning of the poem's last part, Lease considers the
"transparently" assimilationist drive of many U.S. Jews, including
himself among them: "Translucent bodies, / veins inside leaves, //
we have no voices / nor do we believe. // Happily censoring our
children, / we censored ourselves // long ago" (62). If the poet does
not advocate literal belief in Jewish religious tenets, self-"censorship"
includes the refusal of many Jews to provide their children with
a sufficient account of the Holocaust, as though the silence will
"happily" protect both generations from suffering.[41] Such a gesture,
of course, typifying a marginalized group's tacit erasure of the history
of its subjugation, could hardly serve as a shield against a surge of
neo-Nazi mania. Harking back to the troping on the real/false "sun"
in the first section, Lease uses an image of fragmentation to convey
a willed dissociation from ethnic roots: "Inside the vision //
there stood an apartment building torn / into streaks of sun."

Next, the poet reflects on the most dangerous aspect of uncritically
chosen assimilation into a dominant culture: "Here is the friend who
/ betrayed me, he returns to wind: now pick // a card" (62). When
their "friendship" with the German people returned "to wind"—
especially as Hitler's regime, between 1933 and 1935, created law
after law limiting their access to opportunities accorded citizens and
prepared to engineer their expulsion from Germany (before the
"Final Solution" was attempted)—the Jews discovered that they had
been dealt the worst possible "card": "Wrong again."[42] The speaker's
assertion, "I lift a bruise from my leg," suggests the persistence of the
psychic wound left by this betrayal.

In the concluding five couplets of "Slivovitz," the poet returns to
the haunting absence that animates the poem:

> My lips move when I sleep.
> When I think in sleep
>
> where is the broken friend?
> And there was no one
>
> on the hillside, no eyes were dark,
> no one interrupted

the movement toward a belief
    offering no hope.

    Actually, I own the future, I sunbathe
in it, I write it down.

                             (62)

As the series of negations following the question of location pointedly asserts, not even dream-thoughts can re-present the effaced Holocaust victims, "the broken friends" who were, literally, never even acquaintances. Lease cannot report that a hopeful expectation—for example, in the global eradication of anti-Semitism, in an impregnable Jewish solidarity, or in the consolations of a blissful afterlife—has somehow "interrupted" or displaced the hopelessness that the Holocaust seems to "teach."

While he might appreciate Lawrence Langer's point that "the Holocaust still mocks the idea of civilization and threatens our sense of ourselves as spiritual creatures," as well as leaving "wide open the unsettled and unsettling question of why this should be so" (184), Lease posits "the movement towards a belief / offering no hope." As he finishes re-tracing this terrible history, he validates efforts to improve human circumstances, no matter how immense the obstacles are. In echoing the optimistic, fascistic rant of the epigraph of section III, the ironic parting couplet reminds individuals and groups that too much "sunbathing" in utopian dreams, lacking a tempering awareness of complex historical actualities, can lead to inoperable cancers. The representative "I" knows the dangers of presuming that he can "write . . . down" the future and, in fact, the devastating erasures of the Jewish past thwart earnest attempts at historical transcription. The poem's ritual process explores how the *Shoah* continues, despite repression, to haunt, and this process opens a passageway between the original event and its uncanny recurrence.

In each of Martín Espada's five books of poetry, including *The Immigrant Iceboy's Bolero* (1982), *Trumpets from the Islands of Their Eviction* (1987), *Rebellion Is the Circle of a Lover's Hands* (1990), *City of Coughing and Dead Radiators* (1993), and *Imagine the Angels of Bread* (1996), the histories of Puerto Rico, Latin America, and Puerto Ricans on the mainland comprise a prominent focus. (With Camilo Pérez-Bustillo, Espada is the translator of *The Blood that Keeps Singing: Selected Poems of Clemente Soto Vélez* [1991], a widely respected poetic innovator and a champion of the Puerto Rican indepedence movement.)[43] A Puerto Rican born in Brooklyn, New York, in 1957, Espada is the winner of two NEA fellowships, the PEN/Revson Fellowship, the Paterson Poetry Prize, and other honors.

In his essay "Documentaries and Declamadores," Espada asserts that "the most important context for contemporary Puerto Rican poetry" is "the great migration from the island in the 1950s and 1960s, a migration so massive that approximately one-third of the population left Puerto Rico during this time."[44] In turn, the migration must be seen in the context of Puerto Rico's status as a colony (now commonwealth) of the United States, after the U.S. wrested it from Spain in 1898. To a greater or lesser extent, various scholars, including Gordon K. Lewis, Frank Bonilla and Ricardo Campos, and Clara E. Rodriguez,[45] emphasize the oppressive power relations between the United States and Puerto Rico that the dominant U.S. historical narrative has striven to efface. Rodriguez notes that the U.S. takeover "made Puerto Rico . . . politically" and "economically dependent," since the island's "diversified, subsistence economy around the turn of the century with four basic crops produced for export" became "a sugar-crop economy, with 60% of the sugar industry controlled by U.S. absentee owners" (11). This industry's "decline . . . (combined with no reinvestment and continued population growth) in the 1920s resulted in high unemployment, poverty, and desperate conditions in Puerto Rico."

This problem caused "the first waves" of migration from the island. While in the forties "a series of government-owned enterprises were established" that would have fostered "greater economic independence" for Puerto Rico had they been given the time and support to succeed, Congress resisted them on "ideological" grounds, and "between 1947 and 1951, . . . a changeover from government development to promotion of private investment" called "Operation Bootstrap" took place. The plan, as Rodriguez states, was to lure "foreign companies, primarily from the United States, to Puerto Rico with the promise of low wage and tax incentives" (11–12). Although Operation Bootstrap may have brought various technological improvements in the quality of life on the island, Rodriguez points out that "the industry attracted" there "turned out to be increasingly capital intensive, to have little commitment to the development of the island, and to be integrated into sourcing and distribution networks in the United States or other countries, not in Puerto Rico" (12). Thus, "indirect employment effects" were scarce, and "the industrialization path chosen did not provide sufficient jobs."

Espada's pithy, "Operation Bootstrap: San Juan, 1985," a poem in *Trumpets*, finds a highly suitable, cuttingly ironic image for the effects of Puerto Rican underdevelopment that Rodriguez describes:

> Man with one crutch
> staggering between lanes of traffic
> begging coins
> for the other crutch.

(24)

Journalist Anne Nelson presents an extreme example of the trade imbalance and its crippling effect on Puerto Rico: "By the 1970s, 80 percent of the island's food was being imported from the mainland while Puerto Rico's own agriculture languished and died."[46] "Coca-Cola and Coco Frío," a poem in *City of Coughing and Dead Radiators*, addresses the insidious nature of the imbalance, the absurdities it sanctions, and the brainwashing of Puerto Ricans about the superiority of U.S. culture: "On his first visit to Puerto Rico, / island of family folklore, / the fat boy" from Brooklyn is baffled that his "great-aunts" all foist Coca-Cola on him: "One even sang to him, in all the English / she could remember, a Coca-Cola jingle / from the forties" (26). Later, "at a roadside stand off the beach, the fat boy" experiences the delight of "coco frío, a coconut / chilled" and realizes "suddenly, Puerto Rico was not Coca-Cola / or Brooklyn, and neither was he." His own outsider's insights, unfortunately, cannot undo the brainwashing and waste of resources suffered by many who had remained; "for years afterward," he is left to lament the strangeness of "an island / where the people drank Coca-Cola / and sang jingles from World War II / in a language they did not speak, / while so many coconuts in the trees / sagged heavy with milk, swollen / and unsuckled" (27).

To return to what Espada calls "the great migration" to the U.S. mainland in the fifties and sixties, Rodriguez observes that this exodus was spurred by conditions of "increased population growth and displacement from traditional labor pursuits"; the "growing surplus population . . . could not be accommodated in Puerto Rico's new industrial order" (12). According to Anne Nelson, "Puerto Ricans were urged to emigrate to the mainland with cheap airfares and flyers advertising work for harvesters in New Jersey and positions for maids in New York—English preferred but not required" (98). Diana L. Vélez perceives the migration as "an important component" of Operation Bootstrap, because the transfer of " 'excess population' " to the U.S. was "a way of reducing unemployment figures," and so "government planners, both Puerto Rican and North American, could celebrate the economic miracle of" Puerto Rico's "solution" of "its poverty problem."[47]

As various Espada poems suggest, those "evicted" from Puerto Rico during the Operation Bootstrap era do not magically shrug off the debilitating effects of colonial rule. The title-poem of *The Immigrant Iceboy's Bolero* narrates the movement of a boy—who the dedication indicates is the poet's father—from the natural and familial pleasures and edifications of his native Puerto Rico to a disorienting rupture of these deep satisfactions. Catching "lizards in the afternoon / face to the strong sun / and cold water over stone" while learning "grandfather's dignity / from aged men and the coarse-leaf mountains," the boy is full of contentment until the "the belly throbbed, / skin stretched hunger over bone," and he "and the family / joined the father / sweating in New York" (8).

Migration has brought massive frustration and alienation. "Feeling in the head / the city's drill-press rhythms," the poet's father has reaped no profit or psychic sustenance from all his "sweating in New York": "he cannot send money / back to the family," those who have returned, "packing welfare-department clothes" and "the bewilderment / of the cheated" (8). Ironically, he feels that he cannot follow them, because the paradisal Puerto Rico he knew has been desecrated by U.S. capitalist conquest: "Refugee's words. / 'I can't go back. / They poisoned the country.' // And the chemical gas that dissolved in the grain of mountain leaf / has dissolved in the grain of his tongue, / so that he furies at the landlords" like "General Electric" and "Union Carbide" (8–9). The poet's searing images strenuously challenge the blithe disregard of colonial power relations in mainstream representations of Puerto Rico and Puerto Ricans.

One of Espada's most salient and humorous poetic acts of resistance to the distortion of Puerto Ricans' history is "Bully," a poem in *Rebellion Is the Circle of a Lover's Hands*. "Bully" plays upon the irony that a statue of Theodore Roosevelt is situated in the auditorium of a U.S. urban school attended by many Puerto Rican children. When, in 1898, the U.S. wrested colonial control over Puerto Rico from Spain through its victory in the Spanish-American War, Theodore Roosevelt, leader of the "Rough Riders," played a starring role in the U.S. triumph. As assistant secretary of the navy, the jingoistic Roosevelt, later McKinley's second vice president and successor upon the latter's assassination, was active in the shaping of the prewar policy that led to the "annexation" of Puerto Rico, as Arturo Morales Carrion suggests.[48] Espada imagines the "statue" of Roosevelt "nostalgic

/ for the Spanish-American war, / each fist lonely for a saber / or the reins of anguish-eyed horses, / or a podium to clatter with speeches / glorying in the malaria of conquest" (38).

As president, Roosevelt strengthened the grip of colonial rule and rebuffed Puerto Rican leaders who sought self-government for the island.[49] Carrion reports that in a 1906 visit to Puerto Rico "on his way back from the Panama Canal," Roosevelt "had much to say about the beauty of the land and, as a naturalist," its "splendid tropical flora," but spoke of "'something pathetic and childlike about the people'" (163). According to the president, the "'scheme'" of U.S. rule was of "'great benefit to the island'" and resulted in "'no injustice of any kind'" (164). Almost seventy years after Roosevelt's death, in a Boston school now "pronounced Hernandez," shifting demographics dismantle the Rough Rider's vestigial gringo supremacism and matter-of-factly inscribe (or transcribe) cultural difference: "Puerto Rico has invaded Roosevelt / with its army of Spanish-singing children / in the hallways, / . . . children painting Taino ancestors / that leap naked across murals" (38). The frozen trace of the "Victorian," racist "bully" seems about to be subject to playful "bullying" by inheritors of the victimization of his colonialist ideology:

Roosevelt is surrounded
by all the faces
he ever shoved in eugenic spite
and cursed as mongrels, skin of one race,
hair and cheekbones of another.

Once Marines tramped
from the newsreel of his imagination;
now children plot to spray graffiti
in parrot-brilliant colors
across the Victorian mustache
and monocle.

(38)

Converted into a figure of fun, this "serious" hero of U.S. military and political history must now "see" through a monocle imprinted with a Puerto Rican "perspective," the "parrot-brilliant colors" that clash egregiously with the somber hues of Victorian propriety. For the graffiti artists, the ironic play, of course, occurs within an extremely circumscribed social space; even as it affirms group solidarity, it merely provides a temporary respite from the daily disillusionment of second-class citizenship.

Concentrating on the dilemma of urban housing in no fewer than six poems in *City of Coughing and Dead Radiators,* Espada illustrates one important aspect of the post-Bootstrap history of Latinos in the urban U.S. In the title-poem, we hear of "tenants in the city of coughing and dead radiators" who "bang the radiators / like cold hollow marimbas; / they cry out / to unseen creatures / skittering across their feet / in darkness; / they fold hands over plates / to protect food / from ceilings black with roaches" (39). Even as the tenants, for whom "the city" lacks "warmth" in all senses, make anguished "music," they and their lawyers' protests are all but drowned out by the cacophony of a crowded, disordered, disorienting court system, prevaricating landlords, indifferent, racist, and corrupt judges. Indeed, from those who are supposed to dispense justice impartially, they fear violence: "the creases of the judge's face / collapse into a fist" (41).

"The Broken Window of Rosa Ramos," subtitled "Chelsea, Massachusetts, 1991," features the sufferings of a woman who "could spread her palm / at the faucet" of her mice-infested apartment "for hours / without cold water / ever hissing hot" (46). Rosa Ramos must rely for her proof of "identity" on her husband's driver's license, and the fact of her widowhood is substantiated solely by the mocking, ghoulish visibility of his photograph in "a sensationalist newspaper" ("Notes," 87) from Puerto Rico:

> Her husband was dead.
> She knew this
> from *El Vocero* newspaper,
> the picture of his grinning face
> sprayed with the black sauce of blood,
> a bullet-feast.
> Rosa shows his driver's license,
> a widow's identification,
> with the laminated plastic
> cracking across his eyes,
> so that he watches her
> through a broken window.
>
> (46)

The word-play of "widow" and "window" does not lighten the poem's tone; it emphasizes the distorted visual framing that oppresses Rosa Ramos. The term and status of widow are a "(window)-frame" that contextualizes her in a limiting way. The illusion of her husband's surveillance serves as a trope for the "broken window" through which the "majority" tend to see the "mass" of poor Latino immigrants of which Rosa is an "anonymous" part. By developing assertiveness in an alien language, she can combat how she is perceived and treated. She tells the lawyer (perhaps the "real" Espada) [50] helping her to protest conditions in her apartment about the perverse surveillance of the very person who is responsible for it, the "spy / clicking his key in the door unheard / to haunt the living room, / peeking for the thrill of young skin, / a pasty dead-faced man still hungry" (46), and the attorney teaches her "new words in English / for the landlord: 'Get out. Get out. Get out'" (47). In insisting upon her right to private space, she resists objectification and exploitation.

In Espada's poetry the multiple meanings of "eviction" are central to an understanding of Puerto Rican history on the mainland. The title-poem of *Trumpets from the Islands of Their Eviction* represents the struggle against various forms of eviction in U.S. cities, but it also alludes to the original dislocation from Puerto Rico during the time of Operation Bootstrap. In the poem's opening strophe, there is a conflictual swarm of mainland urban cacaphony and the "resistant" strains of Puerto Rican (salsa) music, which serves the effort to diminish the ravaging effects of multiple displacements:

> At the bar two blocks away,
> immigrants with Spanish mouths
> hear trumpets
> from the islands of their eviction.
> The music swarms into the barrio
> of a refugee's imagination,
> along with predatory squad cars
> and bullying handcuffs.
>
> (17)

In a rhetorical strategy typical of Espada's work, the intensity of fear produced by the cumulative impact of literal and figurative evictions is evoked by the metonymic investment of the vehicles and instruments of police authority with inherent menace, apart from their users. Nevertheless, these menacing effects do not overwhelm the music of beloved origins.

The next strophe speaks of the "evictions" of Puerto Ricans through a catalogue of brief narratives. First, Mrs. Alfaro represents those who are literally evicted from their apartments. She loses her home for "daring" to make her intolerable slum conditions visible: "evicted / when she trapped ten mice, / sealed them in plastic sandwich bags /

and gifted them to the landlord" (17). If her "gift" signifies a refusal to pay the rent, this is deemed a rupture of a legal contract, whereas the landlord's tacit refusal to make her apartment safe and sanitary is not. Later in the poem, the speaker reports that "Mrs. Alfaro has thirty days / to bundle the confusion of five children / down claustrophobic stairs / and away from the apartment."

The second character, Daniel, a victim of the prebilingual education era, is evicted from ordinary treatment by an absurdly arbitrary labeling: "stockaded / in the back of retarded classrooms / for having no English / to comfort third-grade teachers" (17). Since Daniel's linguistically "alien" presence makes teachers "uncomfortable," his own discomfort in an "alien" school setting is unjustly ignored. Next, Espada relates how, "thirty-five years ago," his own father was punished for a rejection of the social ritual intended to enforce his visibly constituted invisibility: "brown skin darker than the Air Force uniform / that could not save him, seven days county-jailed / for refusing the back of a Mississippi bus," just as Rosa Parks in Alabama took a visible stand against the segregationist eviction of African Americans from humane treatment. This incident gives the lie to the conservative notion that military service is an ultimate "seal" of one's patriotic Americanness, and it emphasizes the common struggle of African Americans and "brown-skinned" Latinos against obdurate white racism. In "Documentaries and Declamadores," while noting that "Puerto Rican poetry has an oral tradition which antedates its contact with the black community in the United States," Espada approvingly cites Sandra Maria Esteves's remarks about the "merging" of "the Puerto Rican community . . . with the black community in terms of how [they] are treated by the dominant society" (259), as well as her observation that the "reality of Puerto Rican culture" involves "a mixture of Indian, white, and black, even within one family" (261).

The fourth narration in Espada's catalogue presents a uniquely imaginative challenge to the stupidity of segregationist "eviction." The action of a "nameless Florida jíbaro / the grocery stores would not feed / in spite of the dollars he showed" deflates racist stereotyping of Latinos as petty criminals: he "returned with a machete, / collected cans from shelves / and forced the money / into the clerk's reluctant staring hand" (17). Using the threat of violence— the only means of budging the clerk's intransigence—to establish the common "privilege" of being a legitimate consumer, the jíbaro "robs" the clerk of his ability to distinguish arbitrarily between customers and "non-persons." The customer at least temporarily recovers a stolen, inalienable right, even if the clerk's "staring hand" and mind refuse to understand the justice of his claim.

Contesting the reduction of his people to "the ones identified by case number" (17), Espada returns in the poem's last strophe to the affirmative opening image of "immigrants with Spanish mouths" hearing "trumpets / from the islands of their eviction," and he concludes by articulating the trumpets' protective function: "The sound scares away devils / like tropical fish / darting between the corals" (18). In an article on Espada included in *Trumpets*, Diana L. Vélez observes that "Latinos" are "vaguely distasteful to some members of the dominant group" because of "their spicy foods, their loud Spanish voices, their music" (72–73). Annoyed by the "trumpets," "devilishly" prejudiced gringos who might otherwise harass Puerto Ricans leave the area to avoid having to listen. According to Vélez, Espada invests salsa music with "decolonizing" power; the "joyous metallic celebration" of "las trompetas—metonymic for the orchestra's brass section"—enables "the tropics" to "invade the space with sound" (75). In "the chain of signification salsa-trumpets-resistance," she adds, "the trumpets always return with a blast," and "so do the evicted, . . . with the full force of their loud ghetto blasters." When they take the stance of "refusing eviction, effectively taking over the space with their music," as Vélez puts it, Puerto Ricans are utilizing an auditory means of expressing their pride in self-representation, regardless of how others might seize and distort such representations.

Espada is a poet who consciously and consistently speaks on behalf of a collectivity, not only a "nationalist" group of Puerto Ricans (opposed to U.S. socioeconomic domination), but a broader potential coalition among Latino groups whose autonomy is curtailed by similar forces. He often strives to encourage his constituencies' belief in the future efficacy of their own struggles, in the possibility that current hegemonies are not impervious to challenge, through historical representations of the courageous, resourceful resistance of individual figures and groups to oppression. "The Firing Squad Is Singing in Chile," a poem in *Trumpets*, exemplifies this kind of effort. Taken "to the stadium, where thousands of the suspected stood / waiting for a bullet," "Victor Jara, / alleged communist, a singer" refuses to bow to an all-encompassing censorship; he insists on "singing for" the other martyrs-to-be, "and they, neck-bruised, / heartbeat drumming / in the forehead, / fear-eyed they, / they sang" (46). His persistence in the face of unspeakable torture and imminent death suggests, of course, that the murderously oppressive right-wing junta cannot stamp out the movement to bring democratic self-determination to the people of Chile. Taken up by countless other voices, this "song," the poet believes, will endure beyond and eventually triumph over seemingly insurmountable repression:

> And he sang,
> sang after the gun-butts
> fractured his hands
> to stop the guitar,
> sang though they pried the tongue
> from his head
> so that a mouth-cavern of red
> was his song,
> sang till the guards
> pointed metallic snouts
> and punctured his chest
> with machineguns' iron insect sting.
>   (46)

> And years later,
> exiles in cafes sing,
> smuggled tape recordings sing,
> night watchmen late in warehouses sing,
> labor camp prisoners anally raped cry and sing,
> the wives and mothers of the disappeared in protest sing,
> guerrilleros assembling rifles in a clandestine basement sing,
> as if a butchered tongue
> could stop Chile from singing.
>   (48)

Espada refuses to regard "Chile" as the domain of terroristic regimes like Pinochet's, but as a currently fragmented, dispersed collectivity of those in solidarity with Victor Jara's song of freedom. Implicitly, images of "smuggled tape recordings" and "guerrilleros . . . in a clandestine basement" that accompany the persistence of singing seem to prophesy a gradual movement from the necessary secrecy of small groups to increasingly public, mass action. In each of the above passages, the Whitmanian accumulation stemming from the catalogue and the epiphora of forms of the verb "to sing," along with a tone of determination reminiscent of Pablo Neruda's political poetry, permits revolutionary optimism to have some affective force.

The hopeful notion of "multiplication" that animates "The Firing Squad Is Singing in Chile" is central to Espada's concept in various poems of how oppositional strategy has been and can be developed. For example, in "Cockroaches of Liberation," a poem in *City of Coughing and Dead Radiators,* the poet praises the "dramatic" performance of a "student strike" in Puerto Rico against the U.S.'s economic stranglehold on the island. The demonstrators, he observes, display a guerillaesque prowess at becoming "invisible" at the right time. They know the "secret for dissolving / between the grillwork of balconies / and fire escapes, down hallways / with a single dead bulb, basement steps" (23–24) when police appear on the scene. Their talent for reappearance "after the flashlights / and battery-charged eyes of the cops / had dimmed" is also outstanding. As with the multiplication of "cockroaches," the "breeding" of collective resistance to harsh social conditions cannot be halted by typical repressive measures:

> . . . they crept back onto the plaza,
> calling to each other . . .
> multiplying in the dark
> like cockroaches of liberation
> too quick for stomping boots
> that circle back on the hour,
> immune to the stink
> of government fumigation.
>
> (24)

Similarly, in "The King of Books," a poem in *Rebellion Is the Circle of a Lover's Hands* honoring the courage of the book's translator into Spanish, Camilo Pérez-Bustillo, Espada speaks of the "multiplication"—the paradoxically healthful "infestation"—of Pérez-Bustillo's "books" which "traveled with [him] / everywhere, like wrinkled duendes [restless demons or goblins] / whispering advice" (66). In the next strophe, Espada characterizes the books as "bandits, / bootlegging illicit words / like Che and insurrection" into beleaguered El Salvador, where Pérez-Bustillo's own U.S. government during the Reagan era was—as noted in my brief discussion of Forché's *The Country between Us*—essentially condoning atrocious right-wing repression in the name of anticommunist "national security."

Salvadoran military proponents of "rational facist philosophy," "cousins" of Forché's "Colonel," have done their violent best to frighten the left-wing bibliophile into surrendering his books. They used such strategies as "a rifle jabbed in his spine/ . . . electrical wires slowly waving, / branches of cruel sparks," and an agonizingly long, repetitive "interrogation" (66), even as U.S. marines tried, through their actions in the area, to give credence to the effort to halt the flow of Pérez-Bustillo's ideological messages to the Salvadoran populace. Not only did these strategies fail to halt his resistance, but, when he was able to extricate himself from the ordeal, textual evidence grew and grew: "In his apartment books breed, / an infestation of books, / piling, spilling, / a horde of printed words like grasshoppers / blackening the nightmares / of treasury police and armed captains / in El Salvador" (68). This healthful "plague commanded / by Camilo, / the King of Books" figures any such dissemination of forms of political education that vigorously counter the rationalized class interests of those in power.

For Espada, one of the most potent examples of the resistance to oppression in recent times is the triumph of the Sandinista forces in Nicaragua in 1979 and their subsequent eleven years in power. In his poetry about Nicaragua, he seeks to articulate a perspective on history-in-process markedly different from the negative one promulgated by the Reagan administration and its allies. He promotes the recognition of limited, tenuous and yet remarkable success against great odds by the people of an embattled nation; he depicts their arduous struggle toward a version of an egalitarian society. As Robert Creeley notes in his foreword to *Trumpets*, Espada made "a three-part documentary . . . in 1982 from materials gathered in Nicaragua and broadcast on National Public Radio and elsewhere" which served as "an early national advice of circumstances there" (11). This series, "Nicaragua: Three Years After Somoza," earned the recognition of the National Federation of Community Broadcasters.[51]

In considering the context of Sandinista-era Nicaragua, one must recognize that years of U.S. support for the Somoza family's corrupt, tyrannical regime, going back to the time of President Franklin D. Roosevelt,[52] set the stage for the Reagan administration's undeclared war on the small nation's new leadership. In a 1983 address, President Reagan asserts that, despite the Carter administration's "emergency relief and recovery aid" totaling $118 million, "the government of Nicaragua has treated" the U.S. "as an enemy" and "rejected [its] repeated peace efforts."[53] According to Reagan, "a small clique" of Sandinistas, directly after ending Somoza's regime, "ousted others who had been part of the revolution from having any voice in government," and "the Minister of Defense, declared Marxism-Leninism would be their guide, and so it is" (151). The president sees the 1979 shift in power in Nicaragua as "an exchange of one set of autocratic rulers for another," because "the people still have no freedom, no democratic rights and more poverty." The new Nicaraguan leadership, he insists "is helping Cuba and the Soviets to destabilize our hemisphere." In a 1982 address, President Daniel Ortega cites numerous examples of covert action sanctioned by the Reagan government, such as "training camps for Somozist counterrevolutionaries" in Florida and in Nicaragua's neighbor, Honduras, and "a budget of $19 million" approved by the U.S. National Security Council "to promote . . . economic sabotage, attacks, training and arms shipments to Somozist . . . groups."[54]

Thus, Espada's "Grito for Nicaragua," a poem in *Trumpets* that utilizes anaphora and long lines reminiscent of Whitman's declamatory free verse, registers an implicit protest against the Reagan administration policy, as well as one against the continued threat of violent, reactionary forces from Nicaragua's former ruling class. (The poet states in the notes to *City of Coughing and Dead Radiators* that a *"grito,"* which is "literally, a cry or shout . . . has connotations of political uprising, for example, the Grito de Lares, the Puerto Rican rebellion against Spain in 1868"[86].) First, emphasizing how utterly destabilized Nicaragua has been by the civil war and by decades of despotic rule, Espada in "Grito for Nicaragua" gives the lie to the notion that such a ravaged country could currently muster the resources to "export revolution":

> After years of land stripped brown and humiliated as a slave's back,
> after the living flailed by the Guardia into crematorium-volcanoes,
> the corpses dragged through funeral-slow clouded rivers,
> after tree-hidden boys trembled quickly in the waiting of ambush,
> the first killed soldier and vomiting in the humid secrecy of night,
> after rifles kicking again with the force of slaughtered cousins,
> after airlift evacuation of the general's family over caving city walls.
>
> (42)

In a 1980 analysis called "the Somoza legacy," the EPICA Task Force offers what can be viewed as a statistical ballast for the compelling imagery of the above passage. The "incredible price" paid for Nicaragua's "liberation" included "40,000 dead—1.5 percent of the population, some 100,000 wounded, 40,000 children orphaned, 200,000 families left homeless, and 750,000 dependent on food assistance," as well as "an infant mortality rate higher than India's and an illiteracy rate of 53.3 percent."[55] Also thanks to the departed Somoza, "the major cities had been razed and the treasury systematically looted, leaving more than one-third of the labor force out of work" (299). Along with its "deeply depressed economy," Nicaragua suffered from "a neglected social service area" deficient in all major respects, "and an insurmountable external debt totalling $1.5 billion."

Facing these enormous problems, Nicaragua's Junta for National Reconstruction in 1982 stressed the goals of breaking "economic dependence on the transnational corporations and the countries that support these corporations to the extent possible given that" Nicaragua is "a poor, underdeveloped, and small country" and of favoring "changes in the distribution of the national income in ways that benefit the majority of the population," even as survival in the global economy dicatated the promotion of "joint investments with the private" as well as "public sectors."[56] When Reagan looked at the Sandinistas, he did not see a government which combined a mixture of capitalist expedients and socialist principles, nor could he understand how poorly countries like Nicaragua had been served by unbridled multinational capitalist influence in the past; he could only "see Red."

In the next two strophes of his "Grito," a poem consisting of one long sentence, Espada spotlights, not only the faith of common people in such efforts of the Sandinistas, but their joyous, voluntary collaboration to begin the overwhelming task of stabilizing their war-torn nation (and not, as Reagan put it, of destabilizing surrounding countries). The poet lauds their determination to construct a peaceful, thriving environment where the dispossessed can gain a measure of autonomy:

> the shacks grow on stripped land, resurrection of planks,
> the unsteady spine of nails, wounds grafted with cardboard patch,
> the dark backs pushing together, becoming one back to lift long pipe,
> the shovel's iron hungry for the dirt of latrine digging;
>
> then the remains of shacks and fields charred by raiders
> will be raised again in the arms of those left unburned.

(42)

The image of a unification of "the dark backs pushing together" is especially charged, because it simultaneously recalls the abomination of slavery and signifies something close to its opposite, the Nicaraguans' release from socioeconomic bondage into the possibility that hard work will help them raise their standard of living.

Nevertheless, Espada's imagery in the poem also addresses the precariousness of every act of "resurrection." There is the continuing menace of "invading squadrons," "mercenaries and military advisors" of the opposition, and "border patrol snipers" (42). In the "Grito's" closing lines, however, the poet asserts—perhaps too confidently and too lyrically—that the Sandinistas' military force, fueled by deep political conviction, will annihilate the opposition's violent designs with its own (defensive) violence: "then their bone fragments will be strewn like smashed pottery / with the dwindling reminder of their stench / for the curiosity of flies and children."

In "The Meaning of the Shovel," a poem in *Imagine the Angels of Bread* with the subheading "Barrio René Cisneros, Managua, Nicaragua, June-July 1982," Espada gives reasons for coming to Nicaragua fourteen years earlier to "dig latrines" (53). He wished to pay tribute to the ultimate sacrifice of many Nicaraguans in the struggle for their freedom from the Somoza regime and to help combat the dire poverty he saw all around him, typified by the "woman" he saw climbing "into a barrel of water / to wash herself and [her] dress / at the same time, / her cupped hands spilling" and "the boy" who, "in a country / with no glass . . . kept the treasured bottle" of "orange soda" that the poet had been drinking "and poured the liquid into a plastic bag / full of ice, then poked a hole with a straw" (54). Espada happened upon another reason, a desire to honor the richness of Nicaraguan history when his "shovel / struck a clay bowl centuries old, / the art of ancient fingers / moist with this same earth, / perfect but for one crack in the lip" (54). This reminder offers a stark contrast with the attitude of President Reagan, who may only bother to pay attention to such a small country as Nicaragua because, as the Great Communicator puts it, "Central America, bordering . . . on the Caribbean—our lifeline to the outside world" of commerce—holds "strategic importance" to the U.S. (147).

Since Espada published "The Meaning of the Shovel" six years after Nicaraguans voted the Sandinistas out of power and months before the latter lost a second presidential election, the poem can be read as an abiding declaration of solidarity with the Sandinistas. Most likely, Espada believes that the majority of voters' failure to recognize how corporate interests of powerful nations and wealthy entrepreneurs who remained within the country, and not Ortega's socialist policies, did much to create the worsening of Nicaragua's conditions in the eighties. The poem may also express Espada's faith that the Sandinistas will eventually return to power. In any case, Espada's poems on Puerto Rican, Chilean, Nicaraguan, and other Latino history constitute narrative and lyric representations of imperial, colonial, or otherwise oppressive power relations and the struggles of common people to establish national autonomy and democratic conditions.

Unlike the other poets discussed in this book, Gloria Anzaldúa in *Borderlands* intersperses prose essays with her poems in order to confront glaring distortions in "official" historical narratives, and, in the spirit of rectification, to represent the history of particular configurations of violence and oppression. Sonia Saldivar-Hull calls *Borderlands* "a *mestizaje*: a postmodernist mixture of autobiography, historical document, and poetry collection. Like the people whose lives it chronicles, *Borderlands* resists genre boundaries as well as geopolitical borders."[57] This textual strategy of "*mestizaje*" has strong, positive ramifications for the reception of Anzaldúa's political intentions in the poems. Prose sections (which sometimes include poetry and feature endnotes with scholarly references) provide such an abundance of historical contextualization and cultural analysis that it would be difficult for readers to depoliticize or dehistoricize the poems of Chicano/a experience, to write them off merely as individual(istic) expression.

"Born a seventh generation American" in 1942 on a "ranch settlement" in "South Texas," Anzaldúa "lived in a ranching environment" for the next eleven years.[58] Hector A. Torres relates that "her father died when she was fifteen, and Anzaldúa talks about her family having to support itself from that time forward and having 'to go back into the fields and work'" (9), and this work included migrant labor. Anzaldúa was a field-worker "until the time she earned her B.A. from Pan American University in 1969." Certainly, her effort to challenge the mainstream disregard of her people's history has had much to do with particulars of her family's difficult circumstances.

In *Borderlands*, Anzaldúa's story of the origins and unfolding of what, in retrospect, she can call Chicano/a or mestiza history is provided in the first essay, "The Homeland, Aztlán / El Otro México." Without the various components of this story, the full implications of the narration and analysis of the oppression of Chicanos in the nineteenth and twentieth centuries in various poems are not available, nor is a thorough understanding of the construction of mestiza subjectivity, the consciousness of the borderland resident, in other poems. Anzaldúa's counterhistorical narrative exposes the effacement of history in "the Anglos' " self-serving "image of the West as vacant before their arrival," as John R. Chávez put it in *The Lost Land: The Chicano Image of the Southwest,* a source upon which she relies.[59] Against the view that "Anglos" have had the right and responsibility to lay claim to the "virgin" Southwestern and Western "wilderness" and to annex it to "civilization," Anzaldúa claims, footnoting Chávez, that "the oldest evidence of humankind in the U.S.," which "was found in Texas and has been dated to 35,000 B.C.," points to "The Chicanos' ancient Indian ancestors" (4).[60] "In the Southwest United States," she adds, "archeologists have found 20,000-year-old campsites of the Indians who migrated through, or permanently occupied, the Southwest, Aztlán—land of the herons, land of whiteness, the Edenic place of origin of the Azteca." Anzaldúa dates the migration from the Southwest to "what is now Mexico and Central America" to 1000 B.C.

Emphasizing how the origin of the mestiza/o was caused by the burgeoning of European imperialism during Spain's conquest of Mexico (5), Anzaldúa cites Reay Tannahill's *Sex in History*[61] to tell of how the decimation of the "pure-blooded" Indian population was due to importation of "Old World diseases to which the native had no immunity," while "the *mestizos* who were genetically equipped to sur- vive" these diseases "founded a new hybrid race and inherited Central and South America" (5). Thus, "*en* 1521 . . . people of mixed Indian and Spanish blood" emerged, and "Chicanos, Mexican-Americans, are the offsprings of those first matings." When the Spanish, Indians, and mestizos "settled parts of the U.S. southwest" in the 1500s, the Indians who acted as servants of "every gold-hungry *conquistador* and soul-hungry missionary" were able to "return to the place of origin, Aztlán, thus making Chicanos originally and secondarily indigenous to the Southwest." The intermarriage of all three groups "with North American Indians" created "an even greater *mestizaje*."

Moving to the next crucial time of conquest and political disenfran- chisement, the nineteenth century, Anzaldúa offers a quick sketch of Anglos' illegal migration into Mexico's Texas territory "in greater and greater numbers," their driving of "the *tejanos* (native Texans of Mexican descent) from their lands" and general oppression of these indigenous people, and Mexico's justified pursuit of "a war to keep its Texas territory" (6). She speaks of the establishment of the Republic of Texas in 1836 as a "white imperialist takeover" rationalized by the Battle of the Alamo, which "became, for the whites, the symbol for the cowardly and villainous character of the Mexicans," the U.S.'s incitement of "Mexico to war" (7) and the former's victory, which forced the latter "to give up almost half of her nation, what is now Texas, New Mexico, Arizona, Colorado, and California."

It is interesting to contrast such a narrative, supported by John Chávez's detailed account (29–37), with the slippery use of detail of texts like Ray Allen Billington's *The Far Western Frontier, 1830– 1860* (1956), which could easily have provided a basis for the "official" U.S. version in one of Anzaldúa's school history textbooks. Deeming most U.S. citizens who "had been crowding" into Texas "since 1821" (as opposed to earlier "illegal aliens") "sober and law-abiding" and "devotedly loyal to the Mexican government," Billington asserts the inevitability of the escalation of conflict between the Mexicans and Anglos leading to the point where "revolution and Texan independence followed as naturally as day follows night."[62] These antagonists, like "lions and lambs . . . penned together," could hardly be expected to "maintain harmony" (116); Billington supports this contention by painting Mexican culture as wholly authoritarian and "American" culture as tied to a belief in the "natural right" of self-government and the enjoyment of "the blessings of religious and political freedom" (120). Part of that "natural right," it turns out, was to hold African slaves, something that Mexico had outlawed in 1832 (122).

Billington ignores not only the U.S. settlers' *un*democratic establishment of a "democracy" on *others'* territory, but their original violations of the conditions of allegiance to Mexico and its laws that sanctioned their migration to Texas. As Anzaldúa clarifies, their subsequent behavior toward the Mexican "minority" was anything but democratic. Indeed, when the Treaty of Guadalupe-Hidalgo in 1848 ended the U.S.-Mexico War and "left 100,000 Mexican citizens on this side," Anzaldúa states, "the land established by the treaty as belonging to the Mexicans was soon swindled away from its owners"—without any subsequent attempt at "restitution" (7).

After that point, "the Gringo, locked into the fiction of white superiority, seized complete political power, stripping Indians and Mexicans of their land while their feet were still rooted in it" (7), and the *tejanos,* "ignored" and often "penalized" when they sought justice from "the courts, law enforcement officials, and government officials, . . . had no other recourse but armed retaliation" (8). By 1915, there were incidents of "Anglo vigilante groups . . . lynching Chicanos," and organized forms of Chicano resistance were crushed in a variety of ways. One can imagine how Billington and similar apologists for Texan "democracy" would rail against the "exaggerations" and "distortions" of an Anzaldúa poem like "We Call Them Greasers," the title of which respectfully echoes Arnoldo de León's revisionary history, *They Called Them Greasers: Anglo Attitudes toward Mexicans in Texas, 1821–1900* (1983).[63]

In this chilling dramatic monologue, the quintessentially racist and male supremacist Anglo speaker ridicules the *tejanos/as*' farming methods, their gestures of courtesy, their communal spirit, and their "cowardice" in the face of the invaders' overwhelming political power and greater access to deadly weapons. The "greasers'" lack of facility with English is also subject to scorn. As Sonia Saldivar-Hull observes in her analysis of the poem, "For the Anglo-American imperialist literacy in Spanish or any other nonstatus language is by their definition illiteracy" (214). Anzaldúa's masterful use of believable speech and concrete detail perceived through pathologically prejudiced eyes captures the speaker's conviction that "Manifest Destiny"[64] and the *tejanos/as*' character "defects" justify *any* act of violence against them:

> They knew their betters:
> took off their hats
> placed them over their hearts,
> lowered their eyes in my presence.
>
> Weren't even interested in bettering themselves,
> why they didn't even own the land but shared it.
> Wasn't hard to drive them off,
> cowards they were, no backbone.
> I showed 'em a piece of paper with some writing
> tole 'em they owed taxes
> had to pay right away or be gone by *manana*. . . .
>
> Some loaded their chickens children wives and pigs
> into rickety wagons, pans and tools dangling
> clanging from all sides.
> Couldn't take their cattle—
> during the night my boys had frightened them off.
> Oh, there were a few troublemakers
> who claimed we were the intruders.
> Some even had land grants
> and appealed to the courts.
> It was a laughing stock
> them not even knowing English.

Still some refused to budge,
even after we burned them out.

(134)

In the poem's closing strophe, recalling a scene in which he raped a *tejana* after having "her man" tied to a tree, the speaker savors his dominance by stating that while "thrusting and thrusting," he "felt" the lynched man "watching from the mesquite tree / heard him keening like a wild animal" (135). In actuality, of course, the rapist himself is thinking and behaving animalistically and has done so in *all* his dealings with the *tejanos*. Anzaldúa's challenge to contemporary racist whites in "*La conciencia de la mestiza*" is precisely what the speaker cannot and will not do: "To say you've split yourself off from minority groups, that you disown us, that your dual consciousness splits off parts of yourself, transferring the 'negative' parts onto us. . . . To say that you are afraid of us, that to put distance between us, you wear the mask of contempt" (86). Not realizing, it seems, that Mexicans have at least 50 percent "Indian" blood, the speaker compares his female victim to a member of "another" group against whom he wears this "mask": ". . . in that instant I felt such contempt for her / round face and beady black eyes like an Indian's" (135). At the poem's end, contempt and brutality reach their ultimate expression:

Afterwards I sat on her face until
her arms stopped flailing,
didn't want to waste a bullet on her.
The boys wouldn't look me in the eyes.
I walked up to where I had tied her man to the tree
and spat in his face. Lynch him, I told the boys.

(135)

Indicating how Anzaldúa extends Arnoldo de León's and other male Chicano historians' investigations of "lynching as an institutionalized threat against Tejanos" by fleshing "out the ramifications of the lynch law to Chicanas" (214), Saldívar-Hull states that the rapist's accomplishment of "total control over the Tejano through the violation of his woman" brings about the former's utter "contempt for her"; "the woman occupies a position below the already inferior brown man" (215). She adds that the poet's "reluctance to condemn the passive observers, 'the boys,' " constitutes "an implicit recognition of the power of the class structure even in nineteenth century Texas where the rich land barons controlled all their workers, regardless of race or ethnicity" (215–16).

Turning to the next phase of Anzaldúa's historical account in "The Homeland, Aztlán," we find that "Anglo agribusiness corporations" attained hegemony and further exhausted the Chicanos' economic possibilities in the 1930s, when they "cheated the small Chicano landowners of their land" and "hired gangs of *mexicanos*" (9) to clear the land for the implementation of the most technologically "advanced" farming methods. Typical of Chicanos of his generation, Anzaldúa's father was forced into a sharecropper's life: "Rio Farms Incorporated loaned him seed money and living expenses. At harvest time, my father repaid the loan and forked over 40% of the earnings. Sometimes we earned less than we owed, but always the corporations fared well" (9). In her earlier autobiographical essay, "La Prieta," Anzaldúa notes that her family "only migrated once when [she] was seven," because her father, disturbed by the fact that she had "missed a few weeks of school," "decided this should not happen again."[65] Before 1965, when Cesar Chávez led the National Farm Workers Association strike and nationwide boycott of California grapes, the horrendous exploitation of Chicano migrant workers was invisible to most U.S. citizens.[66] Anzaldúa, active in Chávez's movement in the sixties, includes several poems in *Borderlands* that testify to the horrible conditions of field labor and its physical and mental effects.

"A Sea of Cabbages," dedicated to "those who have worked in the fields," represents the experience of one such worker. Despite being "on his knees, hands swollen / sweat flowering on his face," and suffering from "arthritic arms," this man manages to fix "his gaze," not on the ground that he cultivates but "on the high paths / the words in his head twining cords / tossing them up to catch that bird of the heights" (132). Comparing this hopeful yet oppressed worker to "a worm in a green sea / shaken by the wind," the poet implies how the absence of protection from pesticide residue, physical overwork, and the numbing quality of repetitive labor "unleaf" the worker; in addition, the sun, sustainer of life, is his inadvertent torturer:

> Century after century flailing,
> unleafing himself in a sea of cabbages.
> Dizzied
> body sustained by the lash of the sun.
> In his hands the cabbages contort like fish.
> Thickened tongue swallowing

the stench.

The sun, a heavy rock on his back,
cracks,
the earth shudders, slams his face
spume froths from his mouth spilling over
eyes opened, face up, searching, searching.

(133)

Energetic gerunds amid precise visual description, tropes found in concrete, "natural" situations, the muscular progress of the accentual free verse (if not the line lengths and strophe patterns), enjambment and caesuras, and depiction of suffering recall early short poems of William Carlos Williams, himself half Puerto Rican, but the more pronounced political urgency and advocacy in Anzaldúa's lines are hard to miss. While the trope of the sun as "heavy rock" might allude to Camus's use of the Sisyphus myth to articulate existential "absurdity," the transformation that the trope undergoes turns interpretation in a somewhat different direction: elements of nature itself register a powerful "response" to the field workers' pain.[67]

Although one might admire the spiritual strength that enables the worker to seek salvation amid such oppression, Anzaldúa perceives the component of this longing for a mystical, externally based rescue as partly playing into the hands of his exploiters: "Swinging in a mucilage of hope," the man is "caught in the net along with *la paloma*" [the dove] (132), the dream of freedom and tranquility. The poem's closing lines return to a similar trope of entrapment: "He cannot escape his own snare— / faith: dove made flesh" (133). This is not to say that Anzaldúa frowns upon mystical spirituality, which is affirmed as a vital part of Chicano and Mexican culture and in her own life in the *Borderlands* essays, "*La herencia de Coatlicue* / The Coatlicue State (41–51) and "*Tlilli, Tlapalli*: The Path of the Red and Black Ink" (65–75); she believes that such impulses should be accompanied by "worldly" political action.

In "*sus plumas el viento*" [its feathers the wind], the protagonist is a woman suffering similar hardships as the man in "A Sea of Cabbages," except that her gender increases her vulnerability. Possessing "swollen feet / tripping on vines in the heat, / palms thick and green-knuckled, / sweat drying on top of old sweat" (116), Pepita finds that, after "twelve hours" of strenuous labor, "roped knots cord her back" (117). Like the raped woman in "We Call Them Greasers," she is forced "on her back / grimacing to the sky"; this time the

Anglo intruder is "the field boss" who buzzes "around her like a mosquito, / landing on her, digging in, sucking. / When Pepita came out of the irrigation ditch / some of the men," the workers, "spit on the ground" (116). The "irrigation ditch" not only serves as a reminder of the clash between white agribusiness farming methods and the more ecologically appropriate methods that the Chicanos would still be using if their lands had not been stolen, but it signifies how the woman is a receptacle for the misogynistic boss's lustful rage.

In her realistic conversation with herself, represented—as Rafael Pérez-Torres states in a trenchant analysis of "interlingualism"[68] in the poem—by "the use of Spanish" and English both signaling "the hardship of . . . conditions" (235) in the field, Pepita summarizes the components of her burden, fully understands how difficult escape from her situation would be and how severely limited her current options are, and prays for her own children's deliverance from this oppression:

> *Como una mula,* [like a mule]
> she shifts 150 pounds of cotton on her back.
> It's either *las labores*
> or feet soaking in cold puddles in *bodegas*
>
> cutting   washing   weighing   packaging
> broccoli spears carrots cabbages in 12 hours   15
> double shift the roar of machines inside her head.
> She can always clean shit
> out of white folks toilets—the Mexican maid.
> You're respected if you can use your head
> instead of your back, the women said.
> *Ay m'ijos, ojalá que hallen trabajo* [Oh, my children, I hope you find work]
> in air-conditioned offices.

(118)

To learn to "use your head" the way that workers "in air-conditioned offices" are thought to do, of course, requires educational opportunities routinely denied to most Chicanos of Pepita's generation. Midway through the poem, which is dedicated to Anzaldúa's mother, there is a brief mention of a Chicano woman from the same background— someone like the poet herself—who serves as a kind of model for Pepita's wish for her children: "If she hadn't read all those books / she'd be singing up and down the rows / like the rest" (117).

Pérez-Torres points out that "Spanish" in the poem signals "the dream of something better" (235), as in the workers' singing, "which helps alleviate the brutality of the fieldwork" (236). In "A Sea of Cabbages," *la paloma,* the dove, had been the major symbol of the "transcendence" of unbearable conditions, but here, as Pérez-Torres states, it is "the mention of hummingbirds [*chuparrosas*] in both Spanish and English" in the middle of the poem and at the end:

> *Que le de sus plumas el viento.*
> The sound of hummingbird wings
> in her ears, *pico de chuparrosas.*
>
> She looks up into the sun's glare,
> *la chuparrosas de los jardines*
> *en dónde están de su mamagrande?*
> but all she sees is the obsidian wind
> cut tassels of blood
> from the hummingbird's throat.
>
> (116–17)

> She sees the obsidian wind
> cut tassels of blood
> from the hummingbird's throat.
> As it falls
> the hummingbird shadow
> becomes the navel of the Earth.
>
> (118)

Paraphrasing the Spanish lines in the first of the passages above, Pérez-Torres states that the speaker "dreams that the wind would give her its wings. She hears the buzzing sound of hummingbirds and remembers the hummingbirds of her grandmother's garden" (236). This link with "female ancestors" echoes Anzaldúa's dedication of the poem to her mother. For Pérez-Torres, the reference to the hummingbird's cut throat alludes to the Toltecs' sacrifice of these birds, which was ended by "the incursion of the Mexica and their imposition of male deities such as the god of war, Huitzilopochtli"; thus, the displacement of a benign matriarchal power structure by a bellicose patriarchy "in pre-Cortesian Mexican societies" is suggested. I would add that the trope also signifies the brutality of Anglo patriarchy against Chicanos during the nineteenth and twentieth centuries in the Southwest. The poem ends with an affirmative image of the

hummingbird. Pérez-Torres asserts that "out of the sacrifice and brutality comes . . . the potential for centering and rebirth," as signified
by "the navel" which "connects . . . the poet with her mother" and
effects a "transmission of hope from mother to daughter" (237).
Thus, Anzaldúa provides an emblem of the remarkable survival of
Chicana collectivity in a harsh environment.

In *"El Sonavabitche,"* another poem about the exploitation of Chi-
cano/a farm laborers, some measure of concrete social change seems
much more plausible, because the poem narrates a resistance to
oppression that is at least temporarily successful. *"El Sonavabitche's"*
speaker, who could be Anzaldúa herself, is acting as an advocate for
Mexican "illegals" and other Chicano migrant workers. Once placed
in a similar situation as those she seeks to help, she finds that her
visit to the site of their exploitation triggers her anguished memory
and rage:

> Car flowing down a lava of highway
> just happened to glance out the window
> in time to see brown faces bent backs
> like prehistoric boulders in a field
> so common a sight no one
> notices
> blood rushes to my face
> twelve years I'd sat on the memory
> the anger scorching me
> my throat so tight I can
> barely get the words out.
>
>   (124)

The simile of "prehistoric boulders" exposes how the image of Mexicans in these situations is so commonplace to many U.S. citizens,
unaware of Chicano history, that it renders the actual individuals
and the *un*natural injustice of their social context invisible.

Toward the end of "The Homeland Aztlán," speaking in prose of
her people's "tradition of long walks" from the sixteenth century to
the present and providing an important aspect of the context of the
pre-NAFTA *"El Sonavabitche,"* Anzaldúa seeks to restore what has been
erased by elucidating the political dimension of the current return of
"ten million people without documents . . . to the Southwest" (10).
She traces the crisis of the Mexican poor in the 1980s to a trend begun
at the end of the last century, when "powerful landowners in Mexico, in partnership with U.S. colonizing companies," expropriated

land from "millions of Indians" (10). Since then, U.S. corporate dominance has intensified. Anzaldúa notes that "the Mexican government and wealthy growers . . . in partnership with . . . American conglomerates . . . own factories called *maquiladoras*" that employ "one-fourth of all Mexicans," including a disproportionate number of "young women" (10).[69]

Given "the devaluation of the *peso*," unemployment assailing "half of the Mexican people," and the fact that "in the U.S. a man or woman can make eight times what they can in Mexico," many Mexicans perceive crossing the border as the only alternative to starvation (10). The "illegals" take astounding risks to cross, and, once having done so, undergo horrendous hardship to remain in the U.S. and to find work. Upon arriving at "that migrant camp / north of Muncie, Indiana" (125), the advocate/speaker in "*El Sonavabitche*" hears that the "illegals" there—thirteen of them—had spent "five days packed in the back of a pickup / boarded up tight / fast cross-country run no stops / except to change drivers, to gas up / no food they pissed into their shoes," and, in fact, "one smothered to death on the way here" (126). In the two weeks that the twelve workers have been at the farm, "the *sonavabitche*" has worked "them / from sunup to dark—15 hours sometimes," has refused their request for a Sunday "off / . . . to pray and rest, / write letters to their *familias*" by turning away and spitting, and has stated that he would "hold back half their wages / that they'd eaten the other half" (125), as if it were possible. On payday, "*la migra* [immigration officials] came busting in" because of an "anonymous" call: "Guess who? That *sonavabitche*, who else?" (126). He had used this duplicity to acquire "free labor, *esclavos*" [slaves] repeatedly. When the speaker sees "tall men in uniforms / thumping fists on doors / metallic voices yelling Halt! / their hawk eyes constantly shifting" and the Mexicans' desperate flight and hiding, her "knees"—in sympathy with the latter—are "like aspens in the wind" (124). Seeing "that wide cavernous look of the hunted / the look of hares" on the illegals, the poet acutely renders the impact of merciless forces on them: "The bare heads humbly bent / of those who do not speak / the ember in their eyes extinguished" (125).

Simultaneously much more visible than they want to be at the moment and yet invisible, the "illegals" are so exploited and harassed that they seem drained of the energy and perspective to resist these injustices. In *The Illegals* (1978), Grace Halsell, whom Anzaldúa cites as a source for information in "The Homeland, Aztlán" about the situation of Mexican illegal immigration (93), glosses the cha-

rade involving the immigration patrol, the growers, and the "aliens."
She declares that the U.S. spends "by a conservative estimate, . . .
about $250 million each year to wage the war on our doorstep"
and that "over 90 percent of those arrested are recycled—that is,
sent back to Mexico the same day—and they appear in the statistics again and again."[70] Instead of waging this absurd "war" and
continuing to support Mexico's crippling economic dependence on
"industrialization . . . mostly for consumer goods," a process "controlled by foreign-owned multinational corporations" (211), Halsell
believes that the U.S. should assist the Mexican government in plan-
ning "village-based" solutions (210) that enable villagers to keep
farming (212), and spend tax dollars "more profitably in creating
jobs to keep" Mexicans "in Mexico" (215). Many major U.S. players, not to mention smaller operators like "*El Sonavabitche*," would
find the economic empowerment of the entire Mexican nation so
antithetical to their own perceived interests that the costly "failure" of the border "war" may be a perfectly acceptable long-term
"investment."

While these larger structures of exploitation seem impossible for
small political organizations to contest directly, the speaker in "*El
Sonavabitche*" strives for changes on a local level. She describes her
nervousness at confronting the kind of "boss" she may have feared
twelve years ago and the way she summons her resolve before insisting
that he give the workers precisely the recompense they had originally
been promised—but for their actual "15 hours a day" and fourteen
days rather than ten (127). The boss's rejoinder is predictable: the
idea that "wets work for whatever you give them," that "the season
hasn't been good," and that he hasn't "broken no law [*sic*]." Rising
above the fear of confrontation and calling upon her passionate conviction, the speaker threatens exposure of his scam to "neighbors,"
"the mayor," and even "Washington" (128).

Even though she "didn't know anyone in D.C. / now," the gambit
works, and the *sonavabitche*'s absurd implication of extortion, the
insinuation that she intends to pocket the money herself, earns a
response containing the moral basis for her cultural/racial solidarity:
"Sweat money, Mister, blood money, / not my sweat, but same blood"
(128). In her final pronouncement to the *sonavabitche*, she ironically
reverses the kind of Anglo machismo[71] displayed in "We Call Them
Greasers" with her own trope of lynching: "If I ever hear that you
got illegals on your land / even a single one, I'm going to come
here / in broad daylight and have you / hung by your balls." The

advocate has triumphed, for now, but she must remain wary of the man's chicanery. The strain of resistance has taken its toll: "Knees shaking, I count every bill / taking my time."

In an untitled poem that follows the two opening citations of "The Homeland, Aztlán," Anzaldúa develops a description and social analysis of the material trope, the border of *Borderlands,* used to occlude the complex history discussed later in the essay and, thus, to produce conditions suffered and resisted in *"El Sonavabitche."* Jack D. Forbes, author of the essay's second citation and a Native American, sets a point of departure for this poetic analysis by calling into question the notion of *any* Mexicans being labeled "illegal aliens" in the U.S.: " 'The *Aztecas del norte* . . . compose the largest single tribe or nation of Anishinabeg (Indians) found in the United States today. . . . Some call themselves Chicanos and see themselves as people whose true homeland is Aztlán' " (1).[72]

Beginning the poem, an individual Chicana, "wind tugging at [her] sleeve / feet sinking into the sand," places herself at the center of the borders that divide "Aztlán": "I stand at the edge where earth touches ocean / where the two overlap / a gentle coming together / at other times and places a violent clash" (1). Not only a lyrically compelling material presence, a reminder of cosmic forces beyond human will, nature here is also a trope for the psychopolitical condition of the borderland dweller, who understands the potential for a "gentle" confluence or "a violent clash" of cultural beliefs, linguistic strategies, ideologies, and personal desires. The first of the next two strophes, which break into the progression of an incrementally indented left-hand margin that suggests an effect of cascading, examines the "other" side of what had once been unified, and the second returns to the equally vexed "center":

> Across the border in Mexico
> stark silhouette of houses gutted by waves,
>> cliffs crumbling into the sea,
>>> silver waves marbled with spume
>>>> gashing a hole under the border fence.
>
>> *Miro el mar atacar* [I see the sea attack]
>>> *la cerca en* Border Field Park [the fence in . . .]
>>>> *con su buchones de agua,* [with its buckets of water]
>> an Easter Sunday resurrection
>> of the brown blood in my veins.

(1–2)

The "houses" that stand for the desired economic stability of Mexicans in close proximity to what is now labeled Texas, New Mexico, Arizona, and California are "gutted" by waves of U.S. economic influence. Cumulative socioeconomic violence creates the "hole" through which impoverished Mexicans "illegally" enter the "promised land" that had belonged to their ancestors. The sea's attack, which the speaker witnesses, is a surge of fervor to break free of oppression, and the poet sanctifies it with the conflation of a Christian image and a central trope of her cultural identity.

Although the mestiza speaker, born a U.S. citizen, can cross the border freely, her desire to unite with the would-be "illegal aliens" leads her to imagine herself enacting their mode and position of crossing as she experiences the "rust" on the trope/instrument of a history of spatially instituted domination: "I walk through the hole in the fence / to the other side. / Under my fingers I feel the gritty wire / rusted by 139 years / of the salty breath of the sea" (2). While, for the "illegals," crossing can be seen as a game—"Beneath the iron sky / Mexican children kick their soccer ball across, / run after it, entering the U.S."—it is a deadly serious, extremely dangerous one. As Anzaldúa puts it in the prose of "The Homeland, Aztlán," "without benefit of bridges, the '*mojados*' (wetbacks) float on inflatable rafts across *el río Grande*, or wade or swim across naked, clutching their clothes over their heads" and praying to *la Virgen de Guadalupe* (11).

Far from being a nourishing blanket of food, the "Tortilla Curtain" is a knife inflicting a wound upon the tissue of collective identity. In Anzaldúa's description, a tone of lyrical grandeur collides with bitter social significations of the trope under scrutiny. The clash between natural beauty and the manmade oppressiveness of "chainlink fence" and its "barbed wire" resounds:

> I press my hand to the steel curtain—
> chainlink fence crowned with rolled barbed wire—
> rippling from the sea where Tijuana touches San Diego
> unrolling over mountains
> and plains
> and deserts,
> this "Tortilla Curtain" turning into *el río Grande*
> flowing down to the flatlands
> of the magic valley of South Texas
> its mouth emptying into the Gulf.
>
> 1,950 mile-long open wound

> dividing a *pueblo,* a culture,
> running down the length of my body,
> staking fence rods in my flesh,
> splits me   splits me
> *me raja me raja.*

(2)

The awe-inspiring vastness of the nearly two thousand miles underscores the enormity of a series of cultural lacerations from the time
of Cortes to the present that, by now, amount to one devastating
"split." The "stigmata" on the mestiza subject's psychosocial "body"
are at once a product of externally induced alienation from self and
world and an actual location of what is most familiar, homelessness
as "home": "This is my home / this thin edge of / barbwire" (3).

Arguing in *"La conciencia de la mestiza"* that *"la mestiza* undergoes
a struggle of flesh, a struggle of borders, an inner war," Anzaldúa
indentifies the *"choque"* or "cultural collision" caused by "the coming
together of two self-consistent but habitually incompatible frames
of reference" (78). Anzaldúa asserts: "The whites in power want us
people of color to barricade ourselves behind our separate tribal walls
so they can pick us off one at a time . . . ; so they can whitewash and
distort history. Ignorance splits people, creates prejudices."

In the poem's last three strophes, Anzaldúa refuses to succumb to
the "open wound," the terrible pain of her fundamental "split." More
thoroughly and emphatically than in *"sus plumas el viento"* and "A Sea
of Cabbages," she rhetorically situates the counterforce of the drive
for liberation, the defiance of tyranny, in primal elements of nature.
She voices a prophecy of reparation based on faith in the rectitude
of her culture:

> But the skin of the earth is seamless.
> The sea cannot be fenced,
> *el mar* does not stop at borders.
> To show the white man what she thought of his
> arrogance,
> *Yemaya* blew that wire fence down.

> This land was Mexican once,
> was Indian always
> and is.
> And   will be again.

Yo soy un puente tendido
    del mundo gabacho al del mojado,
lo pasado me estira pa' 'trás
    y lo presente pa' 'delante.
Que la Virgen de Guadalupe me cuide
Ay ay ay, soy mexicana de este lado.
                              (3)

[I am a stretching bridge
from the European world to
    the wetback,
the past stretches past
and the present forward,
May the Virgin of Guadalupe
    watch over me.
Yes yes yes, I am Mexican of
    this side.]

When the poet proclaims her Mexican identity—beyond the fact of residing (legally) on this (U.S.) side—in Spanish, she prays for the spiritual guidance of *la Virgen de Guadalupe*. In a later essay in *Borderlands*, she identifies this figure as "a synthesis of . . . the religion and culture of the two races in our psyche, the conquerors and the conquered" and "the symbol of our rebellion against the rich, upper and middleclass; against their subjugation of the poor and the *indio*" (30).

"*Yemaya*," the wind, has not literally "blown" the entire, vast "wire fence down," but Anzaldúa anticipates the eventual, *natural* destruction of oppressive boundaries. In asserting a past, present, and future *Indian* identity of the land, she perceives Spanish and Anglo invasions and displacements, however historically factual and hence debilitating, as contrary to a natural order. Secure in the moral conviction that mestiza Indians have been borne out by history as original inhabitants of the land, those who nurture and are nurtured by it, she affirms a creed of restoration based on cosmic justice. For the author of *Borderlands*, to be a "stretching bridge" is to call arbitrary borders into question as she embodies and records effects of history.

3

Probings of Coalition and Broad Community: Melvin Dixon, Joseph Lease, Stephen Paul Miller, and Gloria Anzaldúa

In "I'll Be Somewhere Listening for My Name," a speech delivered at "the 1992 OutWrite Conference for Gay and Lesbian Writing in Boston" shortly before his death from AIDS and printed as an afterward to his posthumous second book of poetry, *Love's Instruments* (1995), Melvin Dixon draws a parallel between discrimination suffered by African Americans and that suffered by homosexuals.[1] Noting that members of his audience with white skin "protection and privilege" may not have previously "been treated like second-class disposable citizens," he declares: "As gay men and lesbians, we are the sexual niggers of our society" (73). The trope's relevance is confirmed by the relationship of (predominantly Euro-American) movements for gay and lesbian empowerment in the U.S. with African-American struggles during the time when Dixon was coming to maturity. Describing a "decisive break" by militant members of the "homophile movement" in the mid-sixties "with the accommodationist spirit of the 1950s" (as exemplified by the Mattachine Society and the Daughters of Bilitis), John D'Emilio states that the militants' leaders were able to "model their response" to discrimination "on the direct-action techniques of the headline-making black civil rights movement."[2] After the celebrated Stonewall riot of October 1969, the "reformist" homophile movement gave way to a much larger, more visible, "radical" Gay Liberation movement, which, D'Emilio notes, appropriated much of its political rhetoric and tactics of protest from the New Left (233–35). Since the New Left itself was deeply influenced by the Black Power movement, one can attribute a direct influence of Black Power on the Gay Liberationists.[3]

Unfortunately, however, as Dixon observes in his OutWrite speech, "black gay men" are extremely vulnerable "to the disposal or erasure of [their] lives" (77), because there is a "racially exclusive image of gay reality" projected by "white gays," as they "become more and more prominent—and acceptable to mainstream society" (77–78). Another gay African-American poet, Essex Hemphill, insists that the sole interest of the 1980s "post-Stonewall white gay community" in "black gay men" involves sexual objectification.[4] Citing Robert Map-plethorpe's photographs of sexually charged black male anatomy as symptomatic of this tendency, he remarks that, "at the baths, certain bars, in bookstores and cruising zones, black men were welcomed because these constructions of pleasure allowed the races to mutually explore sexual fantasies," while "open fraternizing at a level suggest-ing companionship or love between the races was not tolerated in the light of day" (xix).

In *Gay and Lesbian Politics*, Mark Blasius writes that, when "lesbian and gay people of color . . . feel excluded because they perceive that the 'community' reproduces the patterns of prejudice and discrim-ination based upon ethnicity, race, and class present in the larger society," they "understandably are sometimes reluctant to" take "the social risks of coming out," and thus, "patterns of exclusion . . . un-dermine the possibility of collective identity and any attempts based upon it to eliminate oppression of gays and lesbians."[5] Dixon in his OutWrite speech also notes that, "as white gays deny multiculturalism among gays, so do black communities deny multisexualism among its members" (78). While acknowledging the relative tolerance of Black Panther Party leader Huey Newton, Hemphill argues that the sixties Black Arts and Black Power movements promoted homo-phobia; their "literature most often condemns homosexuality, . . . and positions" it "as a major threat to the black family and black masculinity" (xxiii). This view tends to posit "white racism (or . . . exposure to white values)" as the cause of black homosexuality "and overlook[s] the possibility of natural variance in the expression of human sexuality."

As a member of the African American and gay communities strong-ly committed to the welfare of each, Dixon in his poetry strives to address both and, thus, help them achieve an understanding of each other that could lead to coalition. As *Love's Instruments'* first epigraph and explanation for its title, Dixon takes lines from the seventh sec-tion, "*voice in the wilderness,*" of Robert Hayden's 1970 poetic sequence "Words in the Mourning Time." The speaker exhorts, "Oh, master now love's instruments— / complex and not for the fearful, / simple and not for the foolish," and then seeks authority for his utterance by declaring, "I who love you tell you this, / even as the pitiful killer waits for me."[6] Uncannily, this passage from a self-styled elegy for Martin Luther King Jr. and Robert Kennedy, both slain in 1968, as well as the nation itself (90), retains its original significance within African-American culture and American politics and acquires additional layers of meaning—as Dixon the PWA's (person with AIDS) hearfelt apostrophe to his recently dead European-American lover of twelve years, Richard Horovitz, *and* his insistence that the "blues poetry" of AIDS must foster the gay community's self-affirmation and self-love.

Without obscuring differences between the socially validated and "sexual niggers," Dixon's poetry about AIDS in *Love's Instruments* allows African-American and other heterosexuals who might otherwise wish to distance themselves from the issue to perceive the commonality of human suffering and, perhaps, progress toward solidarity with the afflicted. It must be recalled that the refusal to acknowledge the humanity of gay and intravenous-drug-using PWAs, the influence of ties to fundamentalist Christianity, and adherence to "social Darwinism" shaped the Reagan administration's (non-)policy (dis-)regarding AIDS and made for insufficient correction of this neglect in the Bush years. As Randy Shilts notes in *And the Band Played On,* Reagan broke his public silence about AIDS as late as 1987 and, even then, provided "little talk of education and a lot of talk about testing" without reference to "civil rights protection"; he mentioned "hemophiliacs who got AIDS, transfusion recipients, and the spouses of intravenous drug users, but the G-word was never spoken."[7] In the information display of its window exhibition, *Let the Record Show* (1987), at New York's New Museum, ACT UP (the AIDS Coalition to Unleash Power) includes the statements that "The Pentagon spends in one day more than the government spent in the last five years for AIDS research and education" and "In June 1986, $47 million was allocated for new drug trials to include 10,000 people with AIDS. One year later only 1,000 people are currently enrolled. In that time, over 9,000 Americans have died of AIDS."[8] Dixon's various references to his fears about "the loss of our entire generation" (74) in the OutWrite speech imply a grim allusion to the political context as a horizon for whatever he writes about PWAs and AIDS.[9]

The chillingly specific "Heartbeats," written before Dixon tested HIV positive, represents the progress of a gay male PWA's awareness of

AIDS and physical deterioration.[10] The title and the unnerving shifts in the narration of the speaker's condition (as the poem moves from couplet to couplet) indicate the swiftness of his recognition of imminent mortality. Here, the poet's strategy of allusion once again elicits the attention of both the African American and gay communities. The use of couplets that house a succession of very brief sentences and fragments suggests that Dixon is "revising" Gwendolyn Brooks's much briefer anthology piece, "We Real Cool," which records the collective voice of a group of "cool" young working-class African-American men who "left school," immerse themselves in nightlife pursuits such as "sin," "gin," and "jazz june" (sex), and expect to "die soon."[11] On the other hand, "Heartbeats' " protagonist seeks consciously to prolong his life.

Before his diagnosis, the speaker engages in the disciplined cultivation of the body and responsibly takes precautions against the transmission of AIDS: "Work out. Ten laps. / Chin ups. Look good. // Steam room. Dress warm. / Call home. Fresh air. // Eat right. Rest well. / Sweetheart. Safe sex" (67). If the gym, as Blasius states, has long been considered a gay "sexual/social institution" (108), the "steam room" is not now a place for anonymous sex. Noting that the "invention of safe sex in the context of the AIDS epidemic" is to be credited to the gay and lesbian community, Blasius argues: "Negotiating erotic activities, the ongoing consent and establishment of limits by the participants, and the . . . community's debate, valorization, and publication of such sexual responsibility . . . puts the lie to the image of one's loss of control within the sexual saturation of everyday life" (92). Aside from indicating how the mid-eighties gay man, encouraged by his community, takes personal responsibility, the poet also suggests that his careful regimen does *not* separate him from Brooks's "real cool" men; he, too, will die soon. Of course, one can draw a parallel between institutional racism and the institutional homophobia that drastically delayed appropriations for AIDS research during the Reagan years.

In the fourth couplet of "Heartbeats," symptoms typical of HIV infection like a "long flu" and "hard nodes" appear, and the blood test comes back positive: "Reds thin. Whites low" (67). More debilitating infirmities follow. Formerly able to do "ten laps," the speaker is now exhausted without having exercised. The externally induced sweat of the "steam room" at an athletic club is replaced by AIDS-related "night sweats" and dangerous "weight loss." The prior reference to the need for "fresh air" is replaced by the awareness of horribly constricted respiration: "No air." "Safe sex" gives way to "no sex." The importance of the reiterated imperative "dress warm" is magnified a thousandfold: currently, even a small cold can bring on devastating complications. Likewise, the repeated commands to eat and rest properly are no longer a healthy person's sensible guidelines but desperate measures to prevent an increasingly unstable condition, characterized by a movement toward emaciation, from turning irreversibly critical. Now, when the speaker "call[s] home," he is relating life-and-death information.

Recording these changes, the speaker sketches various aspects of response: "Get mad. Fight back. / . . . // Don't cry. Take charge" (67). The former ability to do "chin ups" is mocked by the empty advice, "Chin up." Coupled with the worsening and multiplication of symptoms, an impersonal hospital atmosphere and medical care in general undermine the PWA's determination and "take-charge" attitude:

> Mouth wide. Drink this.
> Breathe in. Breathe out.
>
> No air. Breathe in.
> Breathe in. No air.
>
> Black out. White rooms.
> Head hot. Feet cold.
>
> No work. Eat right.
> CAT scan. Chin up.
>
> (68)

As Blasius notes, "AIDS activism and patient self-help and empowerment" practiced by gays have "problematized domination over people's bodies by medical power, and its corresponding subjection through the doctor-patient relationship, as well as the direction of the medical research agenda itself" (223). In addition, even before the extremity of his physical deterioration makes continued employment unfeasible, the PWA might experience discrimination at the workplace that leads to his firing.

Thus, in various ways, the PWA is seen to be at the mercy of inexorable external forces and directives. The second reiteration of "chin up" casts further irony on the previous uses in the poem: the patient must mechanically adjust to the hospital equipment that records his physical deterioration. How can he maintain a sense of personal confidence and autonomy in this condition and in such a reifying ambience? Repetitions of "no air" underscore the futility (despite the probable necessity) of his attempts to comply with his own and the health care providers' instructions to inhale and exhale. Shortness of breath is underscored by the poem's dimeter, which can sometimes be scanned as iambic but more often as a spondee, which conveys constriction and tense imperatives.

As "Hearbeats" draws to a close, the speaker is acutely conscious of impending death: "Six months? Three weeks? / Can't eat. No air. // Today? Tonight? / It waits. For me" (68). By now, the commands about eating well mean little, since the immune system is so damaged that food cannot be digested properly. Despite this awareness— including the realization that the ravages of the body have damaged the mind ("Mind gone.")—the speaker clings desperately to whatever life is left: "Sweet heart. Don't stop. / Breathe in. Breathe out" (68). Even as the "sweetheart" mentioned in the poem's third couplet has died or is too ill himself to help, the PWA urges his "sweet" (homosexual and valued) "heart" to endure. Dixon's linguistic compression, his traditional form in dialogue with the precursor poem by Brooks, keeps pathos from "flooding" the reader's reception and thus permits the attentive interpreter to think about the unpalatable sociopolitical context of this dying. Furthermore, Dixon's linguistic economy calls attention to how much his representation necessarily leaves out; the reader is not led to believe that s/he is getting "the whole story." It is obvious, too, that the last moment of life exceeds rendering.

Like Thylias Moss in "Tribute to Jesse and Then Some," Melvin Dixon invokes Jesse Jackson as an emblem of community in one of his most remarkable poetic performances in *Love's Instruments*. "Aunt Ida Pieces a Quilt" uses the interpretation of a symbolic action to foster the imagining of a broad, culturally diverse coalition or collectivity whose goal would be to make institutional heterosexism and, with scientific good fortune, AIDS, things of the past. Dixon combats an apocalyptic scenario by using an uninfected, heterosexual, female African-American figure who mourns a gay grandnephew to appeal to a "common ground" and diffuse damaging polarization.

Jesse Jackson is the only presidential candidate in 1984 and 1988 who actively supported gay and lesbian rights. (Indeed, organizations like the Gay and Lesbian Victory Fund have adopted "Rainbow Coalition"-style strategies of appeal to various relatively disenfranchised groups in order to gain electoral victories for gay and lesbian candidates.) The first epigraph of "Aunt Ida Pieces a Quilt" comes from a refrain in Jackson's speech at the 1988 Democratic National Convention in consonance with his reiterated plea for "common ground": "You are right, but your patch isn't big enough" (63). Leading up to this refrain, Jackson argues that "America is not a blanket, woven from one thread, one color, one cloth," but a quilt like the one his mother made out of diverse "pieces of old cloth—patches . . . barely good enough to shine your shoes with."[12] In Jackson's catalogue of American political groups that are "right" yet lack a "patch" that is "big enough," "gays and lesbians" who "fight against discrimination and for a cure for AIDS" are included with "farmers," feminist "women," and "blacks and Hispanics." According to Jackson, to "bring the patches together, make a quilt, and turn to each other and not on each other" would enable "we the people" to "win."

Against the notion of a "melting pot," the trope of the "quilt" suggests that each group's particular aims and truths would not be compromised out of existence in the larger community's program. However, most activists know that such a balancing of unity and diversity is remarkably difficult to sustain. Even as Jackson declares, later in his speech, that PWAs "deserve resources for research, expedited approval of drugs, a coordinated offensive to stop AIDS now" (18), a gay cultural producer might wonder how even a "rainbow coalition" can be immune to a homophobia that may surface without warning to marginalize gay and lesbian concerns with tropes of "isolated patches." To ensure that Jackson's rhetoric is interpreted in a (double) context that would discourage such marginalization, the poet juxtaposes it (and thus gives it equal emphasis) with a citation from Cleve Jones, who initiated the Names Project Quilt three years before Jackson's speech: "When a cure is found and the last panel is sewn into place, the Quilt will be displayed . . . as a national monument to the individual, irreplaceable people lost to AIDS—and the people who knew and loved them most" (63).[13]

At the beginning of Dixon's poem, Aunt Ida, one of "the people who knew and loved" her grandnephew Junie "most," is struggling to come to terms with the loss. Confronted with a disconcerting pile of Junie's possessions, including "the hospital gown. / Those too-tight dungarees, his blue choir robe / with the gold sash," she declares: "What am I gonna do with all this stuff? / I can remember Junie without this business" (63). When told by Junie's mother about the national scope of quilting for the Names Project, she responds with physical reasons—like poor eyesight, "arthritis," and a bad back—for her not to try to assemble "all this stuff" into a form of remembrance.

However, Francine is able to coax her aunt out of her hesitations through good-natured teasing, an indication, couched in disarmingly casual terms, of the recuperative power of quilted signifiers, and a reference to her much admired talent:

> Francine say ain't I a mess carrying on like this.
> I could make two quilts the time I spend running my mouth.
>
> Just cut his name out the cloths, stitch something nice
> about him. Something to bring him back. You can do it,
> Francine say. Best sewing our family ever had.
>
> (63)

Finally relenting, Aunt Ida stresses the difficulty of quilting, regardless of one's age, and of the project of memory, as well as the communal nature of the undertaking: "Y'all got to help me remember him good." Indeed, in the fourth strophe, she speaks of her training in quilting as part of a (matrilineal) family tradition. As noted in my discussion of "Fingering the Jagged Grains" in the introduction, it is an African-American tradition, and one that sometimes seems in danger of disappearing:

> Most of my quilts was made down South. My Mama
> and my Mama's Mama taught me. Popped me on the tail
> if I missed the stitch or threw the pattern out of line.
> I did "Bright Star" and "Lonesome Square" and "Rally Round,"
> what many folks don't bother with nowadays. Then Elmo and me
> married and came North where the cold in Connecticut
> cuts you like a knife. We was warm, though.
> We had sackcloth and calico and cotton, 100% pure.
> What they got now but polyester-rayon. Factory made.
>
> (64)

Artfully representing Aunt Ida's voice, Dixon points to the satisfactions of a tradition of discipline and thus responds cogently to those who perceive quilts merely as "a marker of women's oppression" and those who find the Names Project an indulgence in "kitsch" and even a passive reaction to the AIDS crisis.[14] After establishing the historical significance of quilting in her family, Ida confides the "secret / nobody knows": she stitches her name "on the backside" of all her quilts "in red thread" (64). She places her individual stamp on each creation, but less overtly than most fine artists do, and she connects her aesthetic panache to Junie's:

When he got the Youth Choir standing up and singing
the whole church would rock. He'd throw up his hands
from them wide blue sleeves and the church would hush
right down to the funeral parlor fans whisking the air.
He'd toss his head back and holler and we'd all cry holy.

(64)

Discussing James Baldwin's fiction in *Ride Out the Wilderness,* Dixon
perceives the dictates of the novelist's African-American church and
gay male desire as warring forces.[15] Here, however, given Junie's aesthetic talent and spiritual energy and devotion, as well as his catalytic
impact on the congregation, Aunt Ida finds antigay prohibitions and
homophobia in general superficial and irrelevant: "Who cared where
he went when he wanted to have fun. / He'd be singing his heart
out come Sunday morning" (64). Ida harbors no double-standard
about the "fun" pursued by gay and straight youths. From this elder's
perspective, it is natural for young people to seek "fun" on their own
terms; it is not to be confused with "sin." Indeed, her acceptance is
stronger than her mild and humorous chiding of his "exhibitionism":
"I caught him switching down the street one Saturday night / and
I seen him more than once. I said, Junie / You ain't got to let the
world know all your business." The misprision that switches "swishing"
to "switching" turns out to be felicitous. Junie was adept at code-
switching; he moved smoothly and precisely between the worlds of
the African-American church's dominantly heterosexual community
and the local gay social scene through the donning and doffing of
sartorial, gestural, and linguistic codes.

Ida herself engages in some code-switching or, more properly,
straddling. At first, she is stunned by Francine's announcement that
the quilt would be displayed in church, because, insists the master-
quilter, "a quilt ain't no show piece, // it's to keep you warm" (64–
65). On some level, of course, Ida's prior attention to her signature
reveals her understanding that her creations *are* art-objects as well
as functional objects, but the fact that the sign of identification has
been relegated to the "backside" has kept that knowledge "secret."
Francine, who says "it can do both" (65), persuades her to broaden
her definition, but Ida uses the opportunity of her participation in
the Names Project to ensure through her instruction as well as her
example that the family tradition of quilting is passed on to Junie's
generation. She insists that Francine's daughter join the two of them
in this ritual of memory.

Aunt Ida answers her initial question about what to do with Junie's possessions and her grief—when she uses bits of the materials of his two major sartorial codes and his last "clothing" to construct the material perpetuation of his name and his connection with family: "Cut the J in blue, the U in gold. N in dungarees / just as tight as you please. The I from the hospital gown / and the white shirt he wore First Sunday. Belinda / put the necktie E in the cross stitch I showed her" (65). This work of naming replies to expectations suggested in the dying Dixon's refrain about the dead being "somewhere listening for [their] name[s]" in his OutWrite speech. In affirming the "tight" jeans, Ida definitively endorses Junie's right to have chosen his own form of sexual expression.

When, during the collective process of quilting, unexpected sensory traces of Junie's "Underarm. Afro-Sheen pomade. Gravy stains" unleash vivid memory and, thus, enable her to forget "all about [her] arthritis," Aunt Ida knows that she has accomplished the goal of doing "something to bring" Junie "back." And as she completes the work, alone, with her signature, thus sealing the connection between the visual "elegist" and the subject of her elegy, the visual and olfactory traces create the happy illusion of auditory "presence," as though "Junie [were] "giggling right along with [her]" (65).

Ida now understands why Francine is "gonna send this quilt to Washington / like folks doing from all cross the country, / so many good people gone. Babies, mothers, fathers, / and boys like our Junie" (65). Making no invidious distinctions among PWAs, she learns how the expansion of functional art marks the tragedy of the worsening epidemic, the value of lives lost: "Francine say / they gonna piece this quilt to another one, / another name and another patch / all in a larger quilt getting larger and larger." Ida's positive version of Jackson's negatively posited (but ultimately affirmative) rhetoric points to the need for a growing collectivity to challenge forces of fragmentation and death: "Maybe we all like that, patches waiting to be pieced." The Names Project Quilt embodies a material rejoinder to Jackson's trope. Stemming from a single "issue" involving a "rainbow" constituency, it *exhibits* potential to bring a broad, diverse community together.

Turning away from larger social issues, Ida concludes her dramatic monologue with what is most familiar, the small social unit of extended family: "We need Junie here with us. And Maxine, / she cousin May's husband's sister's people, / she having a baby and here comes winter already. / The cold cutting like knives. Now where did I put that needle?" (65). With the imminent emergence of new life after absurdly premature death, the actual Junie's irreparable absence is acutely felt; his stand-in, the quilted "Junie," is needed to provide physical warmth and emotional solace. "Aunt Ida Pieces a Quilt" shows, however, that claims of sentiment and social critique, of individual family needs and broad collective imperatives, are not opposed, but complementary. The poem contains the hope that symbolic action, grounded in specificity, affirmation of "otherness," awareness of commonality, and empathy, can offer a kind of psychosocial "model" that will lay the groundwork for the eradication of callous indifference, homophobic discrimination, and flagrantly inadequate government policies on AIDS.

In an "Exchange" with David Shapiro, Joseph Lease remarks that Emily Dickinson "answers" Walt Whitman's confidence in American democracy "in this: the absence everywhere of visionary democracy, of real community, is what defines our actual democracies and communities—that is our lyric structure of our myth of origin founded in the present, in the shattered everyday, in the absence of community."[16] In "Apartment," a long sequence in *Human Rights,* Lease confronts this problem, and he honors Whitman's democratic ambitions as much as he subjects them to Dickinson's subtle critique. The poem is dedicated to Robert Creeley, whose poetry has not only influenced Lease stylistically but has persistently attempted to locate and measure the concept of "common ground."[17] (Also relevant is Adrienne Rich's *The Dream of a Common Language.*)

Neither autobiography nor biography, "Apartment" extends a poignant self-awareness toward the poet's need to write (in) a community. Lease defines the American common place as a polis in which creativity and inspiration can eventually engender significant intersubjectivity. Evoking a range of isolated characters—including "the talking person," the man who can't stop gambling, and the "sixty-year old loner"—and defining the task of writing poetry in relation to nature, the reader, and an angelic wanderer, the poet represents social fabric as communication with the promise that relatively isolated Americans can somehow braid themselves into a weave.

"Apartment" begins with a narrative that pointedly manifests the absence of community and the need for communication within the U.S. democratic experiment during the late twentieth century:

A rusting lamp, a pile of mud-caked
        wheels: *in Berkeley*

        seven months ago—someone steps
up to the café railing

to speak—after the words
        rape and *monkey* and *cat*

        I move away fast—but I look back. I
watch a college student notice

what is happening:
        this emaciated man spraying

        a hex at him. But
what I want to know is

different: can the *talking person*
        stop talking? I

        look at his backpack—
was he a grad student

once?—he circles the café's
        perimeter working up

        dialogue . . . with
me—he has noticed me.

                                        (32–33)

Lease's speaker, a traveler seemingly engaged in the "common" activity of dining in a café, witnesses and participates in an unfortunate "commonplace" in contemporary urban America: the hostile and/or anxious "recognition" among members of different socioeconomic classes. Since Berkeley, a center of New Left radicalism in the sixties, is the scene of this recent encounter, the poet reminds us that the sixties dream of an end to egregious economic disparities gave way to the post-Vietnam, post-Watergate anomie of the seventies and the multinational corporate ascendancy and Reagan/Bush policies of the eighties, which saw a dramatic rise in homelessness.[18] The absurdity of homelessness amid uncultivated real estate is manifested at the end of section I: "A pink hacienda, the Berkeley / Motel, locked and chained. // *Apartment complexes / surrounded / by . . . nothing*" (33).

Discussing the situation of the homeless in U.S. urban areas in a 1992 interview, Robert Coles offers the important reminder that " 'the homeless' are a whole potpourri of individuals, some of whom don't have any money and are sane and solid and need some money."[19] While "some . . . have some money but not enough to pay for rent in a city that just doesn't have available housing for them," others "are out-and-out alcoholics and psychotics, or down-and-out people who in the old days" could dwell in an area like New York's "Bowery . . . where they could find some sort of community. And now we've gentrified these places" (186). During the Reagan years, funding for social services was slashed severely, and so many who needed to live in mental institutions were put out on the streets.

The conjecture that the apparently homeless man in the opening section of "Apartment" might have been "a grad student // once" underscores the notion of downward mobility in a brutally capricious economic climate, as well as the marginal cultural position of the humanities. Knowing that the problem of inequitable distribution of wealth and living space could, sooner or later, put a "hex" on people who think they are solidly middle class, Lease's speaker—not quite as determinate a representative "I" as the speaker of "Slivovitz"—finds himself compelled to "look back" at someone who is not "alien," not wholly "other."

Amid the aura of loss, the speaker poignantly wonders whether "the *talking* person," who uses logorrhea to compensate for his cruel marginalization and alienation, can "stop talking"—in other words, whether he can enter a dialogue. Of course, this is not a question merely to *this* "talking man" but to *anyone*: class and individuals' exclusive immersion in their own experience make it hard to risk dialogic openness. While Whitman boldly proclaims opportunities for individuals in extremely disparate circumstances to overcome mutual misrecognition and, through a resonant "common" language, attain a meaningful recognition of the common humanity and solidarity in such poems as "Song of Myself," "Crossing Brooklyn Ferry," and "The Sleepers," here, Lease frankly addresses barriers to such a realization. In the prose section that follows the verse beginning section I, the postmodern representative "I" talks about his own experience while referring implicitly to "the talking man's" situation, and he seeks the common ground of dialogue with the reader:

> Another night: I didn't think my life would be like this but that shouldn't matter to you. Perhaps I thought I would be directing a play—a magical

ritual that would last for three days; perhaps returning to Evanston, walking in a park where I made love with Lynne eighteen years before, or meeting a friend for lunch. I didn't think I would be *famous,* but I thought it would be *obvious* that I had come back from doing something . . . "exalted" (an Anatomy of the Soul). Tonight is the coldest night of the year so far. I didn't go outside at all today—obviously, I am not homeless, but I have no income and I have no job for next year—this apartment is it. I'm just making a sketch. *I'm not even asking questions . . .* What would the question be: *Shouldn't I polish my brown shoes . . .* ? My father's papers—drafts, notecards—would be spread all over the dining room table: most nights we ate dinner in the kitchen. No, you shouldn't care about this; at this point I'm just—*what?*—just trying to understand this instant. And *you.* Think about your own story— (34)

Lease's witty play of narrative and ironic metacommentary gestures toward a promising middle ground between solipsism and the notion of total, unproblematic communication/identification with another. The reference to the ambition to direct "a magical ritual" suggests the desire to unite alienated people through a democratizing, carnivalesque structure. Focusing on how mainstream society's implicit directives exert force on individuals' self-representations, the poet has the speaker glumly situate himself *between* the homeless and the employed. He holds on to "his" apartment as a minimum resource. Though a "common place" shared with many (not all) urban dwellers, the apartment is also a space indicating separation from others. Lease's choice of "Apartment" as the title for a long poem at the center of a book called *Human Rights* underscores the notion that housing issues are a locus for a consideration of the economics of downward mobility and widespread (working and middle class) perceptions of scarcity; ironically, these unfortunate "commonplaces" deepen individual alienation when collective problem-solving is in order. They not only disturb "exalted" dreams but place limits on imaginative and material capacities for self-fashioning.

In section I's third part, written in couplets with two or three stresses per line, Lease moves from the apartment-dweller's troubles, to a depiction of an "uncivilized" being in a natural shelter. As in many other poems, Lease's gifts as an imagist are abundantly evident:

Round as a basketball,
    the box turtle's shell

    has brass-colored marks,
bright compass points.

Orange clay, orange
    rocks, stretches of water

    and the box turtle, indrawn.
Beads of spit

glisten in the creek bed
    and layers of

    rocks, leaves,
branches and roots

take the shape
    water might take rushing—

(35)

Even if the poet must facilitate his description by using tropes involving human-made objects, it is clear from the stately tone of this elegantly simple passage that he is not placing the turtle and his richly "layered" environment at the periphery and (post-) industrial society—and its apartments—at the center. At this juncture, the simultaneity and contiguity of natural forms and urban areas are inescapable. While the movement into nature does not signify the glorious transcendence that it did for British and American Romantic poets of the previous century, there is a bit of natural regeneration, figured by the promise of water's shapeliness.

In the first prose strophe of "Apartment," the bardic "you" makes the poem's directness inclusive of the reader. The second prose strophe, the first part of section II, begins an infinitive mode that resonates with the "you" of the first prose strophe, the verse of section III, and the lyrical vision of the "box turtle" verse passage. The possibility of nature and water renewing the self, and the image of water as inspiration and life, align the poem with Coleridge, Emerson, and Whitman: the communication that either is or is not possible between the "talking person" and others in society must be read in light of nature's power and the American Romantic tradition that relates this power to American democracy and community. The prose beginning section III concentrates on manifestations of tacit and explicit hierarchy and their connection to processes of self-representation. This aspect of the social "commonplace" is complicated, and the prose reflects multiple (at times, competing) hierarchies and fluctuating positions within them:

Square blur of light on concrete behind an Army Reserve billboard. A teenage boy wearing a BURGER KING paper crown. The blurred sounds of language unknown to the hearer. To die from the guts out, to say the word guts, to sit in a bar like Falstaff (the sun a laughing woman in flame-colored taffeta). What happens to the athlete whose body suddenly won't do it? What happens to the sparrow falling? And a guy who can't stop losing his money betting on hoops will never be Michael Jordan, never even be an *angry young working class rocker* playing a local hole Tuesdays: what does he see when he sees greatness at a card show? Why did Frank Sinatra act like a gangster? *Bullying* meant *class* to him? Day before the first day of spring: sunlight crosses a wood house painted mustard, cold rising behind people's backs. Twilight will come *as wet cold* that *lines* bursts of wind like an aftertaste: five of four. Take notes on *everything*, that's one option. A chest of drawers, unvarnished, unpainted, means one thing to a college sophomore, another to a sixty-year-old "loner"; first apartment, meet last apartment. (36)

A late-twentieth-century descendant of an earlier representative "I," Baudelaire's flâneur, Lease's speaker "strolls through" the particulars of linguistically and culturally heterogeneous urban life, practicing a simultaneous immersion and detachment. If big chains like Burger King afford their major stockholders a version of economic royalty, the teenage customer's sign of cardboard supremacy bears an irony that underscores the distance of many young people from privilege and societal validation. Not unlike numerous American entertainers who enjoy Andy Warhol's "fifteen minutes of fame," Shakespeare's Falstaff parlays his buffoonery—his "attitude"—and his particular "flame-colored" poetic vision into an access to royal favor, but once Prince Hal must assume power and change his image, the barfly serves as the perfect scapegoat, and his "sun" sets precipitously.

Despite his "very human" and publicly exposed problems with gambling, basketball luminary Michael Jordan's regal status is never in jeopardy, whereas an anonymous "guy who can't stop losing his money betting on hoops" lacks the minimal talent and charisma to rise in the hierarchy, even to the level of respect (and self-respect) accorded to a rock musician who will not go beyond performances at "a local hole" on the least crowded weekday night. Nevertheless, the hapless gambler tries to gain some personal satisfaction from his proximity to "greatness at a card show." Gazing at an athlete like Jordan, the gambler might construct a mirror-fantasy of his own mastery, or he might play a masochistic game like "naked cowards" and mistake prodigious athletic ability with an absolute scale of human value.

Lease's allusion to the late Frank Sinatra illustrates how a star's hierarchical status can be read in conflicting ways. The pop icon's "classy" singing has consistently enchanted members of various (European-) American economic classes, and yet his "bullying" off-stage behavior "meant *class*" to some, including him, and lowered his status in the eyes of others. Kitty Kelly writes that, while Sinatra presented "himself to the world as a great humanitarian, an inheritor of the American dream" with tremendous "wealth and power and fame," accolades from "polite society and grateful politicians could never wipe out the taint of his Mafia associations or his ties to organized crime."[20] As Sidney Blumenthal notes, after Sinatra served as "the producer of the Inaugural party" for John F. Kennedy and seemed to be forming special ties with the new president's inner circle, "the FBI told Kennedy of Sinatra's association with Mafia figures," and Sinatra's contact with the new administration was "abruptly terminated."[21] This experience turned the life-long Democrat into a staunch Republican, and Sinatra's recovery of Presidential favor was dramatized at Reagan's 1981 inaugural gala, which Blumenthal calls "a celebration of wealth, by the wealthy, for those who wanted to be wealthy (the rest of us)" (251). Sinatra's switch in political allegiance entailed an endorsement of the Reaganomic social "bullying" of the economically disenfranchised.

When Lease's speaker refers to taking "notes on everything," I am reminded of Whitman's catalogues, which usually emphasize American equality transcending class stratification, the dream of national unity, and a splendid diversity. For Lease, however, Whitmanian ideals can be restored in the midst of postindustrial, postmodern anomie, only when a representative poet accounts for the full *specificity* of distinctions among people. (Even in the Clinton era, a reduction in the overall unemployment rate has been offset by a plethora of "temp" jobs and the relative lack of growth in full-time positions.)[22] Lease's "notetaking" discloses that ordinary objects like the "chest of drawers" may "mean" a "college sophomore's" carefree indifference to material appearances, yet, in the eyes of "a sixty-year-old 'loner,'" may stand for his position near the bottom of the social hierarchy. In enabling "first" and "last apartment" to "meet" in the "Apartment" of comparative discourse, the poet takes a step toward the possibility that widespread interpersonal suspicion can be replaced by empathy based on specific knowledge.

In the second part of section II, consisting of six tercets, Lease approaches the issue of common ground from another perspective. He revises Walt Whitman's representation of the power structure and erotics of the poet/reader relationship. Whitman's persona in "Whoever You Are Holding Me Now in Hand," one of the *Calamus* poems, warns the anonymous reader that s/he "would have to give up all else," making the bard the "sole and exclusive standard" in order to "follow" him and gain his "affections," and even then, the deepest significance of Whitman and his "leaves" would elude the reader.[23] Also, the poet speaks in various ways of an amorous encounter with the reader and calls himself "the new husband" (116). Directly quoting Whitman's title, Lease's poet-speaker also issues requests, but they assert the reader's presumed ability to uplift *him* and in no way argue for the poet's dominant status:

> Whoever you are
> > holding me now in hand,
> > > breathe out,
>
> perfect again,
> > give me
> > > dark stretching
>
> laughter,
> > this name,
> > > watch pride
>
> divide in half
> > on the floor
> > > where I was.
>
> (37)

The poet seeks the reader's sensual energy and extensive ("stretching") expenditure of delight. Honoring insights of reader-response criticism, Lease eschews the illusion of the poet's dominance over the reader, who puts the work to uses beyond authorial control and, metonymically speaking, "divides" the writer's ego when the book is opened. The tender apostrophe promotes trust between "sender" and "receiver" that permits the "laughter" of shared understanding. The concluding tercets of this part envision a complex, "layered" negotiation of plural needs, including erotic ones, that "breathe" each other. The poet entertains the possibility that such a vigorous exchange might form a basis for the development of an ethos of community: "force steel splintering, / force breathing, / layer folded heat, // need breathing / need, / ours and our sharp sky" (37).

Continuing the tercet structure of the previous part until the single-lined concluding stanza, section III opens with brief depictions of visionary environments in which a solitary self contends with bracing natural elements:

> Stain of faded storm light.
>   In clear wind
>   I shake like a tight branch.
>
> I have been a surge
>   of heat on a horse's
>   back, a salmon climbing
>
> a tight stream.
>   I shake like a branch
>   in folds of dew.
>
>   (38)

These lines recall the elegantly spare tone and diction and the sensuous exactitude of Wordworth's and Yeats's poems of individual crisis in a natural setting, and yet the sinuous free verse heightens the sense of compression and attains the precision, freshness, and clarity of Williams at his best. The poet communicates an impulse to flower, to move out of the barren, ego-centered confines—the "tight branch" or "tight stream"—of social/spiritual isolation. Proceeding by contraries, the poem offers no blueprint for a movement from a claustrophobic "apartment," compartmentalized existence, to a communion with "nature" and other human beings. "*You, my mirror?*" (38), the unanswerable, italicized question that follows the passage above, implicitly warns that universalizing identifications among different people's experiences—for example, the poet, his beloved, and diverse readers—are not to be assumed so readily, nor should one resort quickly to the oft-abused pathetic fallacy.

Furthermore, moving out of the self into the environment is to pay close attention, not only to nature, but to disturbing aspects of the urban (and suburban) landscape that threaten its (and our) survival: "Kids from Berkeley High / meander past Tiki's // Massages. Speechless heat: / everybody's floating. Square blur / of light, cobalt sky. // Gases from a fuel / processing plant float over / the cemetery, over an interstate: I // know them just as / a child knows / she is dreaming" (38). The heat's impact, the awareness of pollution—not only in the "gases" that "float over" the zone of death but in the chemical associations of the adjective "cobalt," also used earlier, that modifies "sky"—are all actual, but they combine to induce a lulling effect that may mask the realization that a society *could* work to transform the actuality of its landscape.

The "floating," gaseous nightmare of the "unreal city" provides landmarks that serve as "commonplace" tropes of alienation from notions of life-sustaining community. In the poem's concluding stanzas, the return to infinitive clauses brings the reader again to the foreground. A place of ritual, catharsis, and closure is created for both the "you" and the "I." In a crescendo of infinitives, the poet is joining with the reader to seek a way out of the nighmare:

> To forget to have "a personal life."
>> To unnerve animals.
>>> To wander in a drowse.
>
> To stand in icy water.
>> To believe in words.
>>> To believe in words spoken
>
> by an angel;
>> to worry about the angel's
>>> intentions. To open
>
> smoothly, like a hand.

                    (38–39)

Among other possibilities, the neglect of " 'a personal life,' " which probably encourages the tendency of individuals "to wander in a drowse" through a barrage of daily experiences, may signify capitulation to an extreme version of the Protestant work ethic within a corporate structure or consent to invasion of private space by questionable public (i.e., media) images. While rejecting the concept that one can know "the truth about desire, life, nature, body, and so on"—including the "essence" of the "self"—Michel Foucault insists upon the social value of self-making: "[C]ouldn't everyone's life become a work of art? Why should the lamp or house be an art-object but not our life?"[24] According to Foucault, "From the idea that the self is not given to us, . . . there is only one practical consequence; we have to create ourselves as a work of art" (351). In "Apartment," an engagement with culture and politics is accomplished through the reimagining and reshaping of subjectivity as embodied in lyric form.

For Lease, the shock of "icy water"—immersion in or consciousness of harsh particularities—becomes a vital component of the processes of self-making and community-building, and the visionary affirmation of a belief "in words" as potential vehicles of emancipatory communication is equally powerful. This affirmation is qualified. In keeping with Foucault's assertion that every solution to a social problem "is dangerous, which is not exactly the same as bad," and that "the ethico-political choice . . . to make every day is to determine which is the main danger" (343), Lease knows that the "angelic" qualities of idealist(ic) language may not be innocent. Viligance about specific motivations of proposals for change is crucial. Nevertheless, the closure of the ritual process in "Apartment" encourages the "opening" of selves to one another like "hands."

Never separating the sensual and intellectual, "Apartment" makes its meditation accessible and direct through scene, drama, and the poet's ear. With a daunting range of poetic resources, Lease combines music and narrative, traditional lyric grace and social analysis made possible by experimental formal possibilities. Immediacy and reflection, directness and layering, are not opposed. In this dynamic of lyric structuring, Lease's abstractions become acts within narration, or shaping becomes narration, a dramatized entity. "Apartment" offers a representative "I" that meditates intensively on intersubjectivity, the limits of the self, the powers of others and otherness, and movement toward the deepening and broadening of community.

Like Joseph Lease, Stephen Paul Miller in his poetry engages in a productive dialogue with Walt Whitman's representation of the possibilities of American democracy. In "Democratic Vistas," Whitman figures "America" as the future site of the glorious realization of a broadly inclusive democratic community:

> America, filling the present with greatest deeds and problems, cheerfully accepting the past . . . counts, as I reckon, for her justification and success (for who, as yet, dare claim success?) almost entirely on the future. . . . Sole among nationalities, these States have assumed the task to put in forms of lasting power and practicality, on areas of amplitude rivaling the operations of the physical kosmos, the moral political speculations of ages, long, long deferr'd, the democratic republican principle, and the theory of development and perfection by voluntary standards, and self-reliance.[25]

Relatively early in his long (113 pages), skinny poem *Art Is Boring for the Same Reason We Stayed in Vietnam* (1992), after making the somber assertion that "an / institution's / not going / to posit" "a hypothetical integrity" "even if / institutes / do nothing / but posit," Stephen Paul Miller breezily presents what appears to be a miniparaphrase of this passage and others like it: "Whitman / said that / since we'd / taken / democracy / this far / we might / as well / let it go / all the way."[26] Indeed, Miller's poem imaginatively reconfigures some of Whitman's most central tenets about going "all the way" while accounting for the changed epistemological and social landscape of the late twentieth century United States.

Discussing the work of Whitman, Emerson, Hawthorne, Melville, and others, Donald E. Pease argues that these authors strove "to establish an American public sphere in which all citizens could enter into the decision-making process."[27] According to Pease, "Emerson and Whitman returned to the scene of the nation's founding to recover integrity for the principles of liberty and equality and make them available as motives for the actions of all Americans." Thus, "visionary compacts could effect" a "renewal" of the "unfulfilled promises" of those principles (47). Pease notes that "Whitman believed national dissension originated when the founding principles lost self-evidence," since, for example, "Southern slaveowners, abolitionists, secessionists, proponents of expansionism all claimed liberty as the rationale" (115). Whitman considered it his task "to restore liberty to self-evidence" (125) by positing a notion of "nature's laws," which do "not follow men's precedents" (124). Pease asserts that Whitman's method is to put "regeneration to work" (125). In the notion of the congruence between "nature's law" and the ideal of American democracy, "adherents" are released, "not *from* a despotism but *to* a renewal of all that is best in themselves" without authoritarian pressure. The "motive" for full self-actualization "connects the individual . . . with everything else in existence. It puts the individual in relation to what we could call 'mass logic' " (126).

In this era of Walt Whitman Shopping Centers, competing fundamentalisms on U.S. shores and elsewhere, and multinational corporate agendas, forms of rhetoric linking "nature" and "self-evident truth" are routinely put to abusive ends and frequently called into question by poststructuralists, New Historicists, and proponents of cultural studies. Stephen Paul Miller, himself author of *The Seventies Now: Culture as Surveillance* (1999), a sprawling work of cultural criticism that relies on the insights of Derrida and Foucault, knows that he had better not take the risk of following Whitman in using such rhetorical strategies, even if he adds a stiff dose of (not very Whitmanian) irony.[28] Instead, bringing to light competing forms of social construction, Miller in *Art Is Boring for the Same Reason We Stayed in Vietnam* uses the impression of casual (if sometimes lyrical) speech, "common sense," and quirky, humorous perceptions to persuade readers to seek modes of social organization and action leading towards something akin to Pease's version of Whitman's collective "renewal."

However, the issue of "self-evidence" (without reference to "nature") does engage Miller. Throughout the poem, he advocates a democracy based on "power / exercised / in such a / way that / excludes / no one" (38) and open, nonhierarchical dialogue. In a typically jocular and serious passage, Miller refers approvingly of an "open / forum / structure— / something / like / classical / democracy / before the / advent of / the modern / era's first / American / president, / Julius / Caesar" (36). These are hardly complicated or novel ideas; why is it valuable for a long poem to be built on them? Late in *Art Is Boring,* he states: since "all / this seems / obvious, . . . perhaps" this is "why" he "thought / it / necessary / to say it / in a poem, / implanting / a device / that both / distances / and / internalizes / impact" (107).

Thoroughly inclusive democracy may be "obvious" as an ideal for many, but others—including both those committed to struggles against injustice and those committed to a status quo—may find it "obvious" in a different sense: too simplistic to be relevant to the complex arenas of *real politik.* The seemingly pragmatic reasoning of the latter sense of "obviousness" undermines the impression of "self-evidence" that could give the former connotation sufficient psychological impact. Therefore, Miller wishes to use the "device" of a long poem with various defamiliarizing strategies to reverse this trend. The idea is to restore enough credence in the vitality, "self-evidence," *and* viability of idealistic democratic principles that they can pervasively influence sociopolitical processes: " 'Why / should / anyone be / out of the / loop?' / sounds / incredibly / idealistic / but so / much goes / into / repressing / that / question" (54).

Like Whitman, who refuses in "Song of Myself" to establish a moral hierarchy among the remarkably diverse group of people in his catalogues,[29] Miller indicates, through his insistence that all should be included in the communicative "loop," that he does not see immutable negative qualities in individuals or groups. While Whitman tends to bypass negative critique and move directly to the representation of a flowering of positive social energy, the late-twentieth-century poet focuses on "pragmatic" responses to "dangerous" foes as a "repression" of the luminous potential for open conversation and peace. Even if their rhetorical strategies and some of their metaphysical presuppositions differ, Whitman and Miller crave parallel forms of "regeneration" that base the pursuit of individual happiness on thoroughly inclusive communitarian thinking.

Miller admits that he does not know where he is about to go at any stage in the process of producing this meandering poem, but he also suggests that advocacy of democracy is based on a kind of faith rather than a notion of metaphysical proof; he suspects that there is no sure "compass" for assessing "correctness": "Maybe the / values / I've hit / you over / the head / with are / not / obvious / or, for / that / matter, / correct, / but I have / traveled / through / poetry / with them, / meaning / that I / don't know / where I / am" (107–8). Indeed, some conflictual interaction among relatively distinct communities within the larger collectivity of a democratic experiment may be inevitable. While not sharing Whitman's aura of massive confidence, Miller is *not* being pessimistic. He interprets relative uncertainty and lack of confidence, when coupled with democratic impulses, as both a political and aesthetic *opportunity* more than a burden to be endured:

> Not that
> simply
> talking is
> magical
> but the
> context in
> which we
> talk can
> be because
> all
> contexts
> are bound
> to be
> unguarded
> and
> somewhat
> fertile.
>   (54)

Miller's wordplay with "bound" (in relation to "unguarded") wittily identifies the absence of binding or constraining features on contexts as a barrier to the fixing of determinate meaning. Rather than lamenting this situation as a loss of standards of "objectivity" in politics and general human relations, the poet perceives that the "fertility" of plural signification allows "talking" to result in the "magical" discovery of interesting, productive differences. Almost twenty pages later, he speaks of "the / deconstructive / American / jet engine / cross / within this poem" (73); indeed, his notion of "context" here places an optimistic (American?) spin on Jacques Derrida's potentially sobering notion in "Signature Event Context," that the (re)iterability or citationality of all discourse ensures that "a context is never absolutely determinable."[30] According to Derrida, "Every sign . . . can be *cited,* put between quotation marks; thereby it can break with every given context, and engender infinitely new contexts in an absolutely nonsaturable fashion" (320). Therefore, "there are only contexts without any center of absolute anchoring."

Acceptance of Derrida's remarks might lead one to assume that the condition of citationality[31] inevitably spawns endless, bitter struggles over the "correct" interpretation of political situations. Endless re-contextualization in a quest for dominance would overwhelm striving for consensus that can lead to peace and egalitarian social relations. Miller realizes the dangers that Derrida implicitly articulates. Part of the poet's continual drive to revise his quasi-aphoristic formulations is fueled by the fear of his words being subject to negative re-framing. However, Miller also stresses that awareness of interpretation's instability—its lack of "anchoring"—may serve to weaken the unfortunate grip of a fixed ideology on an individual and to enable him/her to attend more carefully and openly to divergent perspectives:

> I
> think that
> seeing the
> point of
> view of
> all manner
> of enemy—
> artistic,
> political,
> or

whatever—
and even
qualifying
oneself in
an
opponent's
light is a
political
action
because it
stresses a
different
sense of
power.
                (42–43)

Intellectual humility and dialogical generosity, the awareness that "politics / needn't / mean / merely / changing / other / people's / minds" (84) but perhaps one's own rigidities, "stresses" the "power" to conserve one's and others' resources—to avert an all-out war with many greater "costs" than protracted diplomacy. To "qualify oneself" is not to abandon one's perspective but to enrich and enlarge it, to make room for possibilities beyond simple binary thinking.

In *Art Is Boring*, Miller applies these insights while developing a critique of the confrontation between Saddam Hussein's Iraq and George Bush's United States (and the U.N. troops) in the early nineties. (As the poem itself repeatedly announces, various sections about the Gulf War were written before hostilities commenced and others during the war itself.) Critical of the psychopolitical interplay that occurred between the U.S. and Iraq's governments before the war began, Miller deplores the kind of "talking / in which / credentials / must be / checked" (37), the assumption that some representatives of political factions possess equal status and others are to be excluded from dialogue: "We'll / talk to / Palestinians / but not / the / P.L.O." (46). (These lines, of course, were a political cliché before the fragile handshake of Rabin and Arafat in 1995.)

At a meeting with the press three days after the Iraqi invasion of Kuwait on 2 August 1990, Jean Edward Smith recalls, Bush "abruptly dismissed" the idea that "Saddam was signaling a willingness to compromise" when he started "to withdraw his troops from Kuwait City," and the president "summarily rejected a suggestion that he talk to the Iraqi leader."[32] The next day, when "Saddam . . . sought to communicate directly with Bush," the latter's "men" would not grant him access (94). Smith reports, that in a speech that October, Bush justified the rejection of dialogue with Hussein as a crucial matter of political principle: "I am more determined than ever to see that this invading dictator gets out of Kuwait with no compromise of any kind whatever," he said. "It isn't oil we're concerned about, it is aggression, and this aggression is not going to stand" (195). Referring to " 'a great, big, thick history about World War II' " that he had been reading, the president insisted that "there is a parallel between what Hitler did in Poland and what Saddam Hussein has done in Kuwait" (195).

In a part of *Art Is Boring* that identifies itself as having been written following Iraq's invasion of Kuwait (but before the Gulf War began on 15 January 1991), Miller counters Bush's inflammatory call to arms, including an aside that provocatively praises the historical symbol of North Vietnam's resistance to U.S. international might, and offers a different perspective on dialogue as an enhancement of opportunities for greater global security. Uncannily, a casual lyricism and common sense coalesce. Acknowledging that "Okay, Hussein / might be / as dark as / Ho Chi / Minh was / light," the poet asks:

> why should
> instituting
> a more
> effectively
> open mode
> of
> communication
> be
> tantamount
> to
> appeasing
> anyone, no
> matter
> what that
> person's
> crimes or
> supposedly
> imminent
> threats?
> Who ever
> tried
> *bullying*
> anyone

into
getting
off a
ledge or
putting
down a
loaded
gun?

(45–46)

The erroneous linkage of conversation and "appeasement" to which Miller calls attention suggests the macho posture that "real men" right wrongs through violent physical force and "wimps" fall back on reason. A refusal to engage in dialogue with one whose "crimes" are widely deplored—and, in fact, as Ramsey Clark observes, one who enjoyed "several years of" the U.S. government's "close diplomatic, economic, and military cooperation . . . during the Iran-Iraq War"—[33] does not necessarily decrease the chance that the "offenders" will continue or intensify the same pattern of behavior. While respectful conversation at least has the potential to help others perceive advantages in transforming their conduct, aggression countering an aggression against another party often expands rather than contains a burgeoning of destruction.

The absurd image of "bullying" someone on a ledge seems to present a strong reading of Saddam Hussein's perspective about his situation. Clark argues that "the U.S. government used the Kuwaiti royal family to provoke an Iraqi invasion that would justify a massive assault on Iraq to establish U.S. dominion in the Gulf" (3).[34] From the end of the Iran-Iraq conflict in 1988 to the invasion of Kuwait, Clark states, the Reagan and Bush administrations encouraged "Kuwait's economic war against Iraq" and "engaged in efforts of its own to isolate and economically imperil Iraq" by pursuing, with the aid of the media, "a propaganda war against Saddam Hussein and, along with other Western countries, a de facto sanctions campaign" (19), even as "the U.S. Department of Commerce was approving shipments of billions of dollars worth of . . . equipment" (used to construct a "supergun") to Iraq (20). It can be surmised that Hussein, whose army was far less impressive than the Pentagon warned (39–40) and whose nation was saddled with an "outstanding $80 billion debt from the war with Iraq" (83), knew that it was suicidal to face the U.S. and its U.N. allies in an air and ground war. However, after so much provocation from the Bush administration, the Iraqi president may have been so concerned with the maintenance of his "heroic," oppositional image and of the power he held in his nation that he refused to withdraw unconditionally from Kuwait and thus put his people's security and welfare at total risk.

Miller's rhetorical question, "When shouldn't there be a peace conference?" (46), cuts through militarist rationalizations with elegant simplicity. In his eyes, all political actions that encourage or effect marginalization, no matter how they are rationalized, are causes of potentially global suffering. Miller asserts that the counterforce of open communication fosters the probability of "less jack / in the / box, less / crisis / potential" (50) and acts as "a / buffer to / the many / across- / the-board / negative effects / that / necessarily / will follow / anyone's / humiliation" (55). The reference to the children's toy underscores the absurdity of a mechanistic stimulus/response pattern of verbal and military aggression among world leaders— including those President Bush successfully goaded to support the Coalition forces—who should wisely control their emotions when global security is at stake.

In some of his poetic commentary on the Gulf War, Miller emphasizes the centrality of a willful ignorance in the development of an antidialogic posture. He uses dramatically different verbs representing physical/psychological contact to ridicule the U.S. government's arrogance: "How could / we *bomb* / Baghdad / when we / haven't / even *scratched* / the / surface of / understanding / that city?" (59–60, emphases mine). "Baghdad," of course, is not only a referent for an actual city, but a trope for a history that those exercising hegemonic power seek to efface from the awareness of those whose tax dollars fund their military incursions into "alien" territory. Thus, Miller's rhetorical question is especially ironic: how could "we" *not* obscure Iraq's history of achievement if "we" wish to justify bombing the capital?

Slipping into the discourse of a persona who clumsily recognizes but nevertheless valorizes problems of social construction, Miller parodies the tendency of some Americans to get their knowledge of other cultures from absurdly stereotyped and simplistic pop culture fictions. Saying that he has "to / get the / *Thief of* / *Baghdad* / out of the / video / store" and immediately insisting that he is "kidding," the speaker goes on to qualify his correction, as he falls prey to the dangerous lure of the decontextualization of violence through aestheticizing perception. He is enthralled by "those / night / sensitive / pictures / of the / bombing of / Baghdad, / literally

/ filtered / with / etched / moonlight / upon the / Baghdadian / mosques, / replete / with / bubble- / like / flares / arcing / up against / the / gravity of / the grim- / reaper / realities / underlying / the whole / fluid / text" (60–61). This fascination persuades him "that / *The Thief* / *of Baghdad* / might be a / good place / to start" (61). With such a focus on the unsettling visual pleasure of "illumination," there can be no full awareness of the actual deaths and the myriad forms of long-term suffering visited upon on the Iraqi people because of such bombings.[35] The speaker then acknowledges that "Babylonian / artifacts / or the / *Koran* or a / twentieth / century / history / of / the region" would "also" be important sites of inquiry.

Unlike Edward Said in *Orientalism,* cited in the introduction, Miller's naïve persona does not ask from what perspective(s) the "history" would be written, or how the reader would be able to account for effects of the skewing of representations by ideological investments. Instead, he pretends that the perusal of written and visual texts is sufficient; he does not stress the importance of dialogue about cultural issues with the human "objects" of study, who might supply previously unavailable contexts. Nonetheless, through his momentary persona, Miller also suggests that even the limited effort to study various texts with some degree of sincerity and thoroughness would have offered more potential for "seeing the / point of / view of" the "enemy" and maintaining peace than the brandishing of ignorant "certainty" found in the Bush administration and mainstream media representations of the war's contexts.

Miller's investigations of ideological representations in *Art Is Boring* indicate that those who wield power coercively are aware, on some level, that the "fertile" "unguardedness" of contexts is epistemologically "truer" than assertions about determinate contextual boundaries. These "leaders," of course, must repress or "censor" this awareness to consolidate their authority. Before turning to a full consideration of this important dynamic in Miller's critique of U.S. government and media representations of its policies and of the Persian Gulf conflict, I will first sketch ways in which Miller uses contextual uncertainty as the basis for his aesthetic.

Naturally, an author whose 113-page—arguably political—poem is prefaced by a title that tells us how "boring" "art" is for political reasons would find aesthetic strategies to minimize the peril of readerly yawns. Concluding a lyrical paean to Magic Johnson's basketball artistry in the last third of the poem, Miller offers his aesthetic recipe. He links Johnson's magic ways of dribbling a basketball with the play of absence/presence that language constitutes (and is constituted by):

> What's
> magical I
> think is
> that dribbling
> continually
> implies
> the loss
> and
> reappearance
> of the
> basketball
> as a kind
> of
> universe
> of
> signification.
> Is that
> why I use
> such
> skinny,
> dribbling-
> like lines
> in this
> poem—to
> weave
> "magic"
> into a
> dead,
> "political,"
> in the
> worst
> sense of
> the word,
> landscape?
>
> (83)

The poem's "dribbling" play of absence/presence is evident in Miller's use of line breaks and large thematic discontinuities. "Dribbling lines" helpfully slow down the reader's processing of Miller's discourse and encourage concentration on the relative weight and weightlessness of particular words, phrases, hesitancies, and ellisions.

Also, in directing attention to the flux of thought, they subordinate the accomplishment of static realizations to the awareness of thinking as a play of various elements: movement toward a provisional assurance, the crystallization of the assurance itself, critique and movement away from it, fresh uncertainty, and whatever unnameable points lie between and among these stages.

This effect is most salient in the short-lined poetry of William Carlos Williams and Robert Creeley, but, apparently, these writers are not primary influences here. As the above passage on Magic Johnson and poetic magic shows, Miller sometimes places a single word or two in a line where additional words might be just as rhythmically or thematically appropriate. For example, the sandwiching of "universe" by two lines consisting of "of" seems both gratuitous and awkward. (The isolation of "the" on a line sometimes seems meaningful, sometimes not.) Whereas Williams and Creeley achieve subtlety and musical power in using these short enjambed lines, Miller—aware of the general effects discussed above—has told me that he followed John Cage in choosing his form arbitrarily and being open to whatever interesting and dull, specific effects ensued: lines were not to be more than an inch long, and when the text was typeset as a book, an inch turned out to be considerably longer than the average line. (Miller's jaunty poetic homage to Cage, which also implicitly traced his debt to Frank O'Hara, can be found in *The Best American Poetry, 1994,* edited by A. R. Ammons and David Lehman.) [36]

The justification of the right-hand margin, ironically, duplicates the principle of arbitrary line breaks in prose, but the difference of roughly five inches per line makes it impossible to confuse *Art Is Boring* with a prose text. The deliberate arbitrariness of Miller's "prosodic" decision encourages the reader to pay different kinds of attention to the word, the line, the clause, the sentence, and transitions between sentences, rather than to focus on only one or two of these units. Aesthetically productive, the uncertainty engendered by these differences echoes the thematic play of uncertainties in the poem.

A meandering meditation, *Art Is Boring* often resembles a record of its author's associative "leaps." Miller's various probable forerunners in the art of "leaping" in the long poem include David Shapiro, one of his teachers and subject of his 1983 M.A. thesis along with painter Jasper Johns, Wallace Stevens, Frank O'Hara, and John Ashbery. [37] Continually coming back to earlier topics, putting a slightly new "spin" on each, and then departing from them, *Art Is Boring*—like long poems by the precursors cited above—keeps the reader slightly off-balance and in a state of anticipation. There is a continual "loss / and / reappearance / of" each topic (and connections among them): "I know / that I / change a lot. / Something / is always / falling / out of the / sandwich" (8–9). "I" here may refer not only to the poet, but to the poem. Ample tolerance of uncertainties, including an apparent trust in the precarious journey of associative thinking, allows Miller to give exploration priority over static understanding and any determinate, paradigmatic "mapping" of process. The "bread" cannot "frame" the "sandwich" in a way that will guarantee the reader the ability to digest it as a discernibly coherent totality.

Leaping back to Miller's analysis of the Bush administration's attempt before and during the Persian Gulf War to suppress "fertile" contextual openness as a foundationless foundation for democratic interaction, we find the poet following Whitman's drift in "Democratic Vistas," in which the bard exhorts young men "to enter more strongly . . . into politics" while disengaging "from parties," which, "owning no law but their own will" are "more and more combative, less and less tolerant of the idea of ensemble and of equal brotherhood, the perfect equality of the States, the ever-overarching American ideas" (966). Ironically, President Bush's Inaugural Address had called for bipartisan cooperation and "a greater tolerance, an easy-goingness about each other's attitudes and way of life,"[38] and yet made an end to the debate about Vietnam a fundamental condition for this rapprochement. Speaking of "a certain divisiveness" in the nation and in "our great parties," he declares: "It's been that way since Vietnam. That war cleaves us still. *But, friends, that war began in earnest a quarter of a century ago; and surely the statute of limitations has been reached.* This is a fact: The final lesson of Vietnam is that no great nation can long afford to be sundered by a memory" (24). Discussion itself is seen as threatening to American "unity."

Miller places his retort to this manipulative effort to re-frame and obscure a vital context of U.S. politics in a long parenthesis at the end of a sentence about a different subject: "(America / the greatest / star of / all—the / whole / recent war / in many / ways was / fought to / undermine / the / validity / of a title / like 'Art / is Boring / for the / Same / Reason / We / Stayed in / Vietnam')" (17). Indeed, on 16 January 1991, in his first address to the nation after the commencement of hostilities, Bush declared that his preparations for the conflict included instructing "our military commanders to take every necessary step to prevail as quickly as possible and with the greatest degree of protection possible for American people so that this will not be another Vietnam"; the president claimed that U.S. "troops" would "have the best possible support in the entire world" and added: "And they will not be asked to fight with one hand tied behind their back."[39] Referring to the changes occurring in Eastern Europe and its relations with the U.S., Bush stated: "We have before us the opportunity to forge . . . a new world order, . . . where the rule of law, not the law of the jungle, governs the conduct of nations" (41). He prudently linked this "new world order," which may actually signify the ascendency of "free-market" multinational capitalism, with the United Nations as a "peacekeeping" organization (that would coveniently validate the U.S. government's effort to strengthen its position in the Middle East).

Miller reads Bush's presidential tone as implying "that his / assertions / of war are / beyond / criticism" and, with his usual whimsical seriousness, concludes: "That's / what Nixon / meant by / 'I am your / President,' / which to / me sounded / like 'Come / on what's / the / problem? / Get on / with the / program. / True, I'm / your / abuser but / how can't / you accept / the New / War Order— / —The Newer / World / Order—for / whose cool / implementation / I / neutralized / China and / Russia, / Man'" (78–79). (As Miller probably knows, the phrase, "I am the President," attributed to Nixon, was popularized by the comic impression of Nixon by David Frye.) Like many of his earlier pronouncements, Bush's own postwar rhetoric encourages this kind of critique. In his 5 March 1991, "victory" speech before a joint session of Congress, Bush asserted, "The recent challenge could not have been clearer. Saddam Hussein was the villain; Kuwait the victim."[40] Miller imagines his "21st / century / sequel" of this poem "entitled / 'Criticism / is Taboo / for the / Same Reason / That We / Bombed Baghdad'" (78).

The repression of criticism is founded on a rhetorical assertion of "self-evidence" about the need for centralization of social control in a chaotic Hobbesian world that paradoxically is said to preserve "freedom" or "democracy." Due to such manipulation, citizens can choose a leader whose centralizing tendencies leave only a vestige or skeleton of democratic process because their attention has been diverted from "self-evident" truths of participatory democracy. This is indicated in the last part of another syntax-busting parenthesis: " . . . okay, / maybe Nixon *was* / the / American / people, / can people / vote / against / democracy? / well, / yeah, it's / eerie and / filled / with / democratic / wonder but / they can)" (26). In Nixon's coverup of Watergate, pseudopious invocations of "national security" are the excuse for attempts to stifle criticism and hence undermine democratic processes: "Maybe / Watergate / was all / about / systems of / abuse / maintaining / themselves / as / necessary / for the / survival / of life / and / security / as we know / it," and yet it also elicited the uncheckable critical "counter-urge / to stop it / all by / going / public" (79–80). Statements of public policy promulgate particular fictions of contextual closure or determinacy, whereas "leaders' " covert strategies prevent citizens from perceiving "fertile" contextual "unguardedness."

Although Antonio Gramsci's characterization of one primary aspect of "social hegemony" in a well-known passage of *The Prison Notebooks* may be rooted in a social analysis of a political context dramatically different from the U.S. of the early nineties, it can be used to explain Miller's notion that "people" can "vote against democracy." Speaking of "the 'spontaneous' consent given by the great masses of the population to the general direction imposed on social life by the dominant fundamental group," Gramsci argues that "this consent is 'historically' caused by the prestige (and consequent confidence) which the dominant group enjoys because of its position and function in the world of production."[41] The Bush administration used media "advertising" to implant "confidence" in its perspective—and hence consent for the war—in much of the U.S. populace. As George Cheney states, the administration developed an "explicit and strong linkage between support for the troops and support for the U.S. war policy"; although "it's all right to oppose a war prior to its outbreak, . . . once the fighting has started, everyone in the country must be 100 percent behind the troops" and "by extension, . . . the president and his policies."[42] Lack of "unanimity" is said to hurt "the morale of our troops" and present a sense of "our" irresolution "to the enemy" (68). This linkage of "patriotism with consent" shifts "the burden of proof away from those who make war to those who object to it."

Another strategy used by the Bush administration and the military during the war was to restrict the flow of information and hence prevent citizens from learning anything that might well have been damaging to their cause. Miller's rhetorical questions allude to this betrayal of democratic process: "Why do / people / want / *censored / news*? / What is / caught in / my throat?" (51). Even if "censored / news / represents the / smoothest / fiction," this fiction is vexingly connected to a form of domination: "But do you / want to / know the / meaning of / everything / based upon / always / knowing / the / winner?" While lamenting the results of "polls" indicating that "the public sides with the military in its so far successful effort to control the press," no less a media figure than Walter Cronkite blasts the "arrogance" of "the U.S. military in Saudi Arabia" for "trampling on the American people's right to know," and he adds that "the military is acting on a generally discredited Pentagon myth that the Vietnam War was lost because of the uncensored press coverage."[43] Cronkite states that the military strove "to control coverage by assigning a few pool reporters and photographers to be taken to locations determined by the military with supervising officers monitoring all their conversations with the troops in the field" (47). Douglas Kellner observes, "Reporters critical of the deployment were not given access to top military brass or allowed to join the pools, while compliant reporters were rewarded with pool assignments and interviews."[44]

Furthermore, as Sydney H. Schanberg notes in another article written during the war, "all stories and footage" gathered by pool members had to "be submitted to a 'security review'—a euphemism for censorship."[45] Arguing that "the press has been crippled, rendered unable to provide the public with a credible picture of what war is like in all its guises," Schanberg speaks of media coverage as "superficial brush strokes across the sanitized surface of war. Bombs fall remotely and perfectly, and no one seems to be bleeding" (50). After the U.S. victory, various reporters were able to cover previously repressed "stories" (in retrospect). However, Ramsey Clark reports that, after he joined with various progressive U.S. organizations to form a Commission of Inquiry for an International War Crimes Tribunal to assess U.S. government responsibility for the devastating effects of its bombing of Iraq, the commission's findings of grave U.S. culpability were almost entirely ignored by the mainstream media (xvii, 143–48).

At various points in *Art Is Boring*, Miller stresses how it is no easy matter for critics of hegemonic structures to shake off their own partial internalization of the rationalizations for censorship. Wondering "if" the censoring of news as it is unfolding is "like / editing in / your / head?—the / way I / *seem* / [italics mine] to / write," Miller's speaker recognizes that this delusion has partly seduced him: "Am / I cut from / the same / cloth as / the / American / media is? / Of course! / Why would / I be / so different? / I'm not / sure what / I'm trying / to hide / though" (49). The irony in the last sentence is that such internalization of dominant ideology by its critic is frequently *unconscious*. While I cannot imagine Whitman as self-styled bearer of "regeneration" admitting any complicity with the undemocratic values he hopes to supplant, Miller—to the degree that he cautiously posits himself as a "representative 'I' "—sees self-critical interrogation as necessary for the process of democratization.

Indeed, Miller questions the strict separation of "inside" from "outside" in the elucidation of context, whether such a rhetorical move is coming from the "right," "center," or "left." For example, in addressing some "left" ideologues who assume that "the Jews" or at least everyone in Israel wants to dominate the Palestinians and subjugate Arab nations in general, he responds that a group's overall morality cannot be discerned from the actions of a particular government at a specific time. Although "livid / about what / a faction / acting in / the name / of Israel / does," the poet, who is of Jewish descent, remarks—perhaps too vaguely—that "the rigidly / anti-/process / oriented / constituency" comprises "only about / half of / Israel" (63). In an article written soon after the Gulf War's end, Edward W. Said observes that, "in Israel, . . . it is possible to speak, write and represent critical views of Israel and to talk about the Palestinian people with affection and respect."[46]

Contrasting the ideal of a self-critical, democratic populism with authoritarian ones of various ideological stripes, Miller seeks

> some room
> for a
> wildly
> interactive,
> inclusive
> loop as
> opposed to
> the rope
> of a
> wicked
> populism
> in the United
> States, Arab
> nations,
> and Israel
> that
> coalesces
> into big
> units
> organized

by
generalizations
derived
from
ethnic
distinctions.

(65)

The juxtaposition of the terms "loop" and "rope" aptly contrasts notions of contextual openness and closure. The association of a "loop" with computer discourse indicates possibilities of adjustment inherent in feedback, whereas a "rope" is often perceived as a metonymy for stricture and, more pointedly, the violent finality of capital punishment. Valorizing some provisional, nonfundamentalist identity-based strategies and critiquing more rigid uses of identity, Miller would applaud an oppressed group's use of identity in an effort to cut through the "rope" of negative representation and to foster an "interactive, / inclusive / loop" that seeks equitable distribution of social power. He is wary of the (paradoxical?) confluence of essentializing and radical relativist justifications for the impossibility of shared understanding among members of different groups and for the categorical demonization of all in "oppressor" groups. In a critique that is insufficiently attuned to salient differences *within* the field of identity politics, sociologist Todd Gitlin nevertheless trenchantly parallels Miller's implicit critique of "the perspectivist *ad hominem*" by asserting that, although "we start with perspectives," it is crucial to ascertain "where we go with (and from) them."[47] Since "perspective may be conducive to . . . accurate observations or distorted inferences," "discussions, arguments, analyses, and reasoning" (204–5) are needed for the evaluation of one's findings. What should count as "reasoning," of course, is open to question. However, the a priori separatism of "the perspectivist *ad hominem*," as opposed to sincere perspectivist inquiry, makes every exchange a show of force/weakness and precludes the chance for fruitful consensus-building.

Lest I suggest that *Art Is Boring* is "about" the Gulf War, which occupies no more than twenty pages, I should point out that it begins with Miller's critique of the dynamics in a relatively trivial personal incident that serves as fodder for the larger concern with authoritarianism and democracy. In a review of a symposium that includes some positive comments, the poet had called upon the sponsoring poetry institution—unnamed in the poem—to utilize "a less / predictably /

academic / format" (1). Figuring "that they / might see / merit in / [his] / criticisms," he "later / applied / for an / editorial / position / within / that institution." However, Miller "received / an angry / letter / from this / organization's / director / condemning / [him] for / ever 'thinking' / of / participating / within an / institution / that [he] had / criticized," even though the director, speaking at the symposium, had posited the gathering and his organization "as / alternatives / to the monolithic / thought / processes / of 'Jesse Helms' " (2). The director's response is "something / like / censorship" (3); it exercises and consolidates power through a counterattacking dismisssal of the critique as a mere attack.

As Steven C. Dubin argues, the bill "known as the Helms Amendment," which "barred the use of Federal funds to 'promote, disseminate or produce obscene or indecent materials, including but not limited to depictions of sadomasochism, homoeroticism, the exploitation of children, or individuals engaged in sexual acts; or material which denigrates the objects or beliefs of the adherents of a particular religion or nonreligion,' " and which reduced appropriations for the National Endowment of the Arts and other arts organizations, reflected, in the eyes of the most conservative wing of the Republican party, "a struggle for the soul of America in the battle over the arts."[48] According to Dubin, Pat Buchanan held "in a series of venomous columns" that "a small band of arts and gay rights radicals, out of touch with most of society," were promoting "filth and degradation in the guise of mediocre art, and a lifestyle that was suicidal, witness Mapplethorpe's death from AIDS" and aimed "to overturn tradition and create a pagan society," while the conservatives "were the stalwart defenders of the good, the true, and the traditional" (175).

Miller points out the irony of how tactics of intimidation and exclusion practiced by conservative polarizers like Helms and Buchanan sometimes backfire in the cultural marketplace by spotlighting, even if pejoratively, such "pagan" "products" that had received little mainstream focus: When "nowadays / government / supports / the arts / by taking / them to / task," this turns out to be "just as / good an / advertisement / for the / artist as / the paltry / sum of / money / given when / the grant / is not / withheld / thus / giving the / upper / middle- / class / M.F.A. / artist a / chance to / be as / self- / righteous / as Jesse / Helms, / Karen / Finley's / curmudgeon / uncle" (10–11). Dubin acknowledges that "in some cases artists' careers seemed to get a lift when Jesse Helms, the Rev. Wildmon and others turned their critical spotlights on them," as when "the market for [Robert] Mapplethorpe and [Andres] Serrano's work heated up, and Finley profited from the addition of an extra (sold out) appearance at Lincoln Center's Serious Fun! in 1990," but he claims that the "'star quality'" of such notorious artists "may rapidly cool," since "nothing is as stale as yesterday's disreputable headline" (272).

Perhaps Miller's barb is not entirely fair, but his point is that, as a member of the larger U.S. collectivity, even the "oppositional" cultural producer helps constitute elements of discursive possibility within the system and, in having her/his work defined variously by those within it, gains opportunities for the work to be circulated. One form of prohibition enables another form of access to a sector of the public. Miller suggests that Jesse Helms's notions of "purity" and "filth" and Karen Finley's transgressive representations require each other as "foils." Miller's reference to "the / upper / middle- / class / M.F.A. / artist" alludes to what Dubin identifies as the view of many artists who had *always* been excluded from the art world: "An enormous clamor was being raised over the predicament of a few artists, whereas the habitual circumstances of others"—for example, working-class, nonwhite, nonheterosexual artists—"continued to be largely disregarded" (275).

In his own conflict with the poetry director, Miller may wish to find a way out of unproductive polarization, but an anxious one-liner indicates how difficult this is: "This poem / may be / self- / righteous / but at / least it's / ending my / career" (15–16). Here, the poet comically "represses" (and hence underlines) the fact that the "material" of his conflict with the director is central to the "launching" of his career—as author of *Art Is Boring*. Also, not long afterward, his elegy for John Cage appeared in *The Best American Poetry* anthology. Joking about these matters, Miller prevents himself from "buying" the "self-righteous" self-flattery of thinking himself entirely oppositional, thoroughly victimized by "the system," and ideologically "pure."

Miller implicitly links tendencies he deplores in the running of the poetry organization with the potential for authoritarianism in a master/disciple relationship. After another poet, later identified as Sparrow, told him "that it is / necessary / for a poet / to receive / poetic / 'secrets' / from one / who knows / them," Miller compares the idea to "the whole / neo- / conservative / Eighties / gallery / system / rap," in which "you have / to buy the / brand secret" (5–6). Highly publicized eighties artists—for example, "Neo-Expressionists" like Julian Schnabel and David Salle, "Neo Geo" artists like Peter Halley, and post-Pop artists like Jeff Koons—enjoyed much greater financial success in a few years than celebrated poets can achieve over several decades, but each of the two "systems" seems to posit a ritual of accreditation based on arbitrarily "purchased" access to a clique.[49]

If one plausible reason for being "attracted / to / masters" is "to / situate / ourselves / beyond / ourselves" (20), Miller believes that instituting "a / beloved / poet" as "master" fosters "a cult- / like / hierarchy / which"—he generalizes with whimsical excess—"is / tantamount / to all the / various / positions / of poetry / today" (21). For the master/disciple relationship to be actualized, according to Miller, the master "has to / convince / others to / place / trust and / power in / her or / him" (21–22). While Miller does not see "any / way to / accomplish / this / except / through / intimidation / and / exploitation / of a / perceived / need" (22), one may argue that a master's generosity and compassion could motivate both the desire to teach and the disciple's main reason for entering into the relationship.

Late in *Art Is Boring*, Miller inserts a letter from his friend Sparrow (in paragraphs, each line occupying about three times the length of the surrounding verse), critiquing "the first / eighteen / or / nineteen / pages of / this poem" (88). Sparrow applauds his friend's "revolutionary thinking" and yet calls it "the argument of a child, who wants to learn from no one." Acknowledging that he is "a passive guru-follower," Sparrow admits wanting to join a "fraternity" of poets while also thinking "that's an evil idea" (88). When Miller responds "Do you / *really* / think it / would be a / better / world if / no one / dissented?" (89), he makes the error of equating the desire not to oppose the tenets of a particular master with a preference for the general banishment of oppositional thinking. Acknowledging, with prompting from Sparrow, that he is a follower of Meher Baba, an Indian spiritual leader (88, 101–2), Miller should recognize that the choice of one master often implies dissent from the teachings of others.

When Sparrow asserts, "You hate authorities, yet while you write, you become one" (88), Miller *seems* to forge a positive link between conceptually based authority and the provisional claim of individual authority inherent in the assumption of the position of "representative 'I' ": "you say / that a / writer / must / become an / authority, / but / doesn't / that / authority / come from / a devotion / to the / writing / process / as it is / constitutive / of / everyone?" rather than "writing as / mere / assertion" (90), which the poet considers neither "a / triumph or / of the / imagination" (91). Using metonymy tentatively, the poet asks a question which may or may not be rhetorical, and he says that if his correspondent insists on labeling him an "authority" as a writer, then from an ethical standpoint, adherence to democratic principles (rather than either a popularity contest or a seizing of power) "crowns" that alleged authority.

Displaying an unequivocally positive view of his authority in his 1855 preface to *Leaves of Grass,* Whitman claims that "the United States . . . will doubtless have the greatest" poets "and use them the greatest," and predicts that "the great poet" will be the people's "common referee," who as "arbiter of the diverse" and "equalizer of his age and land," "freely" uses "the power to destroy or remould" without ever using "the power of attack" (712–13). According to Whitman, the poet's sublime superiority inheres solely in the quality of his perception: "the others are as good as he, only he sees it and they do not" (713). Unlike this great precursor, Miller stresses the human limits of the poet's perception. Finding it undemocratic to establish himself as authorizer of democracy, he would seek solutions through dialogue and act as a facilitator of process: "In a way, / I'm just / moderating / this poem" (23–24). Of course, Miller must know that this "confession" could seem disingenuous in the light of his expression of various strongly held convictions in the course of his text.

A little over ten pages after granting a provisional usefulness to the concept of authority as adherence to intersubjective standards, Miller turns against any positive definition of authority. Countering Sparrow's accusation that he does not want to learn from others, Miller asserts: "I may / learn from / one poet / more than / another / and some / poets do / build up / *mucho* / trust but / no one's / an / authority. / It / belittles / Shakespeare / to think / of him / that way" (102–3). According to this line of thinking, if "devotion" to democratic ideas (as opposed to writing in the service of the will to power) brings respect and trust from others, it confers trust but not authority. Miller equates the latter term with conditions (perhaps even likelihood) of its abuse, authoritarianism. In addition, the poet sees the investment of authority as a denial of an individual's complexity, a pathetic reification of the human being. Indeed, as postcolonial critics have argued, some who have granted "Shakespeare" (as a collection of texts) massive authority "belittled" the writer by using their association with his authority to foster colonial subjects' internalization of the "appropriateness" of British domination of their land.[50]

Miller's persistent skepticism about the functional value of individual manifestations of political authority for the pursuit of egalitarian social relations permeates *Art Is Boring*. Although he points out that "even / enlightened / despots / invite / dissent / for the / good of / everyone / concerned" (89), the retention of the noun "despots" diminishes the impact of the adjective, "enlightened." Miller tries to use the authority of a writer's position as "representative 'I' " to let go of as much authority as possible and coax the reader to exercise autonomy. In keeping with his view of himself as a "moderator," the poet ends *Art Is Boring* coyly with an invitation to the reader to jump in: "Does / anyone / have any / questions / or comments / about this / poem so / far?" (113). As an apostle of open dialogue, Miller wants his poem to be part of ongoing and "magical" "talking" (speech). To be readable, the poem must provide a marking in space/time "so / far," but Miller wishes to subvert the traditional "sense of an ending" as a final, authoritative crystallization. Of course, this concluding effort depends on rhetorical effects that can be (re-) framed variously. Reiterating a sentence used by many classroom teachers, Miller ironically gives himself the last word asking for someone else's word that cannot literally be given in the text's print format. Even if the "Representative 'I' " must in some way conserve his authority or consign himself to silence, he may mark the extent to which his power can be shared and/or usefully displaced.

Though filled with troubling evidence of the blunting and derailing of democratic processes, Stephen Paul Miller in *Art Is Boring* dares to raise the dialogical imperative as a general foundation for the development of coalitions and for the barely imaginable democracy without reserve.

I have chosen to end this chapter on explorations of coalition and broad community (and this book) with a discussion of the concluding poem in Gloria Anzaldúa's *Borderlands,* a poem which, on the surface, seems to reject the possibility that democratic ideals can be realized. However, "Don't Give In, *Chicanita*" is especially interesting because, depending on whether the interpreter reads its closure literally or figuratively, the poem can provide very different ways of speaking to the issue of community.

Dedicated and addressed to Anzaldúa's niece, Missy, "Don't Give In, *Chicanita*," which is presented in the original Spanish and an English translation by the author, elaborates on the prophecy at the end of the first untitled poem in the book that "This land was Mexican once, / was Indian always / . . . / And will be again" (3). In the opening lines, the poet exhorts her niece to "tighten [her] belt, endure" amid the kind of oppression described throughout *Borderlands* and reminds her of her people's claim as nurturers of the land: "Your lineage is ancient, / your roots like those of the mesquite / firmly planted, digging underground / toward that current, the soul of *tierra madre* [mother earth]— / your origin" (202).

Referring again to the effaced history that she has been joining with other Chicanos/as to restore, Anzaldúa declares that Missy "descended from the first cowboy, the *vaquero,* / right smack in the border / in the age before the Gringo when Texas was Mexico" (202). She alludes to the feminist component of her revisionary Chicana/o history in the family context: "Strong women reared you: my sister, your mom, my mother and I." Acknowledging the social fact of dispossession with the admission that "they've taken our lands," including "the cemetery" where the girl's "great-great-grandfather" lies, the poet depicts the heroic character of Chicana/o endurance in the face of these obstacles: "Hard times like fodder we carry / with curved backs we walk." Then, she predicts not only the end of mestiza/o oppression but the inability of the oppressors' culture to endure, precisely because of their bellicose conduct:

> And when the Gringos are gone—
> see how they kill one another—
> here we'll still be like the horned toad and the lizard
> relics of an earlier age
> survivors of the First Fire Age—*el Quinto Sol.* [the Fifth Sun]
>
> Perhaps we'll be dying of hunger as usual
> but we'll be members of a new species
> skin tone between black and bronze
> second eyelid under the first
> with the power to look at the sun through naked eyes.
> And alive *m'ijita,* [my little spawn] very much alive.
>
> (202–3)

It is important to remember that "Don't Give In, *Chicanita*" was published in 1987 and probably written a few years earlier, prior to the dissolution of the Soviet Union and during the height of President Reagan's rhetoric about the "Evil Empire." Anzaldúa's prediction evokes the widespread fear at the time that one of the two major superpowers might use nuclear weapons against the other and engender another "Fire Age," and yet her faith in Chicano/a survival against all odds does not permit this "worst case scenario." She goes only so far as to assert that the whites' collective history of violence will bring *them* violent retribution and that the sole remnant of their culture(s) will consist of traces of what they had imposed on the mestizas, who "in a few years or centuries / . . . will rise up, tongue intact / carrying the best of all the cultures" (203). Similarly, in the concluding paragraph of "How to Tame a Wild Tongue," emphasizing the Chicanos/as have kept their language despite living "under the hammer blow of the dominant *norteamericano* culture," Anzaldúa declares that her people "count the days the weeks the years the centuries the eons until the white laws and commerce and customs will rot in the deserts they've created, lie bleached" (63–64). She envisions the survivors—"stubborn, persevering, impenetrable as stone, yet possessing a malleability that renders [them] unbreakable"—walking "by the crumbling ashes as [they] go about [their] business" (64).

However, in "Don't Give In," if figurative implications are entertained, it can be argued that Anzaldúa is *not* espousing a separatist stance based on an article of faith. Perhaps the poet, as she addresses Chicanas in order to encourage endurance and pride, is simultaneously (if tacitly) addressing the dominant white culture and invoking something like a conditional, and not an immutable, curse. In other words, she may be saying to "the Gringos" that if they do not radically transform their ideological presuppositions about race, class, and gender and the social formations and habitual actions informed by this ideology, they will literally perish. On the other hand, Anzaldúa may be presenting an immutable curse on the despicable ideology and not on the literal survival of whites. Certainly, "the Gringos" literally have killed and *do* "kill one another" in senseless wars, and many are therefore "gone," but it is possible that the dissolution of "white laws and commerce and customs" can be distinguished from the death of all "white" people. Anzaldúa may simply wish to communicate that, in the course of human political evolution, "ethical Darwinism" will supplant white supremacism and social Darwinism. If the poet is using her scenario to posit an allegory of the drastic future alteration of the social construction of "whiteness" and other racial categories, it is reasonable to suppose that she concludes that "the Gringos," at some point, will be figuratively "gone," even if the physical features of those of European descent have not changed. The poem's closure may involve another rhetorical strategy for posing the challenge, articulated in "*La Conciencia de la mestiza*" to overcome the "split" within "Anglo" society, the multiple culture of North America, and Chicano/a culture: "Admit that Mexico is your double, that she exists in the shadow of this country, that we are irrevocably tied to her. Gringo, accept the doppelganger in your psyche. By taking back your collective shadow the intracultural split will heal" (86).

Yet another reading is possible. As a greater range and diversity of kinship groups with mestiza/o characteristics continually emerge, it can be predicted that fewer and fewer members of the "white" "race" will exist. As she states at the beginning of "*La Conciencia*," Anzaldúa utilizes the Mexican social philosopher Jose Vasconcelos's vision of "*una raza mestiza, una mezcla de razas afines, una raza de color—la primera raza sintesis del globo*" [a mestiza race, a mixture of bordering races, a race of color—the first synthesized race of the globe] (77) as a springboard for her development of the (feminist and antiheterosexist) concept of "*mestiza* consciousness." Vasconcelos's "cosmic race, *la raza cosmica*, a fifth race embracing the four major races of the world" is a "theory . . . of inclusivity" diametrically opposed to the white supremacist "policy of racial purity," and so, for him and Anzaldúa, this multeity within the unity of individual selves and the consequent diversity within collectivity is a marvelous asset: "At the confluence of two or more genetic streams, . . . this mixture of races, rather than resulting in an inferior being, provides hybrid progeny, a mutable, more malleable species with a rich gene pool" (77).[51] Thus, the statistical decline of any "pure" race, if such an entity exists, is no cause for mourning.

Various literal and figurative interpretations of "Don't Give In" have considerable force; there is no easy way to choose among them. Certainly, at various points in *Borderlands,* Anzaldúa expresses the urgent desire, as in the poem "To live in the *Borderlands* means you," to constitute a speaking subject who is able to "live *sin fronteras* [without borders] / be a crossroads" in order "to survive the *Borderlands*" (195) and help others survive. Furthermore, in "*La conciencia*," she evinces the hope that "the work of *mestiza* consciousness," which "is to break down the subject-object duality that keeps [one] a prisoner" and to transcend it, will hold "the answer to the problem between the white race and the colored, between males and females" and may begin the "long struggle . . . that could, in our best hopes, bring us to the end of rape, of violence, of war" (80). Perhaps the antagonisms among the readings of *Borderlands'* final poem reflect the poet's realization—present in different ways in the work of the other poets discussed herein—that there is neither a clear, decisive road to significant coalitions, much less to an all-encompassing egalitarian collectivity, nor an overwhelming reason for those of good will to abandon the drive for the "utopian" objective of broad community.

Notes

INTRODUCTION

1. See Helen Hennessey Vendler, *The Breaking of Style: Hopkins, Heaney, Graham* (Cambridge: Harvard University Press, 1995); *The Given and the Made: Strategies of Poetic Redefinition* (Cambridge: Harvard University Press, 1995); *Soul Says: Recent Poetry* (Cambridge: Belnap, 1995).

2. See Marjorie Perloff, *The Dance of the Intellect: Studies in the Poetry of the Pound Tradition* (New York: Cambridge University Press, 1985); *Poetic License: Essays on Modernist and Postmodernist Lyric* (Evanston, Ill.: Northeastern University Press, 1990); *Radical Artifice: Poetry in the Age of Media* (Chicago: University of Chicago Press, 1991). See George Hartley, *Textual Politics and the Language Poets* (Bloomington: Indiana University Press, 1989); and Linda Reinfeld, *Language Poetry: Writing as Rescue* (Baton Rouge: Louisiana State University Press, 1992).

Along with Perloff and Vendler, Charles Altieri is the leading critic of contemporary poetry in the U.S. In his many books and articles, Altieri has certainly discussed the work of younger poets, but he has concentrated heavily on the poets of the Ashbery/Rich generation.

3. See Thomas Fink, "Between/After Language Poetry and the New York School," forthcoming in *Talisman*, 2001, and Fink, *The Poetry of David Shapiro* (Madison, N.J.: Fairleigh Dickinson University Press, 1993).

4. Ralph Ellison, *Invisible Man* (1952; reprint, New York: Random, 1972), 1. Further quotations from *Invisible Man* are located in the text and are accompanied by page citation.

5. Edward W. Said, *Orientalism* (New York: Random, 1978), 6. Further quotation from *Orientalism* is located in the text and is accompanied by page citation.

6. Audre Lorde, *Sister Outsider: Essays and Speeches* (Trumansberg, N.Y.: Crossing, 1984), 42. Further quotations from *Sister Outsider* are located in the text and are accompanied by page citation.

7. For an analysis of this tendency in feminist criticism, see Tuzyline Jita Allan, *Womanist and Feminist Aesthetics: A Comparative Review* (Athens: Ohio University Press, 1995).

8. Adrienne Rich, *Blood, Bread, and Poetry* (New York: Norton, 1986), 199. Further quotation from *Blood, Bread, and Poetry* is located in the text and is accompanied by page citation.

9. Gloria Anzaldúa, *Borderlands/La Frontera—The New Mestiza* (San Francisco: Aunt Lute, 1987). All quotations from *Borderlands* in this introduction and in chapters 2 and 3 are located in the text and are accompanied by page citations.

10. See Trinh T. Minh-ha, *Woman, Native, Other: Writing Postcoloniality and Feminism* (Bloomington: Indiana University Press, 1989), 80, 101.

11. Trinh T. Minh-ha, *When the Moon Waxes Red: Representation, Gender, and Cultural Politics* (New York: Routledge, 1991), 65. Further quotations from *When the Moon Waxes Red* are located in the text and are accompanied by page citation.

12. For Said's discussion of the (neo-) colonial penetration of contemporary education in various Arab states and the recent emergence of Arab "native informants" in the service of Orientalist discourse, see *Orientalism*, 322–24.

13. Melvin Dixon, *Change of Territory* (Lexington: University of Kentucky, 1983). For a view of Dixon's sense of the erasure of African-American history, see his "The Black Writer's Use of Memory," in *History and Memory in African-American Culture*, ed. Geneviève Fabre and Robert O'Meally (New York: Oxford University Press, 1994), 19. For a brief but useful discussion of Dixon's poetic representations of Africa, see Anthony O'Brien, "Reading Melvin Dixon's Africa," *Found Object* 4 (fall 1994): 91–93.

14. Ralph Ellison, *Shadow and Act* (1964; reprint, New York: Random, 1972), 78.

15. Ralph Ellison, *Collected Essays,* ed. John F. Callahan (New York: Modern Library, 1995), 685–86. Further quotations from Ellison's *Collected Essays* are located in the text and are accompanied by page citation.

16. Albert Murray, *Stomping the Blues* (New York: McGraw-Hill, 1976), 5. Further quotations from *Stomping the Blues* are located in the text and are accompanied by page citations.

17. Albert Murray, "The Visual Equivalent of the Blues," in *Romare Bearden: 1970–1980,* ed. Jerald L. Melberg and Milton J. Bloch (Charlotte, N.C.: Mint Museum, 1980), 26. Further quotation from "The Visual Equivalent of the Blues" is located in the text and is accompanied by page citations.

18. See Myron Schwartzman, *Romare Bearden: His Life and Art* (New York: Harry N. Abrams, 1990), 167–68, 216. Further quotations from *Romare Bearden: His Life and Art* are located in the text and are accompanied by page citations.

19. See Schwartzman, 20–21, for a relative's recollection of the young Bearden's enthusiasm about trains.

20. For another use of "Ellington's A Train," see Dixon's novel, *Vanishing Rooms* (New York: Dutton, 1991), 194.

21. See Schwartzman, 279–80.

22. See Murray, "The Visual Equivalent of the Blues," 26, and Schwartzman, "A Bearden-Murray Interplay: One Last Time," *Callalloo* 11, no. 3 (summer 1988): 410. As Murray notes, Bearden took the title of *Carolina Shout* from a composition that Johnson popularized.

23. For a biographical treatment of Bearden's early life in Charlotte, North Carolina, and for an interview with Bearden entitled "Of Mecklenberg, Memory, and the Blues," see Schwartzman, *Romare Bearden,* 10–43. *Carolina Shout,* part of the *Of the Blues* series, is a collage with acrylic and lacquer on board, 37 1/2"x 51", and is in the collection of the Mint Museum, Charlotte, North Carolina. *Solo Flight,* from the *Jazz* series, is a collage on board, 6"x 9"in a private collection in Southfield, Michigan.

24. *Patchwork Quilt,* 1970, collage of cloth, paper, and synthetic polymer paint on composition board, 35 3/4"x 47 7/8", collection, the Museum of Modern Art, New York. *Quilting Time,* 1985, maquette for mosaic glass mural installed in the permanent collection of the Detroit Institute of the Arts, paper collage on board, 19 3/4"x 28 1/2".

25. *Ride Out the Wilderness: Geography and Identity in Afro-American Literature* (Ur-

bana: University of Illinois Press, 1987); 74. Further quotation from *Ride Out the Wilderness* is located in the text and is accompanied by page citation.

26. Vincent Harding, "Power from Our People: The Sources of the Modern Revival of Black History," *The Black Scholar: Journal of Black Studies and Research* 18, no. 1 (January/February 1987): 40.

27. Gary Y. Okihiro, "Education for Hegemony, Education for Liberation," in *Ethnic Studies: Volume 1—Cross-Cultural, Asian, and Afro-American Studies*, ed. Gary Y. Okihiro (New York: Markus Wiener, 1989), 3–4. Further quotation from "Education for Hegemony, Education for Liberation" is located in the text and is accompanied by page citation.

28. Carlos Muñoz Jr. *Youth, Identity, Power: The Chicano Movement* (New York: Verso, 1989), 130. Further quotation from *Youth, Identity, Power* is located in the text and is accompanied by page citation.

29. Josephine Nieves, Maria Canino, Sherry Gorelick, Hildamar Ortiz, Camilio Rodriquez, and Jesse Vazquez, "Puerto Rican Studies: Roots and Challenges," in *Toward a Renaissance of Puerto Rican Studies: Ethnic and Area Studies in University Education,* ed. Maria E. Sanchez and Antonio M. Stevens-Arroyo (Highland Lakes, N.J.: Atlantic Research and Publications, 1987), 3. Further quotation from "Puerto Rican Studies: Roots and Challenges," is located in the text and is accompanied by page citation.

30. Darlene Clark Hine, *Speaking Truth to Power: Black Professional Class in United States History* (Brooklyn, N.Y.: Carlson, 1996), 6–7. Further quotation from *Speaking Truth to Power* is located in the text and is accompanied by page citation.

31. Sucheng Chan, *Asian Americans: An Interpretive History* (Boston: Twayne, 1991), 181. Further quotation from *Asian Americans: An Interpretive History* is located in the text and is accompanied by page citation.

32. See Muñoz, *Youth, Identity, Power,* 160, for the discussion of how the firing of Ana Nieto-Gomez from the department of Chicano Studies California State University at Northridge catalyzed the Chicana feminist critique of the patriarchal biases of Chicano Studies.

33. Regarding the impact of New York City's 1975 financial crisis on City University, see Nieves et al., 7.

34. Henry L. Minton, "The Emergence of Gay and Lesbian Studies," in *Gay and Lesbian Studies,* ed. Henry L. Minton (Binghampton, N.Y.: Haworth, 1992), 1. For a narrative of the history of Gay and Lesbian Studies in the last three decades, see Jeffrey Escoffier, "Generations and Paradigms: Mainstreams in Lesbian and Gay Studies," in *Gay and Lesbian Studies,* 7–26.

35. Ronald Takaki, "Multiculturalism: Battleground or Meeting Ground?" *Annals of the American Academy of Political and Social Science* 530 (November 1993): 118. Further quotation from "Multiculturalism: Battleground or Meeting Ground?" is located in the text and is accompanied by page citation.

36. Michael Rogin, "'Make My Day!: Spectacle as Amnesia in Imperial Politics," *Representations* 29 (winter 1990): 118, 116. Further quotation from "Make My Day!" is located in the text and is accompanied by page citation.

37. Ronald Reagan, *Speaking My Mind: Selected Speeches* (New York: Simon and Schuster, 1989), 416–17. Further quotation from *Speaking My Mind: Selected Speeches* is located in the text and is accompanied by page citation.

38. Howard Zinn, *A People's History of the United States* (New York: Harper and Row, 1980), 8. Further quotation from *A People's History of the United States* is located in the text and is accompanied by page citation.

39. Zinn's reference to the suppression of the history of gender-based domina-

tion is highly relevant to Reagan's sense of history, as my section on Duhamel in chapter 1 will suggest.

40. Lisa Lowe, *Immigrant Acts: Asian American Cultural Politics* (Durham, N.C.: Duke University Press, 1996), 68. Further quotations from *Immigrant Acts: Asian American Cultural Politics* are located in the text and are accompanied by page citations.

41. Judith Butler, *Gender Trouble: Feminism and the Subversion of Identity* (New York: Routledge, 1990), 14. Further quotations from *Gender Trouble* are located in the text and are accompanied by page citations.

42. Charles Altieri, *Subjective Agency: A Theory of First-person Expressivity and Its Social Implications* (London: Blackwell, 1994), 128. Further quotation from *Subjective Agency* is located in the text and accompanied by page citation.

43. Cornel West, *Race Matters* (Boston: Beacon, 1993), 105.

44. bell hooks, *Killing Rage: Ending Racism* (New York: Henry Holt, 1995), 271. Further quotation from *Killing Rage: Ending Racism* is located in the text and is accompanied by page citation.

45. For a position similar to hooks's, see Manning Marable, *Beyond Black and White: Transforming African-American Politics* (New York: Verso, 1995).

46. Sheila D. Collins, *The Rainbow Challenge: The Jackson Campaign and the Future of U.S. Politics* (New York: Monthly Review, 1986), 86. Further quotations from *The Rainbow Challenge* are located in the text and are accompanied by page citations. For a view of Jackson's differing representations of race in his two campaigns, see Michael Omi and Howard Winant, *Racial Formation in the United States from the 1960s to the 1990s* (New York: Routledge, 1994), 142–43.

47. *Straight from the Heart,* ed. Roger D. Hatch and Frank E. Watkins (Philadelphia: Fortress, 1987), 313. Further quotations from *Straight from the Heart* are located in the text and are accompanied by page citation.

48. Thylias Moss, *Small Congregations: New and Selected Poems* (Hopewell, N.J.: Ecco, 1993), 121. Further quotations from the poem are located in the text and are accompanied by page citation.

49. See *Straight from the Heart,* 232–45, for a 1979 speech and Jackson's address to the 1984 Democratic National Convention, in which he characterizes "our present relationship with South Africa" as "a moral disgrace" (14).

50. Immanuel Wallerstein, *Historical Capitalism* (London: Verso, 1983), 18.

51. I have not located this passage in Jackson's speeches. In a 1986 sermon, he refers to Mary's denigration by the innkeeper who would not welcome her (126) and the notion that "Jesus was rejected from the inn and born in the slum" (18) in his 1984 convention address.

52. In a 1986 conversation with Charles Murray, Jackson recalls being in an "inner-city Washington" high school and challenging "those who had taken drugs to come down front. About three hundred came down" (269). After the *Washington Post* used "the headline 'Jackson does phenomenal thing—kids admit drug usage' " and an editorial suggested he succeeded only because of his "special way with black kids," Jackson went on to produce a similar result at a "97 percent white" school "in one of the richest counties in America" (270).

53. *Straight from the Heart,* 22. A perusal of the speeches in this collection will indicate that Jackson uses many other rhymes in speaking to a variety of audiences. See Collins, 125–31, for an account of differing attitudes among voters toward Jackson's brand of charisma.

54. This exhortation was a refrain near the end of Jackson's speech to the

Democratic National Convention on July 20, 1988. Jesse L. Jackson, "A Call to Common Ground," *The Black Scholar* 20, no. 1 (January/February 1989), 15.

CHAPTER 1. PROBLEMATIZING VISIBILITY: THYLIAS MOSS, JOHN YAU, AND DENISE DUHAMEL

1. *Hosiery Seams on a Bowlegged Woman* (Cleveland: Cleveland State University Press, 1983); *Small Congregations: New and Selected Poems* (Hopewell, N.J.: Ecco, 1993); *Last Chance for the Tarzan Holler* (New York: Persea, 1998); *Tale of a Sky-Blue Dress* (New York: Avon, 1998). Quotations from *Pyramid of Bone, Last Chance for the Tarzan Holler,* and *Tale of a Sky-Blue Dress* are located in the text and are accompanied by page citations. All other quotations of Moss's poetry are from *Small Congregations*; these quotations are accompanied, when necessary, by page citations. For Moss's analysis of her movement as a poet from what she terms the construction of "bleak moments," influenced heavily by Ai's poetry, in her first three books to the full "range of human emotion and endeavor," including "the architecture of joy" (254), see *Tale of a Sky-Blue Dress,* 219–20, 232–37, 251–55. While I identify Moss as African American, the poet acknowledges in *Tale of a Sky-Blue Dress* that hers "are blended people" (9). See *Tale,* 9–11.

2. W. E. B. DuBois, *The Souls of Black Folk* (1903; reprint, New York: Vintage, 1990); Toni Morrison, *The Bluest Eye* (New York: Holt, Rinehart, and Winston, 1970).

3. *Pyramid of Bone* (Charlottesville: University Press of Virginia, 1989).

4. In *Breaking the Magic Spell: Radical Theories of Folk and Fairy Tales* (Austin: University of Texas Press, 1979), Jack Zipes notes that *Snow White,* like other "folk tales gathered by the Grimm Brothers," begins "with a seemingly hopeless situation and . . . the narrative perspective is that of the folk in sympathy with the exploited protagonist of the tale" (6). According to Zipes, "*Snow White and the Seven Dwarfs,* produced in 1936 as Walt Disney's first full-length animated feature" (113), ignoring these aspects, promotes "the image of America as one happy family pulling together to clean up the economic mess" of the Great Depression, so that "capitalism" could "remain the dominant form of production in the society" (114).

5. Patricia A. Turner, *Ceramic Uncles & Celluloid Mammies: Black Images and Their Influence on Culture* (New York: Doubleday, 1994), 110. Further quotations from *Ceramic Uncles & Celluloid Mammies* are located in the text and are accompanied by page citations.

6. *At Redbones* (Cleveland, Ohio: Cleveland State University Press, 1990).

7. In *George Sidney: A Bio-Bibliography* (Westport, Conn.: Greenwood, 1994), Eric Monder speaks of Buckwheat's role in the *Our Gang* shorts. While he holds that "the democratization of the Gang itself results in a non-discriminatory attitude toward Buckwheat, the only African-American member" (89), Monder points out various cases in which Buckwheat is depicted with "stereotypical character embroidery" (25), including one short featuring his "appearance as a cannibal" (95) and another in which he is reduced to playing [a] doorman" (96).

8. *The Signifying Monkey: A Theory of Afro-American Literary Criticism* (New York: Oxford University Press, 1998), 71. Further quotations from *The Signifying Monkey* are located in the text and are accompanied by page citations.

9. *Rainbow Remnants in Rock Bottom Ghetto Sky* (New York: Persea, 1991).

10. See Leonard Maltin, *Movie and Video Guide* (New York: Signet, 1996), 217–19 for his listing and summaries of the Charlie Chan films. Between the penultimate Charlie Chan movie, *Sky Dragon* (1949), and the final *Charlie Chan and the Curse of*

the Dragon Queen, which Maltin calls a "boring comedy" that "wastes its talented cast" (218), thirty-two years elapsed.

11. *Toms, Coons, Mulattoes, Mammies, and Bucks: An Interpretive History of Blacks in American Films* (1973; reprint, New York: Continuum, 1989), 73. Further quotation from *Toms, Coons, Mulattoes, Mammies, and Bucks* is located in the text and is accompanied by page citation.

12. See Eugene Franklin Wong, *On Visual Media Racism: Asians in the American Motion Pictures* (New York: Arno, 1978), 105–9.

13. Wong, 107. Wong's citation is from Chris Steninbrunne and Otto Penzler, eds. *Encyclopedia of Mystery and Detection* (New York: McGraw-Hill, 1976), 72.

14. For an account of economic necessities and social configurations that led many nineteenth-century Chinese immigrants to enter the laundry business, see Ronald Takaki, *Strangers from a Different Shore: A History of Asian Americans* (Boston: Little, Brown, 1989), 92–94.

15. Moss's signifying on Frost's oft-memorized "Stopping by Woods on a Snowy Evening," *Selected Poems* (New York: Holt, Rinehart, and Winston, 1962), 140, is not merely apt because of its dark/light imagery and its canonical status in "Caucasian" literature taught to U.S. elementary students, but because of Frost's highly questionable treatment of African Americans and the racist sentiments he sometimes expressed. Questions of race, however, rarely enter his poems. See Aldon Lynn Nielsen, *Reading Race: White American Poets and the Racial Discourse in the Twentieth Century* (Athens: University of Georgia Press, 1988), 37–40.

16. See Takaki, *Strangers from a Different Shore,* 14, 84–87.

17. For an account of the importance of the third party in the communicative structure of the *Signifying Monkey* tales, see Gates, 55–58.

18. "Poetry Chronicles," *Hudson Review* (spring 1994): 159. Further quotation from "Poetry Chronicles" is located in the text and is accompanied by page citation.

For Moss's discussion of the problematic aspects of her own experience in an (African-American) Christian church in her youth, her father's anti-institutional perspective and its influence on her thinking, and her critique of Christian theology, see *Tale of a Sky-Blue Dress,* 26–27, 99, 212, 214.

19. *Papa Jack: Jack Johnson and the Era of White Hopes* (New York: Free, 1983), 152. Roberts describes how Johnson was absurdly convicted of violating "the White Slave Traffic Act, better known as the Mann Act," which "forbade the transportation of women in interstate or foreign commerce 'for the purpose of prostitution or debauchery, or for any other immoral purpose' " (144). To escape a prison sentence Johnson, still champion, fled the U.S. and returned in 1920, five years after losing the title to Jess Willard. Johnson then served a year-long sentence. See Roberts, 144–84, 214–19.

20. Chris Mead, *Champion: Joe Louis, Black Hero in White America* (New York: Scribner's, 1985), 52.

21. Unlike Johnson, Louis apparently enjoyed extramarital dalliances with black *and* white women with utmost discretion. See Mead, 82.

22. See Mead, 62–65, 67–68, 72–74, for examples of racist sportswriting. For an account of Dempsey's negative views of Louis, expressed after the first Schmeling fight, see Mead 98–99.

23. See Mead, 222–26, 230–32.

24. *The Fiery Cross: The Ku Klux Klan in America* (New York: Simon and Schuster, 1987), 169. Further quotations from *The Fiery Cross* are located in the text and are accompanied by page citations.

25. Many examples of Christian rhetoric can be found in Wade, appendices B and

C, 419–42. See especially questions 1–17, 20, and 24 in appendix C-3, "*Questionnaire for Prospective Members: White Knights of the Ku Klux Klan of Mississippi*," 438–41. Note, for example, the language and use of capitalization of question 11, which speaks of "the Fact that man is absolutely helpless before Satan until he truly and humbly Accepts the Living Christ as his own Personal Savior" and insists that "all of man's" positive attributes are "worthless against Satan, UNLESS there is an Absolute, Primary Foundation of an undying Belief in, Acceptance of and Reliance upon The Living Christ at the root-center of each man's Being" (440). Through an allusion to Christian doctrine, question 24 implicitly provides a rationalization for the Klan's uses of violence: "If the letter of the Law conflicts with the Spirit of the Law, WHICH will you adhere to, obey and enforce?" (441).

26. Frantz Fanon, *Black Skin, White Masks*, trans. Charles Lam Markmann (1952; reprint, New York: Grove Weidenfeld, 1967), 188–89. Further quotation from *Black Skin, White Masks* is located in the text and is accompanied by page citation.

27. John Yau, *Crossing Canal Street* (Binghampton, N.Y.: Bellevue, 1976); *Forbidden Entries* (Santa Rosa, Calif.: Black Sparrow, 1996). Quotations from *Crossing Canal Street* and *Forbidden Entries* are located in the text and are accompanied by page citations.

28. *Corpse and Mirror* (New York: Holt, Rinehart, and Winston, 1983).

29. John Gery, "Ashbery's Menagerie and the Anxiety of Affluence," in *The Tribe of John: Ashbery and Contemporary Poetry*, ed. Susan M. Schultz (Tuscaloosa: University of Alabama Press, 1995), 136.

30. Eileen Tabios, "Approximating Midnight: Her Conversation with John Yau and," *Black Lightning: Poetry-in-Progress* (New York: Asian American Writer's Workshop, 1998), 390. Further quotations from *Black Lightning* are located in the text and are accompanied by page citations.

31. John Yau, "Please Wait by the Coatroom: Wilfredo Lam in the Museum of Modern Art," *Arts* (December 1988): 59.

32. John Yau, "An Interview with John Yau" by Edward Foster, *Talisman* 5 (fall 1990): 43–44. Further quotations from "An Interview with John Yau" are located in the text and are accompanied by page citations.

33. Tabios, 383.

34. Yau makes indirect references to his resistance to the strictures of Language Poetry in Tabios, 384, 390, when he speaks of his interest in the problems of identity. He states that he is "not a Marxist," though interested in "the argument that art is a commodity," in Foster, 36.

35. John Yau, *The United States of Jasper Johns* (Cambridge, Mass.: Zoland, 1996), 5–6.

36. Priscilla Wald, "'Chaos Goes Uncourted': John Yau's Dis(-)Orienting Poetics," in *Cohesion and Dissent in American Literature*, ed. Carol Colatrella and Joseph Alkana (Albany: State University of New York Press, 1994), 142.

37. John Yau, *Radiant Silhouette: New and Selected Work, 1974–1988* (Santa Rosa, Calif.: Black Sparrow, 1989). Quotations from *Radiant Silhouette* are located in the text and are accompanied by page citations.

38. John Yau, E-mail to the author, September 24, 1999.

39. See Ephraim Katz, "Anna May Wong," *The Film Encyclopedia* (New York: Thomas Y. Crowell, 1979), 1,246.

40. James Robert Parrish and William T. Leonard, *Hollywood Players; The 30s* (New Rochelle, N.Y.: Arlington, 1976), 532–33.

41. Gina Marchetti, *Romance and the "Yellow Peril": Race, Sex, and Discourse Strategies in Hollywood Fiction* (Berkeley: University of California Press, 1993), 62. Further

quotation from *Romance and the "Yellow Peril"* is located in the text and is accompanied by page citations.

42. Parrish and Leonard, *Hollywood Players*, 534.

43. John Yau, *Edificio Sayonara* (Santa Rosa, Calif.: Black Sparrow, 1992). Quotations from *Edificio Sayonara* are located in the text and are accompanied by page citations.

44. Susan Faludi, *Backlash: The Undeclared War against American Women* (New York: Crown, 1991), 68. Further quotations from *Backlash* are located in the text and are accompanied by page citations.

45. See Faludi, 154–55. She argues that "trend stories" "weren't chronicling a retreat among women" but "were compelling one to happen" (80). According to Faludi, the "trend story" features "an absence of factual evidence or hard numbers," the citation of "only three or four women, typically anonymously, to establish the trend," an emphasis on prediction, and the use of "consumer researchers and psychologists who often support their assertions by citing" similar "stories" (81).

46. Duhamel, unpublished interview with the author, 19 October 1995, New York, N.Y.

47. *Smile!* (Harrisburg, Pa.: Warm Spring, 1993); *The Woman with Two Vaginas* (Anchorage, Alaska: Salmon Run, 1995); *Girl Soldier* (Truro, Mass.: Garden Street, 1996); *Kinky* (Alexandria, Va.: Orchises, 1997); *The Star Spangled Banner* (Carbondale: Southern Illinois University Press, 1999). Quotations from *Smile!*, *The Woman with Two Vaginas*, *Girl Soldier*, and *Kinky* are located in the text and are accompanied by page citations.

48. *The Best American Poetry, 1994*, ed. A. R. Ammons and David Lehman (New York: Simon and Schuster, 1991), 221.

49. Susan Bordo, *Unbearable Weight: Feminism, Western Culture, and the Body* (Berkeley: University of California Press, 1993), 66. Further quotations from *Unbearable Weight* are located in the text and are accompanied by page citations.

50. Bordo, 128–29.

51. See Sonia Parkes's interview, "Denise Duhamel," *Inkshed* 26 (January–June 1994): 16–20, for Duhamel's discussion of the feminist concepts about women's body-image in various Barbie poems before they were published as *Kinky*. The poet declares that "women are silenced in many complex ways," especially in relation to "beauty," and so she finds "Barbie . . . a perfect metaphor" for the situation (16). Since "angry women are still perceived as shrills," "many women"—like Barbie, who "always smiles, even when . . . angry"—"tend to turn their anger inward." This results in "eating disorders, depression, and self-mutilation which," for Duhamel, includes "plastic surgery." The poet attributes women's anger to the idea that they are not told "it is a lie that women can 'have it all,'" but are "expected to 'do it all'—have a fabulous career, raise healthy children, and, most importantly, look damn good (and smell damn good) while doing it" (16). Duhamel states her belief that "women might be able to break the mould—we're a smart and creative lot."

52. Denise Duhamel, "Evelyn Lau, *Fresh Girls and Other Stories*, and *Oedipal Dreams*," *The Poetry Project* 157 (April/May 1995), 17.

53. While my emphasis here is on Duhamel's feminist poetics, much could be said about poems with other foci in *The Woman with Two Vaginas*. There are myths of evolution, tales of abject poverty, entertaining accounts of interactions between giants and human beings, witty, hyperbolic exposures of foibles, stories about the difficulties of parenting and childhood, and tales about tragic consequences of individual male egotism. See Ruth Farmer, "*The Woman with Two Vaginas*: Erotic Eskimo Tales in Poetry by Denise Duhamel," *Harvard Review* (fall 1995); 162–

63, especially her reading of "The Putting Away of Dolls." Farmer observes that "Duhamel subverts gender roles on several occasions" (163), a point on which I elaborate later in this chapter.

54. Jeanne Holm, *Women in the Military: An Unfinished Revolution* (1982; reprint, Novato, Calif.: Presidio, 1992), xiii. Further quotations from *Women in the Military* are located in the text and are accompanied by page citations.

55. Many poems in *The Woman with Two Vaginas* are based on Inuit takes. In the notes, fifty of the fifty-six poems are acknowledged as having sources in Eskimo mythology; the others were invented by the poet. In my interview with her, Duhamel remarked that, in poems based directly on sources, she "did very little, if anything, when it came to changing the 'plots' " but made "changes . . . purely on imagistic grounds." Citing the "bare-bones" quality of many English translations she found and the absence of a "past or future tense" in various Inuit languages, she stated that was able to take "liberties": "I made [the stories] fleshier; I colored them in."

56. Through his *Returning a Borrowed Tongue: An Anthology of Contemporary Filipino and Filipino American Poetry* (Minneapolis, Minn.: Coffee House, 1995) and his own book of poems, *El Grupo McDonald's* (Chicago: Tia Chucha, 1995), Duhamel's husband Nick Carbó has striven to challenge this tendency in U.S. culture.

CHAPTER 2. THE EFFACEMENT, (RE-)TRACING, AND RECONSTRUCTION OF HISTORY: CAROLYN FORCHÉ, JOSEPH LEASE, MARTÍN ESPADA, AND GLORIA ANZALDÚA

1. *Against Forgetting: Twentieth-Century Poetry of Witness* (New York: Norton, 1993), 30. Further quotation from *Against Forgetting* is located in the text and is accompanied by page citation.

2. *The Angel of History* (New York: Harper Collins, 1994). All quotations from *The Angel of History* are located in the text and are accompanied by page citations.

3. *Gathering the Tribes* (New Haven: Yale University Press, 1976). Further quotations from *Gathering the Tribes* are located in the text and are accompanied by page citations.

4. Stanley Kunitz, foreword to, *Gathering the Tribes,* xi. For a strong analysis of several poems in *Gathering the Tribes,* see Martha M. Vertreace, "Secrets Left to Tell: Creativity and Continuity in the Mother/Daughter Dyad," in *Mother Puzzles: Daughters and Mothers in Contemporary American Literature,* ed. Mickey Pearlman (Westport, Conn.: Greenwood, 1989), 77–89.

5. Forché, "A Lesson in Commitment," *TriQuarterly* 65 (winter 1986): 35.

6. Forché, "El Salvador: An Aide-Mémoire," *American Poetry Review* (July/August 1981); rpt. In *Poetry and Politics,* ed. Richard Jones (New York: Quill, 1985), 249. Further quotations from "El Salvador: An Aide-Mémoire" are located in the text and are accompanied by page citations.

7. Forché, *The Country between Us* (New York: Harper and Row, 1981). Quotations from *The Country between Us* are located in the text and are accompanied by page citations.

8. Mary S. Strine, "Protocols of Power: Performance, Pleasure, and the Textual Economy," *Text and Performance Quarterly* 12, no. 1 (January 1992): 65.

For a thorough and incisive account of the Carter and Reagan administrations' El Salvador policies, see Raymond Bonner, *Weakness and Deceit: U.S. Policy and El Salvador* (New York: Times Books, 1984). Like Forché, Bonner believes that "the Salvadoran military was the law and above the law, as much in 1983 and 1984 as it had been in 1932 and 1979"; calling the military "more ruthless and brutal after the coup," he cites the estimate of "the legal aid office" of El Salvador's "Roman Catholic Church" that "between October 1979 and January 1984 at least 40,000 innocent civilians were murdered" in the country (82).

9. "Carolyn Forché," interview by Bill Moyers, in *The Language of Life: A Festival of Poets*, ed. James Haba (New York: Doubleday, 1995), 133. Further quotation from "Carolyn Forché" is located in the text and is accompanied by page citation.

10. As Michael Greer asserts in "Politicizing the Modern: Carolyn Forché in El Salvador and America," *The Centennial Review* 30, no. 2 (spring 1986), Forché struggles in the Salvador poems against effects on North American perceptions wrought by the U.S. media's tendency to treat "events [like] the murders of Monsignor Oscar Romero, Jose Rudolfo Viera, and the thousands of other Salvadoran workers and *campesinos* . . . as if they were spectacles for our own momentary edification" (178).

11. See Theodor W. Adorno, "Commitment," in *The Essential Frankfurt School Reader*, ed. Andrew Arato and Eike Gebhardt (New York: Urizen, 1978), 300–18, for a powerful account of this issue. Adorno declares that "the so-called artistic representation" of tremendous cruelty and suffering "contains, however remotely, the power to elicit enjoyment out of it. The moral of this art, not to forget for a single instant, slithers into the abyss of its opposite" (312–13).

12. David Montenegro, "Carolyn Forché," in *Points of Departure: International Writers on Writing and Politics*, ed. David Montenegro (Ann Arbor: University of Michigan Press, 1991), 64. Further quotations from Montenegro's interview with Forché are located in the text and are accompanied by page citations. For the reading in poststructuralist theory, other critical theory, and literature that helped Forché reach her new insights, see Montenegro, 65, where she mentions Jean-Francois Lyotard in particular, and Jill Taft-Kaufman, "Jill Taft-Kaufman Talks with Carolyn Forché," *Text and Performance Quarterly* 10, no. 1 (January 1990): 61–70.

13. Lyn Hejinian, "The Rejection of Closure," in *Writing/Talks*, ed. Bob Perelman (Carbondale: Southern Illinois University Press, 1985), 270. Further quotations from "The Rejection of Closure" are located in the text and are accompanied by page citations.

14. Walter Benjamin, *Illuminations*, ed. Hannah Arendt, trans. Harry Zohn (New York: Schoken, 1969), 257.

15. In her "Introduction, Walter Benjamin, 1892–1940," in *Illuminations*, Hannah Arendt notes that Benjamin valorized the method of collage to such an extent that he harbored "the ideal of producing a work consisting entirely of quotations, one that was mounted so masterfully that it could dispense with any accompanying text" (47).

Following an epigraph from a poem by Gershom Scholem, quoted toward the end of the long "dialogue" with Ellie in "The Angel of History" (8; see "Notes," 81), the first two sentences of part IX of "Theses on the Philosophy of History" read: "A Klee painting named 'Angelus Novus' shows an angel looking as though he is about to move away from something he is fixedly contemplating. His eyes are staring, his mouth is open, his wings are spread" (257).

16. In "Jill Taft-Kaufman Talks with Carolyn Forché," the poet says of her work-in-progress that it is "in long . . . but not even lines" with "breaks or pauses . . . between sections of it; . . . the lines are not broken," since they "go all the way to the margin, and certain thoughts are completed and certain are not" (64). Forché adds: "There are intruding voices and interrupting voices and interrogating voices and the work seems to float on the page" (64).

17. In the Montenegro interview, Forché reports that, after becoming parents

and feeling "this new responsibility," she and her husband, Harry Mattison, "a war photographer for twelve years" who "had come perilously close to death on many occasions," chose not to subject themselves "to conditions of war voluntarily, as [they] had done for several years." Now an "older" member of "a profession for young men and women who believe in their immortality," Mattison "had lost his sense of immortality, which is . . . a kind of shield" (74).

18. November 1990 postscript to Montenegro interview, 62.

19. Carolyn Forché and William Kulik, trans., *The Selected Poems of Robert Desnos* (New York: Ecco, 1991).

20. Section 17 of the title-poem of Shapiro's *A Man Holding an Acoustic Panel* (New York: Liveright, 1973) is entitled "The Funeral of Jan Palach" (30).

21. Mark Strand and David Lehman, ed., *The Best American Poetry 1991* (New York: Scribner's, 1992), 304.

22. Simone de Beauvoir, Preface to *Shoah: An Oral History of the Holocaust,* by Claude Lanzmann (New York: Pantheon, 1985), vii. Further quotations from *Shoah* are located in the text and are accompanied by page citations.

23. See Lanzmann, 3–4, 12–13.

24. Lifton, *Death in Life: Survivors of Hiroshima* (New York: Random, 1967), 23. Further quotation from *Death in Life: Survivors of Hiroshima* is located in the text and is accompanied by page citation.

25. Forché does not identify the text by Valéry from which the quotation is drawn. In her interview with Moyers, she tells a story about it. While in her study, putting "away boxes of old notes from this book," she found "a piece of yellow legal paper" with the quote she "had copied from Paul Valéry years ago" (141). She then realized that it could serve as an ending to *The Angel of History*: "It just fell to my feet and it closed the book" (141).

26. Lease's first book, much of which is reprinted in *Human Rights*, is *The Room* (New York: Alef, 1994). Lease considers *Human Rights* (Cambridge, Mass.: Zoland, 1998) his first full-length collection. Quotations from *Human Rights* are located in the text and are accompanied by page citations.

27. Donald Revell, "*The Room* by Joseph Lease," *Colorado Review* 21, no. 2 (fall 1995): 199–209; Forrest Gander, "Joseph Lease's *The Room*," *Agni* 42 (1995): 203–5.

28. Lease gave me a copy of this essay in November 1997.

29. The phrase is from Quentin Anderson, *The Imperial Self: An Essay in American Literary and Cultural History* (New York: Knopf, 1971).

30. Deborah Lipstadt, *Denying the Holocaust: The Growing Assault on Truth and Memory* (New York: Free, 1993), 209. Further quotations from *Denying the Holocaust* are located in the text and are accompanied by page citations.

31. Conversation with the author, November 1997.

32. Larissa Szporluk, "Joseph Lease, *Human Rights*," *Poetry Project Newsletter* 170 (June/July 1998):15.

33. David Shapiro, "After," in *Testimony: Contemporary Writers Make the Holocaust Personal,* ed. David Rosenberg (New York: Random, 1989), 457. Further quotation from "After" is located in the text and is accompanied by page citation.

34. Lawrence L. Langer, *Admitting the Holocaust: Collected Essays* (New York: Oxford University Press, 1995), 183. Further quotation from *Admitting the Holocaust* is located in the text and is accompanied by page citation.

35. Saul Friedlander, *Nazi Germany and the Jews: The Years of Persecution, 1933–1939,* vol. 1 (New York: Harper Collins, 1997), 77. Further quotation from *Nazi Germany and the Jews* is located in the text and is accompanied by page citation.

36. Lease, in a conversation with the author in January 1996, stated that he believes that this epigraph closely resembles a line from the Broadway show *Cabaret*.

37. Wolf Dieter-Dube, "Ernst Ludwig Kirchner," *Ernst Ludwig Kirchner, 1880–1938: Oils, Watercolors, Drawings, and Graphics* (London: Marlborough Fine Art, 1969), 9–10.

38. Jahan Ramazani, *Poetry of Mourning: The Modern Elegy from Hardy to Heaney* (Chicago: University of Chicago Press, 1993). Charting the ways in which modern poets criticize facile consolations of traditional elegies *while* composing elegies, Ramazani finds that this antielegiac strain is "wary of the religious and psychiatric norm of 'healthy mourning' " and sees "it as urging the exploitation and betrayal of the dead" (7).

39. Coleridge, *The Complete Poetical Works,* vol. 1 (London: Oxford University Press, 1962), 186–209. See especially part IV.

40. Of course, the story of Jesus' crucifixion has been used differently—as a way of "reading" the "story" of atrocious suffering in the Holocaust. For a critique of this latter tendency, see Langer, 25–30.

41. Numerous contemporary writers have discussed this issue. To cite one example, in her long poem "Sources," *Your Native Land, Your Life* (New York: Norton, 1986), 3–27—most explicitly in section V—Adrienne Rich alludes to this problem of censorship as she experienced it while growing up during and directly after the Holocaust. She perceives this denial in the context of the poem's overall critique of a Jewish-American assimilationist drive to submerge Jewish identity.

42. See Friedlander, 14–72.

43. Martín Espada, *The Immigrant Iceboy's Bolero* (Madison, Wis.: Ghost Pony, 1982; reprinted, Natick, Mass.: Cordilera, 1983; reprinted, Maplewood, N.J.: Waterfront, 1986); *Trumpets from the Islands of Their Eviction* (Tempe, Ariz.: Bilingual, 1987); *Rebellion Is the Circle of a Lover's Hands* (Willimantic, Conn.: Curbstone Press, 1990); *City of Coughing and Dead Radiators* (New York: Norton, 1993); *Imagine the Angels of Bread* (New York: Norton, 1996). Quotations from *The Immigrant Iceboy's Bolero* (Waterfront edition), *Trumpets from the Islands of Their Eviction, Rebellion Is the Circle of a Lover's Hands, City of Coughing and Dead Radiators,* and *Imagine the Angels of Bread* are located in the text and are accompanied by page citations. Martín Espada and Camilio Pérez-Bustillo, *The Blood That Keeps Singing: Selected Poems of Clemente Soto-Vélez* (Willimantic, Conn.: Curbstone, 1991). See Espada and Pérez-Bustillo's foreword to the book, 7–10, and Espada's note about the poem "Hands without Irons Become Dragonflies," in *Imagine the Angels of Bread,* 92. *Imagine the Angels of Bread* is dedicated to Espada's son, who is named after Soto-Vélez, and Soto-Vélez himself.

For a sense of the political poets whom Espada values most, see the anthology he edited, *Poetry like bread: Poets of the Political Imagination* (Willimantic, Conn.: Curbstone, 1994), and his foreword, 15–19.

44. Martín Espada, "Documentaries and Declamadores: Puerto Rican Poetry in the United States," in *A Gift of Tongues: Critical Challenges in Contemporary American Poetry,* ed. Marie Harris and Kathleen Aguero (Athens: University of Georgia Press, 1987), 258. Further quotations from "Documentaries and Declamadores" are located in the text and are accompanied by page citations.

45. See Gordon K. Lewis, *Puerto Rico: Freedom and Power in the Caribbean* (New York: Monthly Review, 1963), especially his extensive treatment of "Operation Bootstrap," 167–213; Frank Bonilla and Ricardo Campos, "A Wealth of Poor: Puerto Ricans in the New Economic Order," *Daedalus* (spring 1981): 133–76; Ricardo Campos, *Bootstraps and Enterprise Zones: The Underside of Late Capitalism in Puerto Rico and the United States* (Beverly Hills, Calif.: Sage, 1982); Clara E. Rodriguez, *Puerto Ricans Born in the U.S.A.*

(Boston: Unwin Hyman, 1989). Quotations from *Puerto Ricans Born in the U.S.A.* are located in the text and are accompanied by page citations.

46. Anne Nelson, *Murder under Two Flags: The U.S., Puerto Rico, and the Cerro Maravilla Cover-up* (New York: Ticknor and Fields, 1986), 122–23. Further quotations from *Murder under Two Flags* are located in the text and are accompanied by page citations. Accompanying his remark about the extent of "the great migration" in "Documentaries and Declamadores," Espada cites Nelson (98) as his source.

47. Diana L. Vélez, "Dancing to the Music of an 'Other' Voice," *Trumpets from the Islands of Their Eviction*, 70. Further quotations from "Dancing to the Music of an 'Other' Voice" are located in the text and are accompanied by page citations.

48. Arturo Morales Carrion, *Puerto Rico: A Political and Cultural History* (New York: Norton, 1983), 134–36. Quotations from *Puerto Rico: A Political and Cultural History* are located in the text and are accompanied by page citations. Carrion writes of Roosevelt's machinations in 1898: "When war broke out, Roosevelt took a strong position in favor of total expulsion of Spain from the hemisphere. As he left to join the Rough Riders, he wrote Cabot Lodge: 'do not make peace until we get Porto Rico [sic], while Cuba is made independent' " (134).

49. Notes Carrion, "in his 1905 message to Congress, Roosevelt asked for American citizenship and for certain economic measures for Puerto Rico" (162). Perceiving the island's problems as "essentially commercial and industrial," the president "found no fault whatever with the political and administrative structure 'since it has inspired confidence in property owners and investors.' " The Puerto Rican "Unionists" like Luis Muñoz Rivera "did not reject American citizenship," but "colonial tutelage" (163).

50. See Creeley, foreword to *Trumpets from the Islands of Their Eviction*, 11–12, for a discussion of Espada's work as a lawyer for "an organization involved with the legal context of civil rights for immigrants and with bilingual education laws in particular" (12).

51. See the biographical note on Espada on the back cover of *Trumpets from the Islands of Their Eviction*.

52. See Ilene O'Malley, "Play It Again, Ron," in *The Nicaragua Reader: Documents of a Revolution under Fire*, ed. Peter Rosset and John Vandermeer (New York: Grove, 1983), 113–19. According to an article in *Time*, 15 November 1948 (43), FDR said of the first Somoza dictator, Anastasio, "He's a sonofabitch, but he's ours" (O'Malley 119).

53. Ronald Reagan, *Speaking My Mind: Selected Speeches* (New York: Simon and Schuster, 1989), 150. Further quotation from *Speaking My Mind* is located in the text and is accompanied by page citation.

54. "Let There Be Peace in Central America," *The Nicaragua Reader*, 10.

55. EPICA Task Force, "The Somoza Legacy: Economic Bankruptcy," *The Nicaragua Reader*, 299; reprinted from the EPICA Task Force, *Nicaragua: A People's Revolution* (Washington, D.C.: EPICA Task Force, 1980). Further quotations from "The Somoza Legacy: Economic Bankruptcy" are located in the text and are accompanied by page citations.

56. The Junta for National Reconstruction, "The Philosophy and Policies of the Government of Nicaragua," *The Nicaragua Reader*, 263.

57. Sonia Saldivar-Hull, "Feminism on the Border: From Gender Politics to Geopolitics," in *Criticism in the Borderlands: Studies in Chicano Literature, Culture, and Ideology*, ed. Hector Calderon and Jose David Saldivar (Durham, N.C.: Duke University Press, 1991), 211. Further quotations from "Feminism on the Border" are located in the text and are accompanied by page citations. See also the discussion

of "borderlands consciousness" (113) in Kim Whitehead, "Survival as Form in the Work of Gloria Anzaldúa and Irena Klepfisz," *The Feminist Poetry Movement* (Jackson: University of Mississippi Press, 1996), 113–54. All quotations from *Borderlands/La Frontera—The New Mestiza* (San Francisco: Aunt Lute, 1987) in this chapter are located in the text and are accompanied by page citations.

It is germane to note that Anzaldúa has been an important anthologist in the last two decades. See Gloria Anzaldúa and Cherrie Moraga, eds., *This Bridge Called My Back: Writings by Radical Women of Color* (1981; reprint, New York: Kitchen Table: Women of Color, 1983); Gloria Anzaldúa, ed., *Making Face, Making Soul*, Haciendo Caras: *Creative and Critical Perspectives by Women of Color* (San Francisco: Aunt Lute, 1990).

Rafael Pérez-Torres has situated Anzaldúa's place in Chicano poetry in *Movements in Chicano Poetry: Against Myths, Against Margins* (New York: Cambridge University Press, 1995), all quotations of which (in reference to his discussion of particular Anzaldúa poems) are located in the text and are accompanied by page citations. For useful surveys of Chicano poetry in general, see two essays (published the year that *Borderlands* appeared) in *A Gift of Tongues: Critical Challenges in Contemporary American Poetry*, ed. Marie Harris and Kathleen Aguero (Athens: University of Georgia Press, 1987): Bruce Novoa's "Chicano Poetry: An Overview," 226–48, which holds that "Chicano literature is a recent phenomenon that coincides with the . . . Chicano movement and the awakening and expression of a cultural consciousness which that movement produced" (226) yet traces literary antecedents back to the 1830s; and Carmen Tafolla's "Chicano Literature: Beyond Beginnings," 206–25, which includes a fuller discussion of Chicana poetry. See also Bruce-Novoa, *Chicano Poetry: A Response to Chaos* (Austin: University of Texas Press, 1982).

58. Hector A. Torres, "Gloria Anzaldúa," in *Dictionary of Literary Biography, Chicano Writers: Second Series* 122, ed. Francisco A. Lomelí and Carl R. Shirley (Detroit: Gale Research, 1992), 8. Further quotations from "Gloria Anzaldúa" are located in the text and are accompanied by page citations.

Anzaldúa, who told Torres that the Chicano image of a "good Chicanita" was a girl who has dropped out of school by the eighth grade, "received her M.A. in English and education from the University of Texas at Austin in 1972," then taught high school, first "for the children of migrant families" and then in Indiana (9). Although Anzaldúa has "encountered considerable resistance to her diverse . . . interests" in the sphere of academia, she has gained various appointments. "Not advanced to candidacy" after working "from 1974 to 1977" in the comparative literature doctoral program at the University of Texas because of her desire "to write a dissertation . . . on some topic in Chicano or feminist studies," she later taught at San Francisco State University, Oakes College at the University of California at Santa Cruz, Vermont College of Norwich University, and, while Distinguished Visiting Professor in Women's Studies at UC-Santa Cruz, she was *rejected* for admission to the History of Consciousness Program there, because, as she told Torres, they considered her "too established" and insufficiently versed in "theory," and because "they already had too many creative writers" (10).

59. John R. Chávez, *The Lost Land: The Chicano Image of the Southwest* (Albuquerque: University of New Mexico Press, 1984), 2. Unless otherwise indicated, further quotations from *The Lost Land* are located in the text and are accompanied by page citations.

60. Chávez, 9.

61. Reay Tannahill, *Sex in History* (Briarcliff Manor, N.Y.: Stein and Day, 1980), 308.

62. Ray Allen Billington, *The Far Western Frontier, 1830–1860* (New York: Harper, 1956), 116. Further quotations from *The Far Western Frontier* are located in the text and are accompanied by page citations.

63. Arnoldo de León, *They Called Them Greasers: Anglo Attitudes toward Mexicans in Texas, 1821–1900* (Austin: University of Texas Press, 1983). See Anzaldúa, *Borderlands* (7) and footnote 9 (92).

64. Billington accounts for how the "pulse-tingling phrase" "Manifest Destiny" enabled the "exuberant belief" that it signified to "be translated into action": "This was provided by the editor of the New York *Morning News*, John L. O'Sullivan, who in December 1945, wrote of 'our manifest destiny to overspread and to possess the whole of the continent which Providence has given us for the development of the great experiment of liberty and federated self-government entrusted to us' " (149). See also Julius W. Pratt, "The Origin of 'Manifest Destiny,' " *American Historical Review* 31 (1927): 795–98.

65. "La Prieta," in *This Bridge Called My Back: Writings by Radical Women of Color,* 202.

66. In *Youth, Identity, Power: The Chicano Movement* (New York: Verso, 1989), which usefully discusses the relation of the Chicano movement of the sixties and seventies to the efforts of the preceding "Mexican American generation" (19) toward "melting pot democracy" and the subsequent "struggle for Chicano studies" (127) and the 1980s displacement of emphasis "from Chicano to Hispanic" (171), Carlos Muñoz Jr. is careful to note the distinction between Chávez's organization and the Chicano movement, which, of course, included La Raza Unida Party in Texas.

67. Albert Camus, "The Myth of Sisyphus," in *The Myth of Sisyphus and Other Essays, 1955,* trans. Justin O'Brien (New York: Knopf, 1961), 88–91.

68. For Anzaldúa's own treatment of "interlingualism," see "How to Tame a Wild Tongue," *Borderlands,* 53–64.

69. See Devon Peña, "Between the Lines: A New Perspective on the Industrial Sociology of Women Workers in Transnational Labor Processes," in *Chicana Voices: Intersections of Class, Race, and Gender,* ed. Teresa Córdova et al. (Albuquerque: University of New Mexico Press, 1990, 77–95, for a trenchant marxist-feminist account of how the Mexican *Maquiladoras* are governed by the strictures of Global Fordism in conjunction with "male-centered, male-controlled supervisory systems which manipulate the gender specifications of Mexican culture" (80).

70. Grace Halsell, *The Illegals* (New York: Stein and Day, 1978), 5. Further quotations from *The Illegals* are located in the text and are accompanied by page citations.

71. See Anzaldúa's claim in *"La conciencia"* about the "Anglo" origins of the concept of machismo and the effect of Anglo discrimination on Chicanos' view of Chicanas (83).

72. Jack D. Forbes, *Aztecas del Norte: The Chicanos of Aztlán* (Greenwich, Conn.: Fawcett, 1973), 13.

CHAPTER 3. PROBINGS OF COALITION AND BROAD COMMUNITY: MELVIN DIXON, JOSEPH LEASE, STEPHEN PAUL MILLER, AND GLORIA ANZALDÚA

1. See Elizabeth Alexander, introduction to *Love's Instruments* (Chicago: Tia Chucha, 1995), 6. Further quotations from Alexander's introduction, Dixon's poems, and his OutWrite speech in *Love's Instruments* are located in the text and are accompanied by page citations.

Aside from *Change of Territory* and *Ride Out the Wilderness,* both cited in my introduction, Dixon published two novels, *Trouble the Water* (Boulder: University of Colorado and Fiction Collective Two, 1989) and *Vanishing Rooms* (New York: Dutton, 1991), and he edited and translated *The Collected Poetry of Leopold Sedar Senghor* (Charlottesville: University Press of Virginia, 1991), and Genevieve Fabre, *Drumbeats, Masks, and Metaphors: Contemporary Afro-American Theatre*, trans. Dixon (Cambridge: Harvard University Press, 1983).

2. John D'Emilio, *Sexual Politics, Sexual Communities: The Making of a Homosexual Minority in the United States, 1940–1970* (Chicago: Chicago University Press, 1983), 174. See also 198 and 223 for a discussion of the Mattachine Society. Further quotations from *Sexual Politics, Sexual Communities* are located in the text and are accompanied by page citations.

3. See D'Emilio, 224–25, 233.

4. Essex Hemphill, introduction to *Brother to Brother: New Writings by Black Gay Men*, ed. Hemphill and Joseph Fairchild Beam (Boston: Alyson, 1991), xvii. Further quotations from Hemphill's introduction are located in the text and are accompanied by page citations.

Hemphill, who makes the claim that "black gay men have" only "been publishing *overt* homoerotic verse since 1977" (xxii), considers the 1980s "a critically important decade for" black gay literature, and he cites a variety of periodicals, "a promising selection of self-published chapbooks and portfolios," and two anthologies, as evidence that "a generation of black gay writers are at work dismantling the silence" (xxiv).

5. Mark Blasius, *Gay and Lesbian Politics: Sexuality and the Emergence of a New Ethic* (Philadelphia: Temple University Press, 1994), 5. Further quotations from *Gay and Lesbian Politics* are located in the text and are accompanied by page citations.

6. Robert Hayden, *Collected Poems* (New York: Liveright, 1985), 96. The centrality of Hayden's influence on Dixon is also to be found in the latter's use of the older poet's phrase "vanished rooms" as inspiration for the title of the novel, *Vanishing Rooms*. The passage from section V of Hayden's "Elegies for Paradise Valley" (*Collected Poems*, 163–70) that Dixon cites as the epigraph of *Vanishing Rooms* has a startling reference to characters with the same first name as Dixon and his gay brother, Christopher (167).

In her introduction to *Love's Instruments*, Elizabeth Alexander notes that she and members of Tia Chucha Press "chose the cover painting, which was done by Melvin's brother, Christopher Dixon. Tragedy sometimes shamelessly compounds itself; Christopher also died of AIDS" (6–7).

7. Randy Shilts, *And the Band Played On: Politics, People, and the AIDS, Epidemic* (New York: St. Martin's, 1987), 595–96.

Of the many accounts of virulently homophobic representations of PWAs and bizarre representations of AIDS, see especially Paula A. Treichler, "AIDS, Homophobia, and Biomedical Discourse: An Epidemic of Signification," in *AIDS: Cultural Analysis/Cultural Activism*, ed. Douglas Crimp (Cambridge: MIT, 1988), 31–70. Also, see Jan Zita Grover, "AIDS: Keywords," in *AIDS: Cultural Analysis/Cultural Activism*, ed. Douglas Crimp (Cambridge: MIT, 1988), 28–30, for the reasons that the term "People with AIDS" (PWA) is valorized over the term "victim."

8. See Douglas Crimp, "AIDS: Cultural Analysis/Cultural Activism," in *AIDS: Cultural Analysis/Cultural Activism*, ed. Douglas Crimp (Cambridge: MIT, 1988), 7–12.

9. See Blasius, 181–82.

10. See "I'll Be Somewhere Looking for My Name," 76.

11. Gwendolyn Brooks, "We Real Cool," *Selected Poems* (New York: Harper and Row, 1963), 73.

12. Jesse L. Jackson, "A Call to Common Ground," *The Black Scholar* 20, no. 1 (January/February 1989); 15. Further quotation from "A Call to Common Ground" is located in the text and is accompanied by page citation.

13. I have not been able to locate the source for Jones's remarks.

14. In "The Quilt: Activism and Remembrance," *Art in America* 80 (December 1992), Jonathan Weinberg acknowledges that "some 19th-century women were able to express their lives in their quilts and . . . even incorporate political messages about contemporary issues," but he also views the quilt as "a marker of women's oppression, a grid that emblematized the regimentation and categorization that kept them in the home" (39).

For a cogent demonstration of the extent to which the nineteenth-century quilt was a vehicle for "political messages," see Cecilia Macheski, ed., *Quilt Stories* (Lexington: University Press of Kentucky, 1994). In her introduction to *Quilt Stories*, Macheski speaks of "'Radical Rose,' according to quilt legend, . . . a name given to a traditional rose pattern by a quilter sympathetic with the abolition movement before the Civil War." The quilter "stitched a black circle into the center of the rose, a glaring symbol of the slavery despoiling the nation" (4). Macheski observes: "Linking the struggle for justice and freedom with spiritual power and Gospel stories, each writer"—for example, Rebecca Cox Jackson—a black "Shaker Eldress . . . treated with inequality by her 'sisters'—finds in her quilt a vehicle for breaking the silence imposed on women by oppression, disenfranchisement, and illiteracy."

Speaking of those "in the AIDS activist movement" who believe that work like the Names Project has deflected "time and attention away from direct political action," Jonathan Weinberg counters, along with other activists, "that the quilt *is* a form of direct action and that there must be a place for mourning within activism" (39). In "Mourning and Militancy," *October* 51 (1989), Douglas Crimp's reconsideration of Freud's notions of mourning in the context of gay men in the era of AIDS supports this position. Crimp stresses the importance of mourning as a recognition of "unconscious conflict" that, if ignored, could lead them to "make decisions—or fail to make them—whose results may be" almost as "deadly" as those of "sinister" government leaders (17–18). Affirming militancy, Crimp asserts that, "if we understand that violence is able to reap its horrible rewards through the very psychic mechanisms that make us part of this society, then we may also be able to recognize—along with our rage—our terror, our guilt, and our profound sadness" (18).

Regarding the charge that the Names Quilt is tainted by "kitsch," Michael Klein, editor of *Poets for Life: Seventy-Six Poets Respond to AIDS* (New York: Crown, 1989), a collection which features three of Dixon's poems, suggests that the social context allows what might be called the "rhetoric" of the quilt to have a transformative impact: "To the ones in America who tried to ignore AIDS or who held contempt for people with AIDS, this American folk-art project would be a stunning reminder that those who are dead, and those who still suffer, are loved" (11).

Similarly, Cleve Jones notes in *Family: A Portrait of Gay and Lesbian America*, ed. Nancy Andrews (San Francisco: Harper Collins, 1994) that, when he was looking at the initial version of the project, cardboard signs in San Francisco, he recognized its resemblance to a quilt, and he immediately envisioned a dramatic juxtaposition that made a subversive use of such "kitschy" associations. "Immediately flooded with memories of [his] grandmother and . . . great-grandmother," whose quilts "have been passed down through the generations in [his] family," Jones thought of this "warm, middle-class, middle-America, nonthreatening, traditional-values sort of image," and he determined that it should be "the symbol to match with this disease that's killing faggots and junkies and black women and children and other people our society has not yet come to value" (unpaginated). It can be said that Aunt Ida, despite the fact that her overall ideological interests have been quite distinct from Jones's, reaches the same perspective in the course of Dixon's poem.

However valid, Jones's personal associations, of course, do not take into account the not entirely "nonthreatening" or "traditional-values" aspect of quilts that Macheski elucidates.

15. Dixon considers "the central paradox in most of Baldwin's fiction"—one that is not addressed—"the inability to reconcile the emotional (affectional) needs of a homosexual artist who expressed himself in a verbal art based in the religion that ultimately condemns him" (135).

16. "David Shapiro and Joseph Lease: An Exchange." *Misc. Proj.* 3 (July 1997), 10. Further quotation from "David Shapiro and Joseph Lease: An Exchange" is located in the text and is accompanied by page citation.

17. See Robert Creeley, in Tom Clark, *Robert Creeley and the Genius of the American Common Place. Together with the Poet's Own "Autobiography"* (New York: New Directions, 1993).

18. Speaking in an interview in 1992, James R. Dumpson in "The Social Welfare," *Beyond Homelessness: Frames of Reference,* ed. Benedict Giamo and Jeffrey Grunberg (Iowa City: University of Iowa Press, 1992) succinctly articulates the problem from a liberal homeless activist's perspective; whereas Reagan and Bush "want (or wanted) government out of everything," eschewing "partnership" and leaving "it to the marketplace," Dumpson advocates a "public-private partnership" involving "equal responsibilities and the provision of opportunities from both sides for individual and community development" (109).

19. Robert Coles, "The Human Context of Homelessness," in *Beyond Homelessness: Frames of Reference,* ed. Benedict Giamo and Jeffrey Grunberg, 186. Further quotation from "The Human Context of Homelessness" is located in the text and is accompanied by page citation.

20. Kitty Kelly, *His Way: The Unauthorized Biography of Frank Sinatra* (New York: Bantam, 1986), 508–9.

21. Sidney Blumenthal, "Reaganism and the Neokitsch Aesthetic," in *The Reagan Legacy,* ed. Sidney Blumenthal and Thomas Byrne Edsall (New York: Pantheon, 1988), 256. Further quotation from "Reaganism and the Neokitsch Aesthetic" is located in the text and is accompanied by page citation.

22. There are telling statistics in "Economic Growth for Whom?" "Action Brief," Michael Harrington Center for Democratic Values and Social Action, no. 1 (1998). "While the overall unemployment rate in November/December 1997, according to the Bureau of Labor Statistics, "was 4.7%," the Harrington Center states that, for black men, unemployment rose and that "nearly 15% of new job growth has been for temporary workers" (1). In fact, "8.1 million persons in December (6.2 percent of the total employed) held more than one job," and "according to the Economic Policy Institute, nonstandard work patterns are becoming more common."

23. Walt Whitman, *Leaves of Grass* (New York: Norton, 1968), 115, 116.

24. Michel Foucault, "On the Genealogy of Ethics: An Overview of Work in Progress," in *The Foucault Reader,* ed. Paul Rabinow (New York: Pantheon, 1984), 350. Further quotation from "On the Genealogy of Ethics" is located in the text and is accompanied by page citation.

25. *Complete Poetry and Collected Prose* (New York: Library of America, 1982), 929.

Further quotation from *Complete Poetry and Collected Prose* is located in the text and is accompanied by page citation.

26. *Art Is Boring for the Same Reason We Stayed in Vietnam* (New York: Domestic Press, 1992), 23. All further quotations from *Art Is Boring for the Same Reason We Stayed in Vietnam* are located in the text and are accompanied by page citations.

Before *Art Is Boring*, Miller, who was born in 1951, authored four poetry chapbooks published as issues of the journal *New Observations* in the eighties. In 1990 Miller assembled a selection of this work for publication by Domestic Press and titled it "Skinny Eighth Avenue." During publication delays, Miller wrote *Art Is Boring*, and the press decided to publish the second manuscript and put the first one on hold. In the emergent poststructuralist explorations of his early poetry, Miller often ponders abstractly and figuratively about the problematics of naming, flux as a constant, randomness, and disjunction as aesthetic method. Wallace Stevens, John Ashbery, and Miller's teacher David Shapiro, the composer John Cage, and the painter Jasper Johns are powerful influences on his elaboration of these concerns. Also, the playful "I do this I do that" poetry of Frank O'Hara is reflected in Miller's affectionate uses of small, idiosyncratic details. All of these figures thematize notions of reader-response from time to time, and Miller is also deeply interested in these issues.

27. Donald E. Pease, *Visionary Compacts: American Renaissance Writings in Cultural Context* (Madison: University of Wisconsin Press, 1987), 45. All further quotations from *Visionary Compacts* are located in the text and accompanied by page citations.

Although Pease offers a strong reading of a crucial aspect of Whitman's poetic project that impinges on Miller's articulation of democratic principles, I believe that Whitman's complex poetic rhetoric is open to conflicting interpretations that are also highly persuasive. For example, in his deconstructive study, *Whitman's Presence: Body, Voice, and Writing in* Leaves of Grass (New York: New York University Press, 1992), Tenney Nathanson analyzes the figuration linking the bard's body and the body politic as a yoking of "archaic satisfactions to social allegiances strictly incompatible with them. The body that incarnates the American polity is also a body whose capacities suggest a refusal of socialization" (485). Thus, according to Nathanson, "a vision of community loosely compatible with a millennial interpretation of the American errand" depends on celebration of "a fantasized immunity to the very solidarity" that readers "are busy praising."

28. Stephen Paul Miller, *The Seventies Now: Culture as Surveillance* (Durham, N.C.: Duke University Press, 1999).

29. See, for example, section 15 of "Song of Myself," *Leaves of Grass* (New York: Norton, 1965), 41–44.

30. *Margins of Philosophy*, trans. Alan Bass (Chicago: University of Chicago Press, 1982), 310. Further quotations from *Margins of Philosophy* are located in the text and are accompanied by page citations. For Miller's most salient observations about Derrida and deconstruction in *The Seventies Now*, see 11, 27, 159, 334, 343, 363.

31. See Thomas Fink, "Citationality and Its Discontents," *American Letters & Commentary* 2 (fall 1989): 53–63.

32. Jean Edward Smith, *George Bush's War* (New York: Henry Holt, 1992), 89. Further quotations from *George Bush's War* are located in the text and are accompanied by page citations.

33. Ramsey Clark, *The Fire This Time: U.S. War Crimes in the Gulf* (New York: Thunder's Mouth, 1992), 29. Further quotations from *The Fire This Time* are located in the text and are accompanied by page citations. While I use Clark's data and interpretations in this chapter and find them to be a refreshing and accurate

departure from information provided by the Bush administration and its many supporters in the media, I find Clark's text insufficiently critical of Saddam Hussein's government's actions in domestic affairs and in foreign policy, and of his military's actions in Kuwait before the Gulf War and its actions during the conflict.

34. See Clark, 12–19, regarding this argument about the Bush administration's use of Kuwait as a provocateur.

35. See Smith, 253, and Clark, 40–54, 59–74.

36. I learned the information about Cage's influence on the poem in a conversation with Miller in June 1995. "I Was on a Golf Course the Day John Cage Died of a Stroke," *The Best American Poetry, 1994,* ed. A. R. Ammons and David Lehman (New York: Touchstone, 1994), 133–35, is a delightful homage to both Cage and its precursor poem, Frank O'Hara's "The Day Lady Died," *Selected Poems,* ed. Donald Allen (New York: Random, 1974), 146, that details the impact of Cage's procedural uses of chance on Miller's aesthetic, as well as ways in which Miller departs from Cage's project.

37. Although the relaxed, colloquial, but frequently abstract meandering of A. R. Ammons's long poems bear some resemblance to *Art Is Boring,* Miller was not acquainted with Ammons's work until a few years after he wrote the long poem.

Miller has written an analysis of Wallace Stevens, "An Ordinary Evening in New Haven," *Collected Poems* (New York: Knopf, 1977), 465–89, in *The Seventies Now,* 188–96. His readings of John Ashbery, "Self-Portrait in a Convex Mirror," *Self-Portrait in a Convex Mirror* (New York: Viking, 1975), 68–83, appear in chapter 4 of *The Seventies Now* and two of his articles: " 'Self-Portrait in a Convex Mirror,' the Watergate Affair, and Johns's Crosshatch Paintings: Surveillance and Reality-Testing in the Mid-Seventies," *boundary 2* 20:2 (summer 1993): 84–115, and "Periodizing Ashbery and His Influence," *The Tribe of John: Ashbery and Contemporary Poetry,* ed. Susan M. Schultz (Tuscaloosa: University of Alabama Press, 1995), 146–67, which also includes a discussion of Shapiro's poetry. See also Miller, "Jasper Johns and David Shapiro, an Analogy," master's thesis, City College of New York, 1983.

38. George H. W. Bush, "Inaugural Address," *Representative American Speeches, 1988–1989: The Reference Shelf,* 61, 6 (New York: H. W. Wilson, 1989), 25. Further quotation from the "Inaugural Address" is located in the text and is accompanied by page citation.

39. George H. W. Bush, "Operation Desert Storm," *Representative American Speeches, 1990–1991: The Reference Shelf* 63, 6 (New York: H. W. Wilson, 1991), 41. Further quotation from "Operation Desert Storm" is located in the text and is accompanied by page citation.

40. George H. W. Bush, "The War is Over: A Framework for Peace," *Representative American Speeches, 1990–1991: The Reference Shelf* 63, 6 (New York: H. W. Wilson, 1991), 44.

41. Antonio Gramsci, *Selections from the Prison Notebooks,* trans. Quintin Hoare and Geoffrey Nowell Smith (New York: International, 1978), 12.

42. George Cheney, "We're Talking War: Symbols, Strategies, and Images," in *Desert Storm and the Mass Media,* ed. Bradley S. Greenberg and Walter Gantz (Cresskill, N.J.: Hampton, 1993), 68.

43. Walter Cronkite, "What Is There to Hide?" in *The Media and the Gulf War,* ed. Hedrick Smith (Washington, D.C.: Seven Locks, 1992), 45. Further quotation from "What Is There to Hide?" is located in the text and is accompanied by page citation.

44. Douglas Kellner, "The Crisis in the Gulf and the Lack of Critical Media Discourse," in *Desert Storm and the Mass Media,* ed. Bradley S. Greenberg and Walter Gantz (Cresskill, N.J.: Hampton, 1993), 43.

45. Sydney H. Schanberg, "Censoring for Political Security," in *The Media and the Gulf War*, ed. Hedrick Smith (Washington, D.C.: Seven Locks, 1992), 50. Further quotation from "Censoring for Political Security" is located in the text and is accompanied by page citation.

46. Edward W. Said, "The Prospects for Peace in the Middle East," *The Politics of Dispossession: The Struggle for Palestinian Self-Determination, 1969–1994* (New York: Pantheon, 1994), 156–57.

47. Todd Gitlin, *The Twilight of Common Dreams: Why America Is Wracked by Culture Wars* (New York: Henry Holt, 1995), 204. Further quotation from *The Twilight of Common Dreams* is located in the text and is accompanied by page citation.

48. Steven C. Dubin, *Arresting Images: Impolitic Art and Uncivil Actions* (New York: Routledge, 1992), 180, 175. Further quotation from *Arresting Images* is located in the text and is accompanied by page citations.

49. See Dubin, 20–24.

50. See, for example, Guari Viswanathan, *The Masks of Conquest: Literary Study and British Rule in India* (New York: Columbia University Press, 1989).

51. Note that the first footnote for *"La conciencia"* reads "This is my own 'take off' on José Vasconcelos's idea. Jose Vasconcelos, *La Raza Cósmica: Missión de la Raza Ibero-Americana* (Mexico: Aguilar S. A. de Ediciones, 1961)" (97). For Vasconcelos's articulation of his theory in English, see Vasconcelos and Manuel Gamio, *Aspects of Mexican Civilization* (Chicago: University of Chicago Press, 1926). He argues that "the mestizo represents an entirely new element in history," because "never before had there come together two races as wide apart as the Indian and the Spanish, and never before had the fusing processes of two such different castes been made on such a large scale" (83). For Vasconcelos, "hybridism in man, as well as in plants, tends to produce better types and tends to rejuvenate those types that have become static" (85). At times, his description of the attitudes of mestizos and Anzaldúa's characterization of mestiza consciousness bear striking similarities in their emphasis on multiplicity and divergent perspectives. Stating that mestizos/Mexicans wish to express "life through . . . a thousand channels" and "are not addicted to local tradition or to the European," he refers to "a plurality of emotion, an almost mad desire to try all and to love life from every point of view and every manner of sense experience"; according to Vasconcelos, this makes mestizos "more truly universal in sentiment than any other people" (92–93).

Apart from Anzaldúa's awareness of postmodern, especially poststructuralist theories, a major difference between her and Vasconcelos, whose works are separated by roughly six decades, can be found in the latter's lack of commentary on gender relations and sexual preference.

My student Pilar Cruz has graciously assisted me in translating various forms of Spanish in the sections on Anzaldúa's work in chapters 2 and 3.

Works Cited

Adorno, Theodor W. "Commitment." In *The Essential Frankfurt School Reader*, ed. Andrew Arato and Eike Gebhardt, 300–18. New York: Urizen, 1978.

Alexander, Elizabeth. Introduction to *Love's Instruments* by Melvin Dixon. 5–7. Chicago: Tia Chucha, 1995.

Allan, Tuzyline Jita. *Womanist and Feminist Aesthetics: A Comparative Review.* Athens: Ohio University Press, 1995.

Altieri, Charles. *Subjective Agency: A Theory of First-person Expressivity and its Social Implications.* London: Blackwell, 1994.

Anderson, Quentin. *The Imperial Self: An Essay in American Literary and Cultural History.* New York: Knopf, 1971.

Anzaldúa, Gloria E. *Borderlands/ La Frontera—The New Mestiza.* San Francisco: Aunt Lute, 1987.

———. "La Prieta." In *This Bridge Called My Back: Writings by Radical Women of Color*, ed. Anzaldúa and Cherrie Moraga, 198–209. 1981. Reprint, New York: Kitchen Table/ Women of Color, 1983.

———, ed. *Making Face, Making Soul* Haciendo Caras: *Creative and Critical Perspectives by Women of Color.* San Francisco: Aunt Lute, 1990.

Anzaldúa, Gloria E., and Cherrie Moraga, ed. *This Bridge Called My Back: Writings by Radical Women of Color.* 1981. Reprint, New York: Kitchen Table/ Women of Color, 1983.

Arendt, Hannah. "Introduction: Walter Benjamin: 1892–1940." In Walter Benjamin, *Illuminations,* ed. Hannah Arendt. 1–55. New York: Schocken, 1969.

Ashbery, John. *Self-Portrait in a Convex Mirror.* New York: Viking, 1975.

Benjamin, Walter. *Illuminations.* Ed. Hannah Arendt. Trans. Harry Zohn. New York: Schoken, 1969.

Billington, Ray Allen. *The Far Western Frontier, 1830–1860.* New York: Harper, 1956.

Blasius, Mark. *Gay and Lesbian Politics: Sexuality and the Emergence of a New Ethic.* Philadelphia: Temple University Press, 1994.

Blumenthal, Sidney. "Reaganism and the Neokitsch Aesthetic." *The Reagan Legacy.* Ed. Sidney Blumenthal and Thomas Byrne Edsall. 251–94. New York: Pantheon, 1988.

Bogle, Donald. *Toms, Coons, Mulattoes, Mammies, and Bucks: An Interpretive History of Blacks in American Films.* 1973. Reprint, New York: Continuum, 1989.

Bonilla, Frank, and Ricardo Campos. "A Wealth of Poor: Puerto Ricans in the New Economic Order." *Daedalus* (spring 1981): 133–76.

Bonner, Raymond. *Weakness and Deceit: U.S. Policy and El Salvador.* New York: Times Books, 1984.

Bordo, Susan. *Unbearable Weight: Feminism, Western Culture, and the Body.* Berkeley: University of California Press, 1993.

Brooks, Gwendolyn. *Selected Poems.* New York: Harper and Row, 1963.

Bruce, Novoa. "Chicano Poetry: An Overview." In *A Gift of Tongues: Critical Challenges in Contemporary American Poetry,* ed. Marie Harris and Kathleen Aguero. 226–48. Athens: University of Georgia Press, 1987.

Bush, George H. W. "Inaugural Address." *Representative American Speeches, 1988–1989: The Reference Shelf.* 61, 6. 18–26. New York: H. W. Wilson, 1989.

————. "Operation Desert Storm." *Representative American Speeches, 1990–1991.* 63, 6. 37–43. New York: H. W. Wilson, 1991.

————. "The War Is Over: A Framework for Peace." *Representative American Speeches, 1990–1991.* 63, 6. 43–50. New York: H.W. Wilson, 1991.

Butler, Judith. *Gender Trouble: Feminism and the Subversion of Identity.* New York. Routledge, 1990.

Campos, Ricardo. *Bootstraps and Enterprise Zones: The Underside of Late Capitalism in Puerto Rico and the United States.* Beverly Hills, Calif.: Sage, 1982.

Camus, Albert. "The Myth of Sisyphus." In *The Myth of Sisyphus and Other Essays.* trans. Justin O'Brien. 1955. 88–91. Reprint, New York: Knopf, 1961.

Carbó, Nick. *El Grupo McDonald's.* Chicago: Tia Chucha, 1995.

————. "Returning a Borrowed Tongue." In *Returning a Borrowed Tongue: An Anthology of Contemporary Filipino and Filipino American Poetry,* ed. Nick Carbó. i–xvi. Minneapolis, Minn.: Coffee House, 1995.

Carrion, Arturo Morales. *Puerto Rico: A Political and Cultural History.* New York: Norton, 1983.

Chan, Sucheng. *Asian Americans: An Interpretive History.* Boston: Twayne, 1991.

Chávez, John R. *The Lost Land: The Chicano Image of the Southwest.* Albuquerque: University of New Mexico Press, 1984.

Cheney, George. "We're Talking War: Symbols, Strategies and Images." In *Desert Storm and the Mass Media,* ed. Bradley S. Greenberg and Walter Gantz. 61–73. Cresskill, N.J.: Hampton, 1993.

Clark, Ramsey. *The Fire This Time: U.S. War Crimes in the Gulf.* New York: Thunder's Mouth, 1992.

Clark, Tom. *Robert Creeley and the Genius of the American Common Place. Together with the Poet's Own "Autobiography."* New York: New Directions, 1993.

Coleridge, Samuel Taylor. *The Complete Poetical Works.* Vol. 1. London: Oxford University Press, 1962.

Coles, Robert. "The Human Context of Homelessness." [Interview with Benedict Giamo and Jeffrey Grunberg.] In *Beyond Homelessness: Frames of Reference,* ed. Benedict Giamo and Jeffrey Grunberg. 177–203. Iowa City: University of Iowa Press, 1992.

Collins, Sheila D. *The Rainbow Challenge: The Jackson Campaign and the Future of U.S. Politics.* New York: Monthly Review, 1986.

Creeley, Robert. Foreword to *Trumpets from the Islands of Their Eviction,* by Martín Espada. 9–13. Tempe: Arizona: Bilingual, 1987.

Crimp, Douglas. "AIDS: Cultural Analysis/Cultural Activism." In *AIDS: Cultural Analysis/Cultural Activism,* ed. Douglas Crimp. 3–16. Cambridge: MIT, 1988.

————. "Mourning and Militancy." *October* 51 (1989): 3–18.

Cronkite, Walter. "What Is There to Hide?" In *The Media and the Gulf War,* ed. Hedrick Smith. 45–47. Washington, DC: Seven Locks, 1992.

de Beauvoir, Simone. Preface to *Shoah: An Oral History of the Holocaust.* iii–x. New York: Pantheon, 1985.

de León, Arnoldo. *They Called Them Greasers: Anglo Attitudes Toward Mexicans in Texas, 1821–1900.* Austin: University of Texas Press, 1983.

D'Emilio, John. *Sexual Politics, Sexual Communities: The Making of a Homosexual Minority in the United States, 1940–1970.* Chicago: University of Chicago Press, 1983.

Derrida, Jacques. *Margins of Philosophy.* Trans. Alan Bass. Chicago: University of Chicago Press, 1982.

———. *Writing and Difference.* Trans. Alan Bass. Chicago: University of Chicago Press, 1978.

Desnos, Robert. *Selected Poems.* Trans. Carolyn Forché and William Kulik. New York: Ecco, 1991.

Dieter-Dube, Wolf. "Ernst Ludwig Kirchner." *Ernst Ludwig Kirchner, 1880–1938: Oils, Watercolors, Drawings, and Graphics.* 8–11. London: Marlborough Fine Art, 1969.

Dixon, Melvin. "The Black Writer's Use of Memory." In *History and Memory in African-American Culture,* ed. Geneviève Fabre and Robert O'Meally. 18–27. New York: Oxford University Press, 1994.

———. *Change of Territory.* Lexington: University of Kentucky, 1983.

———. *Love's Instruments.* Chicago: Tia Chucha, 1995.

———. *Ride Out the Wilderness: Geography and Identity in Afro-American Literature.* Urbana: University of Illinois Press, 1987.

———. *Trouble the Water.* Boulder: University of Colorado and Fiction Collective Two, 1989.

———. *Vanishing Rooms.* New York: Dutton, 1991.

Dubin, Steven C. *Arresting Images: Impolitic Art and Uncivil Actions.* New York: Routledge, 1992.

DuBois, W. E. B. *The Souls of Black Folk.* 1903; reprint, New York: Vintage, 1930.

Duhamel, Denise. "Denise Duhamel." Interviewed by Sonia Parkes. *Inkshed* 26 (January–June 1994): 16–20.

———. "Evelyn Lau, *Fresh Girls and Other Stories* and *Oedipal Dreams.*" [Review] *The Poetry Project* 157 (April/May 1995): 7.

———. *Girl Soldier.* Truro, Mass.: Garden Street, 1996.

———. "Interview with Denise Duhamel," by Thomas Fink, October 19, 1995, New York, unpublished.

———. *Kinky.* Alexandria, Va.: Orchises, 1997.

———. *Smile!* Harrisburg, Pa.: Warm Spring, 1993.

———. *The Star Spangled Banner.* Carbondale: Southern Illinois University Press, 1999.

———. *The Woman with Two Vaginas.* Anchorage, Alaska: Salmon Run, 1995.

Dumpson, James R. "The Social Welfare." [Interview with Benedict Giamo and Jeffrey Grunberg.] In *Beyond Homelessness: Frames of Reference,* ed. Benedict Giamo and Jeffrey Grunberg. 89–109. Iowa City: University of Iowa Press, 1992.

"Economic Growth for Whom?" "Action Brief," Michael Harrington Center for Democratic Values and Social Action, Queens College, City University of New York, no. 1 (1998): 1–2.

Ellison, Ralph. *Collected Essays.* Ed. John F. Callahan. New York: Modern Library, 1995.

———. *Invisible Man.* 1952. Reprint, New York: Random, 1972.

———. *Shadow and Act.* 1964. Reprint, New York: Random, 1972.

EPICA Task Froce. "The Somoza Legacy: Economic Bankruptcy." In *The Nicaragua Reader: Documents of a Revolution under Fire,* ed. Peter Rosset and John Vandermeer. 299–301. New York: Grove, 1983. Reprinted from EPICA Task Force. *Nicaragua: A People's Revolution.* Washington, D.C.: EPICA Task Force, 1980.

Espada, Martín. *City of Coughing and Dead Radiators.* New York: Norton, 1993.

———. "Documentaries and Declamadores: Puerto Rican Poetry in the United States." In *A Gift of Tongues: Critical Challenges in Contemporary American Poetry,* ed. Marie Harris and Kathleen Aguero. 257–66. Athens: University of Georgia Press, 1987.

———. *Imagine the Angels of Bread*. New York: Norton, 1996.

———. *The Immigrant Iceboy's Bolero*. Madison, Wis.: Ghost Pony, 1982; reprinted, Natick, Mass.: Cordilera, 1983; reprinted Maplewood, N.J.: Waterfront, 1986.

———. Foreword to *Poetry like bread: Poets of the Political Imagination*. Ed. Martín Espada. Willimantic, Conn.: Curbstone, 1994. 15–19.

———. *Rebellion Is the Circle of a Lover's Hands*. Willimantic, Conn.: Curbstone, 1990.

———. *Trumpets from the Islands of Their Eviction*. Tempe: Ariz.: Bilingual, 1987.

Espada, Martín, and Camilo Pérez-Bustillo. Foreword to *The Blood That Keeps Singing: Selected Poems of Clemente Soto-Vélez*. Trans. Martín Espada and Camilio Pérez-Bustillo. 7–10. Willimantic, Conn.: Curbstone, 1991.

Fabre, Geneviève. *Drumbeats, Masks, and Metaphor: Contemporary Afro-American Theater.* Trans. Melvin Dixon. Cambridge: Harvard University Press, 1983.

Faludi, Susan. *Backlash: The Undeclared War against American Women*. New York: Crown, 1991.

Fanon, Frantz. *Black Skin, White Masks*. Trans. Charles Lam Markmann. 1952. Reprint, New York: Grove Weidenfeld, 1967.

Farmer, Ruth. "*The Woman with Two Vaginas*: Erotic Eskimo Tales in Poetry by Denise Duhamel." *Harvard Review* (fall 1995): 162–63.

Fink, Thomas. "Citationality and Its Discontents." *American Letters & Commentary* 2 (fall 1989): 53–63.

———. *The Poetry of David Shapiro*. Madison, N.J.: Fairleigh Dickinson University Press, 1993.

Forbes, Jack D. *Aztecas del Norte: The Chicanos of Aztlán*. Greenwich, Conn.: Fawcett, 1973.

Forché, Carolyn. Introduction to *Against Forgetting, Twentieth Century Poetry of Witness*. Ed. Carolyn Forché. 29–46. New York: Norton, 1993.

———. *The Angel of History*. New York: HarperCollins, 1994.

———. "Carolyn Forché." In Bill Moyers, *The Language of Life: A Festival of Poets*, ed. James Haba. 129–41. New York: Doubleday, 1995.

———. "Carolyn Forché" [Interview with David Montenegro] *Points of Departure: International Writers on Writing and Politics*. Ed. David Montenegro. 62–79. Ann Arbor: University of Michigan Press, 1991.

———. *The Country between Us*. New York: Harper and Row, 1981.

———. "El Salvador: An Aide-Mémoire." *American Poetry Review* (July/August 1981). Rpt. In *Poetry and Politics*, ed. Richard Jones. 243–57. New York: Quill, 1985.

———. *Gathering the Tribes*. New Haven: Yale University Press, 1976.

———. "Jill Taft-Kaufman Talks with Carolyn Forché." [Interview] *Text and Performance Quarterly* 10, no. 1 (January 1990): 61–70.

———. "A Lesson in Commitment." *TriQuarterly* 65 (winter 1986): 35.

Foucault, Michel. *The Archeology of Knowledge and the Discourse on Language*. Trans. A. M. Sheridan Smith. New York: Pantheon, 1972.

———. "On the Genealogy of Ethics: An Overview of Work in Progress." [Interview with Paul Rabinow and Hubert Dreyfus.] *The Foucault Reader.* 340–72. New York: Pantheon, 1984.

Friedlander, Saul. *Nazi Germany and the Jews: The Years of Persecution, 1933–1939*. Vol. 1. New York: HarperCollins, 1997.

Frost, Robert. *Selected Poems*. New York: Holt, Rinehart, and Winston, 1962.

Gander, Forrest. "Joseph Lease's *The Room*," *Agni* 42 (1995): 203–5.

Gates, Henry Louis Jr. *The Signifying Monkey: A Theory of Afro-American Literary Criticism*. New York: Oxford University Press, 1988.

Gery, John. "Ashbery's Menagerie and the Anxiety of Affluence." In *The Tribe of John: Ashbery and Contemporary Poetry*, ed. Susan M. Schultz. 126–45. Tuscaloosa: University of Alabama Press, 1995.

Gitlin, Todd. *The Twilight of Common Dreams: Why America Is Wracked by Culture Wars*. New York: Henry Holt, 1995.

Gramsci, Antonio. *Selections from the Prison Notebooks*. Ed. And trans. Quintin Hoare and Geoffrey Nowell Smith. 1971. Reprint, New York: International, 1978.

Greer, Michael. "Politicizing the Modern: Carolyn Forché in El Salvador and America." *Centennial Review* 30, no. 2 (spring 1985): 160–80.

Grover, Jan Zita. "AIDS: Keywords." In *AIDS: Cultural Analysis/Cultural Activism*, ed. Douglas Crimp. 17–30. Cambridge: MIT, 1988.

Halsell, Grace. *The Illegals*. New York: Stein and Day, 1978.

Harding, Vincent. "Power from Our People: The Sources of the Modern Revival of Black History." *The Black Scholar: Journal of Black Studies and Research* 18, no. 1 (January/February 1987): 40–51.

Hartley, George. *Textual Politics and the Language Poets*. Bloomington: Indiana University Press, 1989.

Hayden, Robert. *Collected Poems*. New York: Liveright, 1985.

Hejinian, Lyn. "The Rejection of Closure." In *Writing/Talks*, ed. Bob Perelman. 270–91. Carbondale: Southern Illinois University Press, 1985.

Hemphill, Essex. Introduction to *Brother to Brother: New Writings by Black Gay Men*. Ed. Hemphill and Joseph Fairchild Beam. xv–xxxi. Boston: Alyson, 1991.

Hine, Darlene Clark. *Speaking Truth to Power: Black Professional Class in United States History*. Brooklyn, N.Y.: Carlson, 1996.

Holm, Jeanne. *Women in the Military: An Unfinished Revolution*. Novato, Calif.: Presidio, 1992.

hooks, bell. *Killing Rage: Ending Racism*. New York: Henry Holt, 1995.

Jackson, Jesse L. "A Call to Common Ground." *The Black Scholar* 20, no. 1 (January/February 1989): 12–18.

———. *Straight from the Heart*. Ed. Roger D. Hatch and Frank E. Watkins. Philadelphia: Fortress, 1987.

Jones, Cleve. "Cleve Jones." In *Family: A Portrait of Gay and Lesbian America*, ed. Nancy Andrews. San Francisco: HarperCollins, 1994. Unpaginated.

Jones, LeRoi. *Blues People: Negro Music in White America*. 1963. Reprint, New York: William Morrow, 1970.

Junta for National Reconstruction. "The Philosophy and Policies of the Government of Nicaragua." In *The Nicaragua Reader: Documents of a Revolution under Fire*, ed. Peter Rosset and John Vandermeer. 258–69. New York: Grove, 1983.

Katz, Ephraim. "Anna May Wong." *The Film Encyclopedia*. 46. New York: Thomas Y. Crowell, 1979.

Kellner, Douglas. "The Crisis in the Gulf and the Lack of Critical Media Discourse." In *Desert Storm and the Mass Media*, ed. Bradley S. Greenberg and Walter Gantz. 37–47. Cresskill, N.J.: Hampton, 1993.

Kelly, Kitty. *His Way: The Unauthorized Biography of Frank Sinatra*. New York: Bantam, 1986.

Kim, Elaine H. *Asian American Literature: An Introduction to the Writings and Their Social Context.* Philadelphia: Temple University Press, 1982.

Klein, Michael. Introduction to *Poets for Life: Seventy-Six Poets Respond to AIDS.* Ed. Michael Klein. 9–15. New York: Crown, 1989.

Kunitz, Stanley. Foreword to *Gathering the Tribes,* by Carolyn Forché. iv–ix. New Haven: Yale University Press, 1976.

Langer, Lawrence L. *Admitting the Holocaust: Collected Essays.* New York: Oxford University Press, 1995.

Lanzmann, Claude. *Shoah: An Oral History of the Holocaust.* New York: Pantheon, 1985.

Lease, Joseph. *Human Rights.* Cambridge, Mass.: Zoland, 1998.

———. *The Room.* New York: Alef, 1994.

———. "A Study in 'Counter-Dependence': Language Poetry as 'Collective Voice.' " Unpublished manuscript, 1997.

Lewis, Gordon K. *Puerto Rico: Freedom and Power in the Caribbean.* New York: Monthly Review, 1963.

Lifton, Robert Jay. *Death in Life: Survivors of Hiroshima.* New York: Random, 1967.

Lipstadt, Deborah. *Denying the Holocaust: The Growing Assault on Truth and Memory.* New York: Free, 1993.

Lorde, Audre. *Sister Outsider: Essays and Speeches.* Trumansberg, N.Y.: Crossing, 1984.

Lowe, Lisa. *Immigrant Acts: Asian American Cultural Politics.* Durham, N.C.: Duke University Press, 1996.

Macheski, Cecilia. Introduction to *Quilt Stories.* Ed. Cecilia Macheski. 1–7. Lexington: University Press of Kentucky, 1994.

Maltin, Leonard. *Movie and Video Guide.* New York: Signet, 1996.

Marable, Manning. *Beyond Black and White: Transforming African-American Politics.* New York: Verso, 1995.

Marchetti, Gina. *Romance and the "Yellow Peril": Race, Sex, and Discourse Strategies in Hollywood Fiction.* Berkeley: University of California Press, 1993.

McDowell, Robert. "Poetry Chronicles." *Hudson Review* (spring 1994): 159–60.

Mead, Chris. *Champion: Joe Louis, Black Hero in White America.* New York: Scribner's, 1985.

Miller, Stephen Paul. *Art Is Boring for the Same Reason We Stayed in Vietnam.* New York: Domestic, 1992.

———. "I Was on a Golf Course the Day John Cage Died of a Stroke." In *The Best American Poetry, 1994,* ed. A. R. Ammons and David Lehman. 133–35. New York: Touchstone, 1994.

———. "Jasper Johns and David Shapiro, an Analogy." Master's thesis, City College of New York, 1983.

———. "Periodizing Ashbery and His Influence." In *The Tribe of John: Ashbery and Contemporary Poetry,* ed. Susan M. Schultz. 146–67. Tuscaloosa: University of Alabama Press, 1995.

———. " 'Self-Portrait in a Convex Mirror,' the Watergate Affair, and Johns's Cross-hatch Paintings: Surveillance and Reality-Testing in the Mid-Seventies." *Boundary 2* 20:2 (summer 1993): 84–115.

———. *The Seventies Now: Culture as Surveillance.* Durham, N.C.: Duke University Press, 1999.

Min-ha, Trinh T. *When the Moon Waxes Red: Representation, Gender, and Cultural Politics.* New York: Routledge, 1991.

————. *Woman, Native Other: Writing Postcoloniality and Feminism.* Bloomington: Indiana University Press, 1989.

Minton, Henry L. "The Emergence of Gay and Lesbian Studies." In *Gay and Lesbian Studies,* ed. Henry L. Minton. 1–6. Binghampton, N.Y.: Haworth, 1992.

Monder, Eric. *George Sidney: A Bio-Bibliography.* Westport, Conn.: Greenwood, 1994.

Morrison, Toni. *The Bluest Eye.* New York: Holt, Rinehart, and Winston, 1970.

Moss, Thylias. *At Redbones.* Cleveland, Ohio: Cleveland State University Press, 1990.

————. *Hosiery Seams on a Bowlegged Woman.* Cleveland, Ohio: Cleveland State University Press, 1983.

————. *Last Chance for the Tarzan Holler.* New York: Persea, 1998.

————. *Pyramid of Bone.* Charlottesville: University Press of Virginia, 1989.

————. *Rainbow Remnants in Rock Bottom Ghetto Sky.* New York: Persea, 1991.

————. *Small Congregations: New and Selected Poems.* Hopewell, N.J.: Ecco, 1993.

————. *Tale of a Sky-Blue Dress.* New York: Avon, 1998.

Muñoz Jr., Carlos. *Youth, Identity, Power: The Chicano Movement.* New York: Verso, 1989.

Murphy, Timothy F. "Testimony." In *Writing AIDS: Gay Literature, Language, and Analysis,* ed. Timothy F. Murphy and Suzanne Poirer. 306–19. New York: Columbia University Press, 1993.

Murray, Albert. *Stomping the Blues.* New York: McGraw-Hill, 1976.

————. "The Visual Equivalent of the Blues." In *Romare Bearden: 1970–1980,* ed. Jerald L. Melberg and Milton J. Bloch. 23–30. Charlotte, N.C.: Mint Museum, 1980.

Nathanson, Tenney. *Whitman's Presence: Body, Voice, and Writing in* Leaves of Grass. New York: New York University Press, 1992.

Nelson, Anne. *Murder under Two Flags: The U.S., Puerto Rico, and the Cerro Maravilla Cover-up.* New York: Ticknor and Fields, 1986.

Nielsen, Aldon Lynn. *Reading Race: White American Poets and the Racial Discourse in the Twentieth Century.* Athens: University of Georgia Press, 1988.

Nieves, Josephine, Maria Canino, Sherry Gorelick, Hildamar Ortiz, Camilio Rodriquez, and Jesse Vazquez. "Puerto Rican Studies: Roots and Challenges." In *Toward a Renaissance of Puerto Rican Studies: Ethnic and Area Studies in University Education,* ed. Maria E. Sanchez and Antonio M. Stevens-Arroyo. 3–12. Highland Lakes, N.J.: Atlantic Research and Publications, 1987.

O'Brien, Anthony. "Reading Melvin Dixon's Africa." *Found Object* 4 (fall 1994): 91–93.

O'Hara, Frank. *Selected Poems.* Ed. Donald Allen. New York: Random, 1974.

Okihiro, Gary Y. "Education for Hegemony, Education for Liberation." In *Ethnic Studies: Volume 1—Cross-Cultural, Asian, and Afro-American Studies.* Ed. Gary Y. Okihiro. 3–4. New York: Markus Wiener, 1989.

O'Malley, Ilene. "Play It Again, Ron." In *The Nicaragua Reader: Documents of a Revolution Under Fire,* ed. Peter Rosset and John Vandermeer. 113–19. New York: Grove, 1983.

Omi, Michael, and Howard Winant. *Racial Formation in the United States from the 1960s to the 1990s.* New York: Routledge, 1994.

Ortega Saeevedra, Daniel. "Let There Be Peace in Central America." [Address to U.N. Security Council, March 25, 1982]. In *The Nicaragua Reader: Documents of a Revolution Under Fire,* ed. Peter Rosset and John Vandemeer. 9–11. New York: Grove, 1983.

Parrish, James Robert, and William T. Leonard. "Anna May Wong." *Hollywood Players: The 30s.* 532–39. New Rochelle: N.Y.: Arlington, 1976.

Pease, Donald E. *Visionary Compacts: American Renaissance Writings in Cultural Context.* Madison: University of Wisconsin Press, 1987.

Peña, Devon. "Between the Lines: A New Perspective on the Industrial Sociology of Women Workers in Transnational Labor Processes." In *Chicana Voices: Intersections of Class, Race, and Gender,* ed. Teresa Cordova et al. 77–95. Albuquerque: University of New Mexico Press, 1990.

Pérez-Torres, Rafael. *Movements in Chicano Poetry: Against Myths, Against Margins.* New York: Cambridge University Press, 1995.

Perloff, Marjorie. *The Dance of the Intellect: Studies in the Poetry of the Pound Tradition.* New York: Cambridge University Press, 1985.

———. *Poetic License: Essays on Modernist and Postmodernist Lyric.* Evanston, Ill.: Northeastern University Press, 1990.

———. *Radical Artifice: Poetry in the Age of Media.* Chicago: University of Chicago Press, 1991.

Ramazani, Jahan. *Poetry of Mourning: The Modern Elegy from Hardy to Heaney.* Chicago: University of Chicago Press, 1993.

Reagan, Ronald. *Speaking My Mind: Selected Speeches.* New York: Simon and Schuster, 1989.

Reinfeld, Linda. *Language Poetry: Writing as Rescue.* Baton Rouge: Louisiana State University Press, 1992.

Revell, Donald. "*The Room* by Joseph Lease." *Colorado Review* 21, no. 2 (fall 1995): 199–209.

Rich, Adrienne. *Blood, Bread, and Poetry.* New York: Norton, 1986.

———. *Your Native Land, Your Life.* New York: Norton, 1986.

Roberts, Randy. *Jack Johnson and the Era of White Hopes.* New York: Free, 1983.

Rodriguez, Clara E. *Puerto Ricans Born in the U.S.A.* Boston: Unwin Hyman, 1989.

Rogin, Michael. "'Make My Day!: Spectacle as Amnesia in Imperial Politics." *Representations* 29 (winter 1990): 99–123.

Said, Edward W. *Culture and Imperialism.* New York: Knopf, 1993.

———. *Orientalism.* New York: Random, 1978.

———. "The Prospects for Peace in the Middle East." *The Politics of Dispossession: The Struggle for Palestinian Self-Determination, 1969–1994.* 156–74. New York: Pantheon, 1994.

Saldivar-Hull, Sonia. "Feminism on the Border: From Gender Politics to Geopolitics." In *Criticism in the Borderlands: Studies in Chicano Literature, Culture, and Ideology,* ed. Hector Calderon and Jose David Saldivar. 203–20. Durham, N.C.: Duke University Press, 1991.

Schanberg, Sydney H. "Censoring for Political Security." *The Media and the Gulf War.* Ed. Hedrick Smith. 48–58. Washington, D.C.: Seven Locks, 1992.

Schwartzman, Myron. "A Bearden-Murray Interplay: One Last Time." *Callaloo* 11, no. 3 (summer 1988): 410–15.

———. *Romare Bearden: His Life and Art.* New York: Harry N. Abrams, 1990.

Shapiro, David. "After." *Testimony: Contemporary Writers Make the Holocaust Personal.* Ed. David Rosenberg. 456–74. New York: Random, 1989.

———. *A Man Holding an Acoustic Panel.* New York: E. P. Dutton, 1971.

Shapiro, David, and Joseph Lease. "David Shapiro and Joseph Lease: An Exchange." *Misc. Proj.* 3 (July 1997): 5–10.

Shilts, Randy. *And the Band Played On: Politics, People, and the AIDS Epidemic.* New York: St. Martin's, 1987.

Smith, Jean Edward. *George Bush's War.* New York: Henry Holt, 1992.

Steninbrunne, Chris, and Otto Penzler, eds. *Encyclopedia of Mystery and Detection.* New York: McGraw-Hill, 1976.

Stevens, Wallace. *Collected Poems.* 1954. Reprint, New York: Knopf, 1977.

Strand, Mark, and David Lehman, eds. *The Best American Poetry, 1991.* New York: Scribner's, 1992.

Strine, Mary S. "Protocols of Power: Performance, Pleasure, and the Textual Economy." *Text and Performance Quarterly* 12, no. 1 (January 1992): 61–67.

Szporluk, Larissa. "Joseph Lease, *Human Rights.*" *Poetry Project Newsletter* 170 (June/July 1998): 14–15.

Tafolla, Carmen. "Chicano Literature: Beyond Beginnings." In *A Gift of Tongues: Critical Challenges in Contemporary American Poetry,* ed. Marie Harris and Kathleen Aguero. 206–25. Athens: University of Georgia Press, 1987.

Takaki, Ronald. "Multiculturalism: Battleground or Meeting Ground?" *Annals of the American Academy of Political and Social Science* 530 (November 1993): 109–21.

———. *Strangers from a Different Shore: A History of Asian Americans.* Boston: Little, Brown, 1989.

Tannahill, Reay. *Sex in History.* Briarcliff Manor, N.Y.: Stein and Day, 1980.

Torres, Hector A. "Gloria Anzaldúa." In *Dictionary of Literary Biography, Chicano Writers: Second Series* 122, ed. Francisco A. Lomelí and Carl R. Shirley. 8–17. Detroit: Gale Research, 1992.

Treichler, Paula A. "AIDS, Homophobia, and Biomedical Discourse: An Epidemic of Signification." In *AIDS: Cultural Analysis/Cultural Activism,* ed. Douglas Crimp. 31–70. Cambridge: MIT, 1988.

Turner, Patricia A. *Ceramic Uncles & Celluloid Mammies: Black Images and Their Influence on Culture.* New York: Doubleday, 1994.

Vasconcelos, Jose, and Manuel Gamio. *Aspects of Mexican Civilization.* Chicago: University of Chicago Press, 1926.

Vélez, Diana L. "Dancing to the Music of an 'Other' Voice." In *Trumpets from the Island of Their Eviction,* by Martín Espada. 69–89. Tempe, Arizona: Bilingual, 1987.

Vendler, Helen Hennessey. *The Breaking of Style: Hopkins, Heaney, Graham.* Cambridge: Harvard University Press, 1995.

———. *The Given and the Made: Strategies of Poetic Redefinition.* Cambridge: Harvard University Press, 1995.

———. *Soul Says: Recent Poetry.* Cambridge: Belnap, 1995.

Vertreace, Martha M. "Secrets Left to Tell: Creativity and Continuity in the Mother/Daughter Dyad." In *Mother Puzzles: Daughters and Mothers in Contemporary American Literature,* ed. Mickey Pearlman. 77–89. Westport, Conn.: Greenwood, 1989.

Viswanathan, Gauri. *The Masks of Conquest: Literary Study and British Rule in India.* New York: Columbia University Press, 1989.

Wade, Wyn Craig. *The Fiery Cross: The Ku Klux Klan in America.* New York: Simon and Schuster, 1987.

Wald, Priscilla. "'Chaos Goes Uncourted': John Yau's Dis(-)Orienting Poetics." In *Cohesion and Dissent in American Literature,* ed. Carol Colatrella and Joseph Alkana. 133–58. Albany: State University of New York Press, 1994.

Wallerstein, Immanuel. *Historical Capitalism*. London: Verso, 1983.

Weinberg, Jonathan. "The Quilt: Activism and Remembrance." *Art in America* 80 (December 1992): 37–39.

West, Cornel. *Race Matters*. Boston: Beacon, 1993.

Whitehead, Kim. *The Feminist Poetry Movement*. Jackson: University of Mississippi Press, 1996.

Whitman, Walt. *Leaves of Grass*. New York: Norton, 1968.

———. *Complete Poetry and Collected Prose*. New York: Library of America, 1982.

Wong, Eugene Franklin. *On Visual Media Racism: Asians in the American Motion Pictures*. New York: Arno, 1978.

Yau, John. *Corpse and Mirror*. New York: Holt, Rinehart, and Winston, 1983.

———. *Crossing Canal Street*. Binghampton, N.Y.: Bellevue, 1976.

———. *Edificio Sayonara*. Santa Rosa, Calif.: Black Sparrow, 1992.

———. *Forbidden Entries*. Santa Rosa, Calif.: Black Sparrow, 1996.

———. "An Interview with John Yau." Interview by Edward Foster. *Talisman* 5 (fall 1990): 31–50.

———. "Please Wait by the Coatroom: Wilfredo Lam in the Museum of Modern Art." *Arts* 63, no. 4 (December 1988): 56–59.

———. *Radiant Silhouette: New and Selected Work, 1974–1988*. Santa Rosa, Calif.: Black Sparrow, 1989.

———. *The United States of Jasper Johns*. Cambridge, Mass.: Zoland, 1996.

Yau, John, and Eileen Tabios. "Approximating Midnight: Her Conversation with John Yau and." *Black Lightning: Poetry-in-Progress*. 379–400. New York: Asian American Writer's Workshop, 1998.

Zinn, Howard. *A People's History of the United States*. New York: Harper and Row, 1980.

Zipes, Jack. *Breaking the Magic Spell: Radical Theories of Folk and Fairy Tales*. Austin: University of Texas Press, 1979.

Index